P9-DKE-712

ROCKHURST COLLEGE LIBRARY

0 0006 0092116

Date Due

12/9/98		

BRODART, INC.   Cat. No. 23 233   Printed in U.S.A.

UP IS NOT THE ONLY WAY

PRENTICE-HALL, INC.
ENGLEWOOD CLIFFS, NEW JERSEY 07632

UP IS NOT THE ONLY WAY

a guide for
career development practitioners

BEVERLY L. KAYE

Library of Congress Cataloging in Publication Data

Kaye, Beverly L.
 Up is not the only way.

 Includes bibliographical references and index.
 1. Personnel management. 2. Vocational guidance.
I. Title. II. Title: Career development practitioners.
HF5549.K32   658.3′124   81-12056
ISBN 0-13-939173-8   AACR2

Interior design/Production supervision by Steven Young
Cover design by Lorraine Mullaney
Manufacturing buyer: Ed O'Dougherty

© 1982 by Beverly Kaye

All rights reserved. No part of this book
may be reproduced in any form or
by any means without permission in writing
from the publisher.

Printed in the United States of America
10 9 8 7 6 5 4 3 2 1

ISBN 0-13-939173-8

Prentice-Hall International, Inc., *London*
Prentice-Hall of Australia Pty. Limited, *Sydney*
Prentice-Hall of Canada, Ltd., *Toronto*
Prentice-Hall of India Private Limited, *New Delhi*
Prentice-Hall of Japan, Inc., *Tokyo*
Prentice-Hall of Southeast Asia Pte. Ltd., *Singapore*
Whitehall Books Limited, *Wellington, New Zealand*

ROCKHURST COLLEGE LIBRARY

HF
5549
K32

To Barry,
my greatest source of encouragement

111375

111345

contents

preface

I live in Los Angeles. A transplant from the East Coast. Like all local transplants, I soon realized that Los Angeles is not so much a city in the familiar sense, but rather a car-oriented conglomerate of widely dispersed suburbs. We commonly spend an hour or more each day on an intricately interconnected inner city belt of expressways (called "freeways" because of the absence of those pernicious Eastern Coast highway toll charges) traveling to and from work, dining out, or simply visiting some "close" friends.

To use the freeway system efficiently, we have to refer constantly to a large selection of detailed maps, typically one map per local area, which occupies the greater portion of our car glove compartments. However, when venturing to some distant suburb, before these extensive local maps can be used, we usually consult one chart which provides a concise, compact overview of the entire Los Angeles freeway network, along with some major city thoroughfares. This indispensible six-inch-by-eight-inch aid is treasured above all of the other maps because it provides us with 90 percent of the directions needed to arrive at our intended destinations in an orderly, uncluttered format, devoid of extraneous or tangential information.

Certainly, no one ignores the necessity of the large unwieldly local maps (which I somehow can never quite refold into their original flat states) for completing the final details of our automobile safaris. But I must confess to you, unashamedly, that I would never know where to even begin most of my trips without resorting to that one handy freeway map.

A concise map created for the career development practitioner, this book was written to help you design and implement a career development effort that meets the specific needs of your organization. In an easy-to-read format it provides a general overview of all of the steps required to successfully complete the process—from the initial conceptualization through program implementation. In most situations it will contain enough depth of information to serve as a self-contained guidebook. However, no single reference source can anticipate all of its readers' needs. For those programmatic areas in which you need more detail, it will point you in the right direction and tell you which additional maps are most appropriate. Using it as your primary career development aid, however, you will fall into the habit of consulting it frequently along the road to your program goals, to avoid costly and time-consuming detours over nonproductive pathways.

This book will highlight six distinct stages that together comprise an effective career development effort. Each stage by itself contributes substantially to the organization and to the development of individual participants, but together the stages become synergistic.

The first of these, *Preparation,* will direct you through some painstaking steps in readying your organization for the career development effort. Much of this is done behind the scenes—not much applause here, but if it's well done, the applause will ring loud and clear later.

Profiling, the second stage, will give you some very specific tips on how to assist employees in your organization in identifying and verifying the skills they possess. This is a vital step in producing a realistic career development plan.

The essence of the *Targeting* Stage is alluded to in the title of the book—there *are* more ways to move, grow, and develop in an organization than just vertically. The sooner the practitioner appreciates this and translates it into terms that are meaningful to managers and employees alike, the better.

The fourth stage, *Strategizing,* will remind you of the many nuances existing in the informal organization, as well as in the structured formal one, so that you, in turn, will be able to deliver this information to employees. It also teaches several methods of devising action plans that help program participants take responsibility for their particular career development goals and plot the appropriate course of action.

The *Execution* Stage provides specific ideas which will enable you to properly advise employees of the many options for acquiring the tools and skills required to make their plans materialize. It emphasizes the importance of demonstrating these new skills once they have been duly acquired.

The sixth and last stage, *Integration,* assists you in developing evaluation procedures to demonstrate that all-important return on investment. It also reminds you to consider systems which would reward employees who by this time have changed, moved, or grown in valuable directions. It discusses rewards for managers who have taken particular care in the development of their subordinates.

Human resource activities that are relevant to each stage are also reviewed. They are presented, not to fully educate the practitioner about any one activity, but rather to show how they can reinforce the career development process and become part of a larger integrated whole.

The original delineation of the stages and their components is derived from my dissertation work done at UCLA which was then massaged with many years of practice in the field of career development in business and industry. I hope you use it as a basis on which to build a still clearer framework. Maps change with growth.

Surveying and mapping any terrain is usually not done in isolation or as a solo journey. I have had some very special and necessary assistance in my attempt to provide this map. I am thankful to have had mentors like Sam Culbert, Warren Schmidt and Lena Astin who prodded and pushed the original work, and colleagues like Rosabeth Kanter, Alice Sargent, Caela Farren, Suzanne Bryant, and Betsy Jacobson, who either read chapters, or dialogued with me, and always, always urged me on. I am also thankful (and smart) for having enlisted the superb technical assistance and active encouragement of Katherine Janka and, later, Hugh Taylor, who listened to my ideas and helped me to organize my thoughts in a coherent fashion. The long, tedious work of my support staff, Sandra Marley and Rolanda Irvin, made the final product possible—they worked above and beyond the call of duty.

I am appreciative of the clients who believed in my efforts and basic framework and invited me to work with them on a great variety of career-related interventions.

I am fortunate in having a close loving family. Their weekly telephone calls provided me with much needed reassurance and nurturance.

Most of all, I wish to acknowledge my husband, Barry Levitt, who seemed to know from the start that this project was something I had to do, could do, and would do. His patience and encouragement enabled me to begin—and to continue to completion. His support, understanding, and pride in my accomplishments have been vital underpinnings of my own career development.

UP
IS
NOT
THE
ONLY
WAY

THE PROCESS AND THE PAYOFF

"What we seem to be missing is an integrating framework."

It all used to be so simple. American workers selected a career area, educated themselves to pursue it, settled into an organization that could use their talents, worked to achieve higher rungs on the corporate ladder, and collected a gold watch at the mandatory 65-year retirement age.

Myriad social, economic, and legal changes of recent years have radically disrupted this long-standing pattern; and organizational mechanisms for dealing with accelerating change are still in the early stages of development and experimentation. Many individuals and organizations seem at a loss for means to anticipate and cope with the rapid evolution of their environments. Rather than direct their own progress, individuals and organizations are instead controlled by their environments, with a subsequent loss of power and productivity. It is important that both the organization and the individual develop the ability to manage and direct such change to their own benefit.

Long-range strategic planning is a process that has recently received considerable attention as a possible answer for organizations wishing to regain control over their environment. This process includes closely examining every aspect of the firm—its strengths, weaknesses, opportunities, and threats. It then seeks to carve out a planned and orderly future based upon an honest appraisal of the firm and its present and anticipated future environments. This process includes planning for unexpected possibilities and provides periodic measurement and comparison of reality with the plan, in order to ensure that assumptions are still valid (or that timely revisions are made).

Career planning and development activities are to the individual what strategic planning is to the firm. Career development involves looking realistically at the present conditions and at the career environments of today and tomorrow in order to regain the control necessary to ensure future productivity and job satisfaction. It also includes contingency planning and reality-testing.

But career development is more than this. Not only does it aid the individual in confronting and coping with a rapidly evolving working world, but it can also be a vital link between individual and organizational goals and objectives. It can become the vehicle for implementing the human resource aspects of a company's strategic plan (for such a plan must also look closely at this resource and formulate a framework for its development and use). Career development in this sense, therefore, is not simply another human resource activity, but instead an integrating concept that systematically ties together and builds upon human resource programs that already exist, so that they simultaneously support individual and organizational growth.

This book addresses the rationale and design of such career development efforts and is directed to those individuals who are charged with initiating and implementing those efforts within the organization.

THE EMPLOYEE STIMULUS

The rising interest in career development has been stimulated by new (or at least more vociferously articulated) employee expectations, such as

- increased personal responsibility for their careers
- increased career opportunities
- increased participation in decision making
- more meaningful work leading to a feeling of contribution to society
- increased job challenge and satisfaction
- more opportunities for self-actualization
- more on-the-job learning experiences
- more flexible work schedules
- freedom to immediately experience leisure activities, such as: sabbaticals and community projects
- more openness and honesty from management
- more return on their investment in the organization: wanting an organization that shows that it cares.

Employees who are dissatisfied with any of the above areas or with the "old" motivators of money, status, or other tangible rewards are not hesitating to leave the firm at the first sign of a better offer. And they will leave the second job if conditions are not much better. Job changing, especially among the younger workers who are needed to prime the future management pump, is becoming a common phenomenon. And it is costing management a bundle, especially when the turnover occurs just at the point where the employee is beginning to return some of the initial investment made in training and development. Besides hopscotching from firm to firm, employees of all ages and persuasions are beginning to see "dropping out" as a viable alternative to job stress and dissatisfaction. Men and women, young and old alike, are dropping out, returning to school, touring the country, or changing careers in midstream with increasing frequency.

In addition, employees are prepared to back up their demands for a new lease on working life. The spectacular sales records of self-insight, self-help books, such as *What Color Is Your Parachute?*, point to a population which is ready to assume responsibility for its own career decisions. Today's workers do not show the blind faith or undying loyalty to their employers that those of a decade or so ago demonstrated. Their first loyalty seems to be to themselves.

If this revolution in work attitudes were the only issue with which employers had to deal, some simple resolution, such as sabbaticals or the four-day work week, might help stem the tide. But nothing is ever quite that simple. For while society may have unconsciously developed this attitude revolution, government is also doing all it can to enforce what amounts to a revolution in employment policies.

Beginning with the Equal Pay Act of 1963 and moving quickly along to the Civil Rights Act of 1964, Executive Orders #11141 and #11246, and the Age Discrimination in Employment Act of 1967, this country endorsed the concept of equal employment opportunity, but the concept alone was not sufficient to change the status quo. Affirmative legal action was required for carrying out the spirit of the law, and employers soon found themselves squarely in the middle of the battle.

Beyond simply opening certain job categories to women and minorities, EEO ultimately alters recruitment and selection procedures, paper and pencil tests, physical exams, interviews, and other screening devices, as well as pension plans, compensation systems, seniority systems, performance appraisal processes, job analysis and classification systems, and opportunities for job bidding and training and development. In effect, many businesses have had their personnel systems pulled out from under them. Faced with what boils down to a legislative and judicial imperative, numerous firms have had to change their entire approach to managing human resources. This has meant unanticipated costs for legal fees, internal reviews, validation procedures, policy and procedural changes, labor union disputes, and revisions in selection, promotion, and compensation systems, not to mention back pay awards, reinstatements, and trust funds for minority development.

To further confuse current corporation-employee relations, there are the increasing pressures and expense of keeping up with technological change. Our knowledge base is growing so quickly that individuals will no longer be able to think in terms of career education, but rather of a lifetime of multiple careers. It will be (and in fact already is) the job of the organization to assist its employees in coping with this rapid change. The firm must be prepared to help its employees avoid the erosion of their skills and the onset of individual obsolescence.

Rapid changes in business technology require flexible employees and employers who are receptive to change. Those who cannot meet this demand become difficult to utilize. Management is then faced with a difficult decision: how to maintain productivity levels without having to terminate employees who contributed years of effective performance before reaching obsolescence. Complicating this issue, of course, is the implication of possible age discrimination. It is not an easy decision to make.

THE ORGANIZATIONAL RESPONSE

During the days of a rapidly growing economy, organizations could better bear the burden of retaining some marginal performers. Total revenue was growing fast enough to allow many companies to relax their vigilance on cost control. Under such conditions it was possible to avoid or postpone the ultimate blow to the employee's self-esteem by moving obsolescent employees out of the mainstream of activity and into a less vital position where they could be carried until retirement. Today this option has virtually disappeared.

Economic growth has greatly slowed and inflationary costs are eroding profits. Efficiency, profitability, corporate growth, and perhaps even survival of the firm depend upon maximum utilization and development of all corporate resources, including the individual employee. With legal and regulatory actions, capital costs, and governmental procurement shifts largely beyond the control of individual companies, management has turned to areas within its direct influence and control to improve profitability and assure sustained growth. One of these areas is human resource management. Companies are more than ever coming to see that an investment in developing people, whether they are men or women, minority or majority, old or young, managerial or clerical, is an investment in the future of the organization.

Considerable attention is being directed toward getting maximum benefit from human resources. A company cannot succeed in meeting its corporate goals if it is plagued by high turnover rates and low productivity, or if it has an inadequate base from which to draw fresh management talent. How to attract, keep, and fully use talented, innovative employees who have their own personal concerns has become a basic corporate need.

To meet this need, a variety of personnel-related techniques have evolved. Recruitment programs, performance reviews and appraisals, training programs, and management development seminars are among the key tools of any personnel department. These tools were all designed to better use the talent that a corporation possesses in its employees. Unfortunately many of these programs are less effective than they might be because they are not integrated closely with (or may even be working at odds with) one another, and because they do not take into account the actual career interests of the individual.

A carefully planned and thoughtfully implemented career development program can provide the means to help an organization combat this lack of integration. Such a program pulls the assortment of human resource development activities together into a coherent unit and provides links with the organization's bottom line. A well-designed career development effort can (1) help identify individual talents and desires and place employees in work situations that are personally meaningful because of relevance to those talents and desires, (2) assist employees to view the organization as one that respects their unique abilities and encourages their utilization and growth, (3) involve employees in communicating their needs and aspirations at all levels of the organization, and (4) enable individuals to continually develop their potential and to be challenged by future learning possibilities. In short, a full range of human resource problems, evidenced by symptoms such as frequent turnover, skill deficiencies, low morale, or decreased productivity, may be addressed by a career development effort.

Career development supports the recognition that different individuals are motivated to on-the-job effectiveness by different organizational endeavors. For example, while the security of continually demonstrating talents on the same job may stimulate one person, new experiences or a perceived chance for growth and change may stimulate another. While some employees may be inspired by a sense of organizational "caring" about their well-being, others may want more specific rewards and incentives for continued growth. Career development, with its emphasis on ongoing diagnosis of individuals' unique needs and capacities, allows organizations to discover and direct appropriate means of satisfying a variety of employee preferences, while at the same time meeting organizational needs in the most efficient manner—filling jobs with people best suited to them.

A FRAMEWORK FOR ACTION

There is a need today to define a new relationship between the employee and the corporation, to develop a relationship that blends the individual's career objectives into overall corporate goals. When it is effective in this, career development cuts across traditional organizational boundaries. It cannot be constrained by arbitrary functional designations.

Human resource practitioners who restrict career development to the role of a single event (such as a goal-setting workshop or an annual career discussion) force it to become an isolated end with no particular influence over the organization or any of the other units of which the organization is comprised. Integration of the different aspects of career development and human resource development becomes virtually impossible under these conditions, and the potential effectiveness of the program is lost.

To be effective, then, a new system is in order—one that realigns these boundaries and allows the career development practitioner access to people and information throughout the organization. This can be accomplished by shifting our perspective to focus upon the career development effort as our system of interest, and by looking at other human resource development activities as they might relate to that effort.

The Players

Every career development effort requires the participation of three distinct groups of players: the organization, represented by top management; the individual, represented by those employees who elect (or are selected) to participate in the program; and the practitioner, represented by a professional staff with the responsibility for the career development effort. (In those organizations which may not have professional career development practitioners, the line supervisor will sometimes inherit the practitioner's role. In other situations the supervisor may have a follow-on role that is involved in the later implementation of career development efforts.) These players interact with one another within a common environment containing all the political, legal, social, economic, cultural, and natural forces that influence the program in different ways.

This book is addressed to persons termed practitioners. These practitioners might be full-time career development professionals; they may be human resource staff personnel who are charged with the development and implementation of a career development effort; they might be training and development professionals who find themselves working in the career development field as a result of organizational needs, EEO requisites, or AAP requirements; or they may be line managers and supervisors involved part time in career development programs for their subordinates. No matter what the case this book is aimed at and meant to serve as a guide for whoever is fulfilling the practitioner role at any particular time in the career development program.

The world of career development, then, can be shown to embrace a larger and more complex environment than that of the organization alone, or of a single individual's attempts at development. It is important to understand the interaction and interdependence between the individual and the organization, and the impact of programmatic intervention on each, in order to manage an effective career development effort. Exhibit 1-1 illustrates the interaction between the players and their shared environment. This comprises the formal career development effort elaborated in this book.

The Six-Stage Process

A complete career development effort moves sequentially through six stages and involves separate as well as interactive participation by each of the three players described above. Each of these stages constitutes a vital step in a complete career development effort, yet each has substantial payoff of its own. Although the greatest return on investment comes at the completion of all six stages, there are distinct contributions to both the individual and the organization at the conclusion of each stage. The relative emphasis, discreteness, and interconnectedness of these stages, though, can vary greatly among organizations.

This six-stage career development model can provide the framework by which the practitioner can link the frequently disconnected activities of the human resource department. The same stages also serve as the guiding framework for the design of workshops and individually directed career

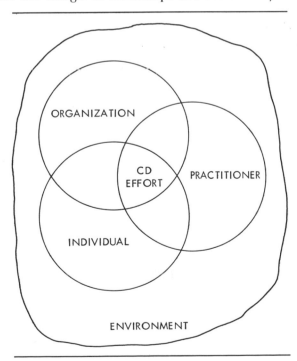

Exhibit 1-1   Interacting Players

counseling sessions. The stages become a checklist to facilitate evaluation—by comparing an existing program to the stages in the model, one can identify areas that have been neglected or areas that have been over-emphasized. Practitioners can also use the model to identify stages within their influence, as well as to understand the broader picture of organizational career development. A clear understanding of the processes involved in each of the six stages will provide a guide to determining which steps must be undertaken to introduce career development as the human resource umbrella. The stages are introduced here and are described in detail in the ensuing chapters.

Stage 1: Preparation.   Preparation, the first stage in the cycle, begins with an organizational response to a perceived need. Two distinct processes are involved: *analysis* and *planning*.

The combined processes involve several tasks: (1) analyzing needs and demands (2) formulating objectives that respond to those needs, (3) developing programming to accomplish those objectives, (4) assigning responsibility for execution of the programs, (5) determining evaluation methodology, (6) outlining the ongoing human resource activities that can be linked to the program, (7) charting new activities that must be accomplished to make the program work, and (8) readying resources necessary for the succeeding five stages. The thoroughness with which this is done will largely determine return on investment that the organization can expect to receive from the program.

While it is more effective to involve all three players at each stage, some clearly dominate others at different points in the cycle. At the Preparation Stage, the organization and the practitioner are the dominant players involved, although it is definitely to the advantage of the program to involve representatives of the target employee population to be addressed.

By the conclusion of the Preparation Stage organization members are introduced to the career development effort. The program design is determined, and resources are committed. These two outcomes—plans and commitment—largely determine the eventual effectiveness of the program.

Stage 2: Profiling.   The Profiling Stage is the first to more actively involve individual employees. The dominant players become the practitioner and the employee who together undertake the processes of *identification* and *reality-testing*.

The *identification* phase poses the question, "Who am I?" The purpose of identification is to consider an individual's capacity (sum of personal skills, values, and interests, as well as work contexts or desired environ-

STAGE 1—Preparation
  Analysis
  Planning
STAGE 2—Profiling
  Identification
  Reality-Testing
STAGE 3—Targeting
  Exploration
  Specification
STAGE 4—Strategizing
  Understanding
  Synthesizing
STAGE 5—Execution
  Resource Acquisition
  Demonstrating Competencies
STAGE 6—Integration
  Evaluation
  Rewards

Exhibit 1-2   The Six Stages of Career Development

ments) in such a way that by verifying, changing, or adding information, the individual's perception of self is strengthened. Individuals are continually appraising themselves and being appraised by others. Identification seeks to make this process conscious and explicit, so that individuals become aware of the assumptions upon which they operate. Only then can positive change be effected.

The *reality-testing* process entails evaluation of personal skills as they are perceived by those who interact with the individual. For example, individuals might discuss the results of the identification phase with their own supervisors. This dialogue between employee and supervisor about overall capacity of the employee should already be a part of the performance appraisal process. Employees who enter this dialogue after working through the identification phase will be better prepared to discuss their own strengths and weaknesses and to evaluate the veracity of their supervisors' reactions. Thus, profiling by employees and their managers should strengthen the performance appraisal interchange.

Profiling culminates in a verified description of the participants' knowledge about their interests, abilities, attitudes, opinions, values, and desired work contexts. As a consequence the participant develops more confidence and is thus willing to consider more development options. As individuals begin to think consciously about identifying and assessing personal characteristics, they will be better able to continue the process on their own.

Stage 3: Targeting. At the Targeting Stage individuals build on the information generated during profiling to select suitable career goals. The two processes involved are *exploration* and *specification*. Although the dominant players are the practitioner and the individual, the involvement of key decision makers is vital. They must share information about the organization's long- and short-range plans so that individuals can develop realistic targets. They must also develop the capacity to utilize the information generated during this stage in succession planning and internal promotion programs.

The *exploration* process involves assisting the individual in choosing a set of simultaneous options for movement within or out of the organization. Six possible career alternatives are available for the individual, including lateral movement and job enrichment as well as traditional vertical mobility. The exploration process is most effective if the individual has an idea about the range of available opportunities and has an understanding of the organization's future plans, so that personal goals may be synchronized with those of the organization. The practitioner's job is to provide employees with a framework for carrying this out.

The *specification* process involves converting the goal from a vague concept into an action-oriented goal statement. This process involves testing each goal for its ease of attainability, relevance, and specificity. It involves using information discovered during the Profiling Stage and knowledge about present and future policies and career opportunities within the organization. This process is facilitated by the practitioner's efforts to provide an arena for teaching the goal-setting process and perhaps by individualized assistance provided by managers or a career development staff, so that goals remain realistic and measurable.

At the conclusion of the Targeting Stage individuals have generated a set of career goals congruent with information about organizational needs and personal abilities, for use in the succeeding stages.

Stage 4: Strategizing. Strategizing involves developing plans to accomplish the goals set in targeting. Because of changes in the organization and in the individual, no one plan is adequate. Therefore, the Strategizing Stage is aimed at developing the contingency capabilities of employees. The dominant player is the individual, with the practitioner often providing technical assistance and parameters for the Strategizing Stage. The role of the organization is to support strategies developed during this process. Strategizing consists of two phases: *understanding the system* and *synthesizing information*.

The first phase involves the individual in an attempt to gain an accurate understanding of the forces that influence life and potential growth in the organization. Individuals come to understand the informal system, with its subtle games of power and politics; gain insight into the culture, with its associated norms and boundaries; and continually attempt to gain insight into their own place within that system.

The second phase, *synthesizing,* involves formulating a specific course of action to reach a particular goal and planning for contingency capabilities. Effective action planning requires having certain organizational information, including knowledge of how people have moved before and of the interim steps necessary to reach certain positions in the organization. This information may be available in the career path progression charts already housed in the organization. By the conclusion of this stage individuals develop a written development plan (with deadlines) for acquiring the skills, training, experience, and resources needed to reach their goals. They also become aware of personal, interpersonal, and organizational forces that may tend to act for or against their plan and consider strategies for coping with them. The practitioner works to provide information, creates opportunities for interaction, and introduces any tools and techniques that might make this stage easier to move through.

Stage 5: Execution.   The Execution Stage involves putting strategies into action. The role of the practitioner is that of facilitator—matching the needs of the individual to the available resources within the organization. Execution involves the acquisition of *specific resources* for goal attainment and the *demonstration* of these new abilities in the organization. Action plans formulated during the Strategizing Stage suggest two types of plans that are pursued during the Execution Stage: (1) plans to acquire the necessary skills, experience, visibility and personal contacts, required for goal achievement, and (2) plans to make new or better use of resources presently possessed by the individual, as actual steps toward goal achievement. The two phases that make up the Execution Stage reflect these categories of action plans.

The Execution Stage delineates the three principal sources of the necessary technical and managerial tools: (1) training and education—gaining skills through training programs sponsored within and outside of the organization, (2) learning based on experience—gaining skills through work on special projects or through on-the-job training, and (3) support-guided development—gaining skills by learning from other people inside and outside of the organization. The individual must select appropriate resources, acquire or master the new skill or knowledge, and demonstrate that new learning within the organization. Although responsibility for the process rests with the individual, organizational support in the form of resources and development dollars can greatly affect the success of the employee during this process.

At the conclusion of the Execution Stage employees will have selected their sources of training. They will have investigated these training sources, decided which seem most appropriate, completed the necessary training, and demonstrated the learned skills. The resulting improvements in performance have been documented by the organization. In addition employees will be aware of additional personal and programmatic resources available to them within the current organizational framework.

Stage 6: Integration. Integration is defined as active movement by individuals toward specific goals they have outlined and as more efficient utilization of human resources within the organization. Although certain earlier processes may be repeated prior to the movement (such as re-verification of a person's capabilities or redirection of one or more career goals), the primary Integration Stage process means productive change for both the organization and the individual.

Integration is the end stage in one complete cycle of the career development process. At this point, both the individual and the organization *evaluate* the efficacy of the career development effort, and *rewards* are appropriately distributed. Individuals examine their own development, while the organization examines and considers the return on investment gained from the process and the degree to which objectives outlined at the Preparation Stage have been met.

The *evaluation* phase involves determining the appropriate evaluation methodology to best address the objectives set during the Preparation Stage. The practitioner must take the lead here in selecting, designing, executing, and reporting results to those organization members who will need to determine the effects the program has had on the bottom line. Although *evaluation* is a continual process and occurs throughout all six stages, it is at the Integration Stage that evaluation must be completed and that results are made visible. Similarly, throughout the process the practitioner has needed to interface with colleagues in compensation and benefits in order to determine appropriate methods for *rewarding* employees who move toward career goals (especially those who move in other than vertical directions) and managers who support that movement. At the Integration Stage these *reward* systems are implemented and made public.

Although the Integration Stage marks the end of the six-stage cycle, it by no means marks the end of developmental planning. For if the effort was successful, individuals should be able to transit the stages again, and the organization and practitioner should be even more prepared to offer continued support and structural assistance.

CHARACTERISTICS OF THE MODEL

Each of the stages previously described constitutes a vital element of a complete career development effort and exhibits important characteristics. Each stage, for example, is integrated with the preceding and succeeding stages to the degree that it absorbs information from the preceding stage and contributes combined information to the succeeding stage. Effective career development occurs only when the program design facilitates progress through all six stages, and when involvement of all three players has been achieved.

Movement between the stages may proceed sequentially or oscillate among stages; yet all six must be traveled at least once for one complete cycle, ending at the Integration Stage. Repetition of any stage is assumed to produce "higher" knowledge or experience, that is, the individual has experienced it once and is, therefore, more sophisticated. For example, on the basis of an action plan formulated in the Strategizing Stage, an individual might return to school to acquire specific skills at the Execution Stage. During that time a different application of those resources might become obvious, prompting a reconsideration of the goals set at the Targeting Stage. The individual's ability to select goals the next time around, however, will be enhanced by previous experience with the process.

Another characteristic is drawn from a law of physics that suggests that movement toward a higher level of order in one system will result in a greater degree of disorder in another system. The more isolated the career development effort, the greater the opportunity for causing disruption in the individual's work or nonwork setting. The practitioner must be aware of the turmoil that can be produced and must design the links necessary to tie the career development process with the routine of the organization and with the personal life of employee participants.

As an employee works toward a higher level position, demanding a greater commitment of time and travel, for instance, the employee's spouse may experience a disruption in the homelife pattern and may not support the move. This negative effect might have been avoided if adequate linkage between the employees' personal world and their career development goals had been established, for example, if spouses were included in the formulation of mutually satisfactory goals during the Targeting Stage. A manager who has not been apprised of or involved in the career development effort may support an employee's participation in a workshop offered on company time but may not be willing to support movement through the Execution Stage, during which the employee seeks to acquire specific skills needed to move toward a particular career goal. The manager may see the career development opportunity as having been provided in the workshop and not in additional hours following that event. The practitioner who sees the necessity of building these vital links prior to the program, and carefully establishes them, will have greater success during program implementation.

While it is not possible to predict every type of disorder that will be generated during career development, understanding potential problems and working through them can help minimize some of the most common disruptions that result from career development efforts.

Because career development efforts exist within organizations whose environments are constantly changing, they are subject to a variety of forces which produce strain, tension, or conflict at each of the stages. The women's movement and accompanying affirmative action edicts for example constitute external forces that have caused tension in many organizations. Practitioners must be aware of the variety of forces that affect the career development effort and must be willing to modify each stage accordingly.

A career development effort is most effective when it is ongoing, integrated in the organization, internalized by the participant, and designed to include all six stages. It is synergistic when it combines all the conditions necessary for each stage in order to provide the maximum benefit to the individual and the organization.

An understanding of the career development framework and accompanying characteristics enables the practitioner to analyze, predict, and manage the processes underlying a career development effort. The framework also provides a mechanism for understanding other isolated human resource activities (described in the next chapter) as they relate to these six stages. The framework additionally accommodates changes in program structure, as required by the process of maturation in each of three players—the organization, the practitioner, and the employee participant.

As long as the functional requirements of each stage are observed, a career development effort can be structured to meet unique needs. It can be simple or sophisticated, use very basic or highly advanced support technology, address secretaries or vice-presidents, and still be successfully described and understood in terms of the six-stage framework.

PAYOFFS: THE BOTTOM LINE

While an organization will not realize every possible payoff from a career development effort, an understanding of what the payoffs might be can help sell the program, by providing managers and career development practitioners with an additional tool for articulating the program's rationale and invoking the commitment of key individuals throughout the organization.

The following lists describe potential payoffs for the organization and for others affiliated with the career development effort.

Payoffs for the Organization

- *Skill building.* Increasing the abilities of employees in their current jobs, as well as enhancing their abilities to adapt to task changes and technological advances.
- *Talent matching.* Providing information about employees' abilities and aspirations, in order to establish a match between organizational needs and individual capabilities.
- *Productivity and morale.* Reducing counterproductive forces—such as high turnover, absenteeism, and grievances—that may result from morale problems

among employees who view themselves as having little opportunity for greater advancement.

- *Motivation.* Stimulating increased employee effectiveness among those who value a climate of growth, challenge, and shared organizational responsibility for personal development.
- *Revitalization.* Creating new challenges and opportunities for those who may have "retired on the job" to use their skills.
- *Advancement from within.* Developing a high-quality group of in-house candidates for promotion to higher positions.
- *Recruitment.* Enhancing the attractiveness of the organizational climate as a place where talented individuals will want to work.
- *Human resource planning.* Providing additional information and resource identification for efforts that assist in determining future needs.
- *Problem identification.* Providing early information about staffing problems, including underutilization and competence deficiences.
- *Image building.* Improving the corporate image as a forward-thinking, contemporary organization that strives to continually improve its operations.
- *Goal commitment.* Clarifying organizational goals for all employees and strengthening employees' understanding of their contributions to those goals.
- *Program integration.* Creating understanding of a system that links career development with other existing human resource processes, such as performance appraisal, pay plans, employee counseling, and career path planning.
- *Equal opportunity.* Helping identify women and minorities with potential for advancement and encouraging development of that potential.
- *Legal implications.* Helping meet legal requirements in areas such as equal pay, equal employment opportunity, and age discrimination.

Payoffs for Managers and Supervisors

- *Communication.* Increasing communication between managers and employees about their current performance and future opportunities.
- *Information.* Providing managers and supervisors with better information about staffing needs, as well as about possibilities for addressing them by developing skills or changing the patterns of using talent.
- *Goal clarity.* Helping managers clarify organizational and unit goals, and how they fit with individual tasks.
- *Developmental responsibilities.* Assisting managers in acquiring skills to counsel and coach employees about developmental concerns.
- *Staffing justification.* Developing information to justify staff increases or cutbacks.
- *Identification.* Supporting efforts to identify employees who can be moved to other responsibilities.
- *Special projects.* Providing inventories of talents that may be called upon when special projects require assembling a task group to meet temporary needs.
- *Personnel decisions.* Helping employees to understand the manager's rationale for making difficult personnel decisions, including selections, promotions, transfers, and discharges.

- *Performance appraisal.* Setting the stage for easier performance review, by enhancing individuals' knowledge of their strengths and weaknesses before their managers formally appraise their work.
- *Motivation.* Establishing commitment and willingness on the part of employees to respond to requests for effective performance and new challenges.
- *Personal development.* Assisting managers to become aware of their own career development needs and to plan strategies for fully developing and using their own talents.

Payoffs for Employees

- *Self-knowledge.* Understanding personal strengths and weaknesses, as well as desires and needs for life and career integration.
- *Organizational knowledge.* Gaining current information that provides greater understanding of personal possibilities and future opportunities within the organization.
- *Sense of purpose.* Focusing on clear multiple goals for the future and developing ways to meet those goals.
- *Self-determination.* Exercising control over aspects of life that may have been felt to be in someone else's hands, gaining a positive, active stance toward life and work.
- *Organizational identity.* Feeling a greater commitment to organizational purposes.
- *Skill building.* Learning new skills that can aid in accomplishing current tasks and also provide wider options for the future.
- *Experimentation.* Seizing opportunities to test new or potential talents and explore different areas of work and learning.
- *Supervisory relations.* Establishing more open communication with supervisors about developmental possibilities, personal performance, and organizational opportunities.
- *Peer relations.* Establishing opportunities for support and feedback from other employees.
- *Personal satisfaction.* Developing self-esteem from growth and learning.
- *Advancement potential.* Enhancing opportunities for advancement into higher positions.
- *Job enrichment.* Recognizing that career growth begins on the current job and that one can increase challenge and stimulation without necessarily moving "up."

Payoffs for the Career Development Practitioner

- *Integration of human resource activities.* Establishing a system that links together a wide range of human resource activities and enhances understanding and use of them in the organization.
- *Information dissemination.* Increasing information flow regarding important organizational issues and practices related to career development and, thus, clarifying to others the role of human resource development work.

- *Image building.* Enhancing professional image and worth by establishing a visible and systematic program that has bottom-line value to the organization.
- *Growth opportunity.* Developing personal talents by undertaking the challenge of planning and administering a far-reaching career development program for the organization.
- *Personal satisfaction.* Gaining a sense of satisfaction from contributing a meaningful service that assists others in personal and professional development.
- *Organizational involvement.* Obtaining involvement and shared responsibility from others—especially managers and supervisors—who may have previously seen human resource development as something "those other folks will take care of."
- *General program support.* Demonstrating success in a major program in a way that can help elicit support for ongoing or future human resource development programs.
- *Personal development.* Becoming more aware of one's personal development, and applying career development processes and strategies to one's own organizational life.

When fully implemented, career development can become the mission that gives meaning to the variety of human resource activities within the organization, and thus can the organization strengthen. Without such a linkage, communication between individual programs and the organization is often sporadic, blocked, or nonexistent. A typical example of this can be seen in organizations that have one department planning future human resource needs and other departments handling training and other personnel functions. Overall corporate human resource requirements may never be conveyed to the people planning an affirmative action program, affirmative action needs may never be conveyed to recruiters, and line managers' training needs may never be conveyed to trainers. As a result programs are likely to be much less effective than they could be, and employees may become frustrated by the lack of coherent information about future career possibilities within the organization.

A career development framework that has clear steps and that links other human resource activities to those steps can be a strong integrating force within an organization. A career development practitioner trained in building this framework can provide a focal point for individual, corporate, and personnel interests. The next chapter will describe the preparation necessary for the career development effort. It will showcase those human resource development activities that can be linked to the stages of the career development cycle and will suggest strategies necessary to preparing for a strong, integrated career development effort.

READYING RESOURCES
the preparation stage

" . . . but when will it look as if we're really <u>doing</u> something?"

The preparation for any new organizational effort typically occurs when someone decides, "Looks like a good idea; could pay off; we can probably find some start-up funds; Harry, you take it." It all looks and sounds so simple: it is merely a matter of deciding to act, making an initial commitment of resources, and assigning responsibility.

But is it really that simple? Do successful programs happen "just like that"? And if they do get started so simply and easily, why devote a full chapter of this book to the Preparation Stage?

Career development efforts are not only complex and long term; they go beyond most other human resource efforts in one important respect: they directly and continually affect the work lives of people at all levels and in all parts of the organization, and, very often, they have tremendous impact upon the actual structure of the organization itself. The practitioner who is going to be involved with career development will be highly visible within the organization and will find that the career development effort touches upon a host of other personnel programs which may be ongoing or planned for the future.

To be successful, therefore, career development must be the most carefully planned, most totally supported, most intricately linked with other efforts, most delicately executed, and most thoroughly monitored and evaluated of all human resource programs. At their best career development efforts are synonymous with human resource development.

At their worst they can disrupt lives and organizations on a scale far greater than anything else.

For these reasons it is imperative that those charged with the design and implementation of career development programs make their preparations as carefully as would an advertising executive planning a crucial campaign.

A MODEL TO MODEL

In the first chapter readers were introduced to a six-stage model of career development. The Preparation Stage is, for the practitioner and the organization, a microcosm of the same model, that is the practitioner in preparation will move through the same steps that the individual will be moving through, once the plan gets underway. The format will be the same but will involve many more people, will require a much greater expenditure of effort, and will take a great deal of time before its rewards and benefits will be seen or felt.

The Preparation Stage alone will require

- *Preparation*—Getting things ready to go.
- *Profiling*—Determining where the organization is (that is, the status quo) and what its needs will be.
- *Targeting*—Establishing goals and objectives to meet those needs.
- *Strategizing*—Developing specific plans to accomplish those goals.
- *Execution*—Providing mechanisms for implementing the plans.
- *Integration*—Designing the means to evaluate the program and tie it into the existing and projected efforts of other parts of the organization.

Practitioners at this stage are very often confronted by a host of feelings: "It's too big!" "It involves too much!" "I cannot do it!" They feel a kinship with and understanding of the sailor who prayed, "Oh, Lord, help me. The sea is so big and my boat is so small."

These fears and feelings are understandable. The task is large. It will require a great deal of effort, but the purpose of this chapter is to provide a way in which that task can be taken on, one piece at a time, in a step-by-step process, which makes it accomplishable. This process will not only make planning the career development effort easier; it will also allow the practitioner to work through the model as a basic planning process and learn its value. (Although the model will be followed, the stages will not necessarily be identified individually. This will be done in order to spare readers from an overly academic treatment and to provide a more informal presentation.)

Exhibit 2-1 will help to identify the two major phases of this stage:

I. Analysis
    A. Preparation
        1. Why Career Development?
        2. Introducing Change
    B. Profiling
        1. Structural Supports: Human Resource Development Links
        2. Individual Supports: Program Approaches
II. Planning
    A. Targeting
        1. Setting Program Goals
        2. Determining Roles and Responsibilities
    B. Strategizing
        1. Building the Plan
        2. Assisting in Implementation
    C. Execution
        1. Getting Underway
        2. Overcoming Resistance
    D. Integration
        1. Evaluation
        2. Avoiding Errors

Exhibit 2-1 Two Major Phases of the Preparation Stage

ANALYSIS

Why Career Development?

The first task of preparation is to determine the scope and nature of the career development effort through analyzing the needs, problems, and activities that led to the career development effort and that will, eventually, determine its objectives. The primary responsibility for this first step rests with the career development practitioner or a generalist manager who has overview responsibilities. There are many reasons why organizations undertake career development programs. The practitioner, especially, must be clear on this issue. Where does the need or demand for career development originate in this organization? What signals are organization members sending to suggest the need for career development? The answers to these questions require an examination of why career development is important, what problems it may help address, and who the beneficiaries of the program may be.

Chapter 1 outlined a variety of social, legal, and technological factors contributing to the current need to reassess the organization's responsibilities to its work force. Underlying all these factors is the pervasive need to develop a work force that is capable of and committed to maximizing organizational effectiveness—and thus to ensure the continued health of the organization. The best of advanced technology, efficient structure, and enlightened leadership is of little avail if individual employees are under-utilized, underskilled, dissatisfied, or disaffected by organizational purposes.

Following the Trend. Addressing future trends can not only assist analysis of the need for career development, but can also provide a valuable aid in selling the program to top management. All too often organizations find themselves fighting fires rather than aggressively plan-ning for future trends and changes. Practitioners who can provide ideas and forums for discussions and problem solving (avoidance) will be providing a valuable benefit to their organizations.

Sixteen major developments, issues, and events that have had an impact on organizations in the last two decades of the twentieth century have been identified. Knowing these trends can provide practitioners with a valuable tool for brainstorming about the need for career development programs and organizational planning. They can be examined in the light of

- How these trends may affect the organization and its employees, and
- How a systemic career development effort could address these problematic situations.

To aid practitioners in generating brainstorming sessions, discussion examples have been included with the first three items. Additional, or different, examples will aid the process.

1. Microelectronics and telecommunications will advance to the point that people will be able to work at home, have access to a wide variety of information/ communication resources, and perform functions formerly requiring travel. The fusion of data processing and telecommunications will also permit the gradual elimination of written records, mail, and related services at the office.

   (Discussion Example: In late 1980 a major insurance company instituted an experiment in which all policyholder paperwork was eliminated and total reliance upon data and word processing and telecommunications was in-stituted. What are possible ramifications of such a policy on an organization's filing, billing, and accounting functions? What new skills will be required of people in those functions if they are to remain productive? What new career paths will open? What career paths will close? What does this suggest for the planning of an organization-wide career development effort?)

2. Technological knowledge will expand to render entire job categories obsolete and allow for increased automation of manufacturing. This will markedly reduce the need for unskilled and semiskilled labor, but should generate new types of jobs as well.

   (Discussion Example: Automated multiple-function welding machines have eliminated a great many welder requirements in the automobile manufacturing industry. What are possible effects of such machines on future needs for skilled welders and solderers in American industry? What developmental actions will be necessary if those currently employed in those career fields are to remain

profitably employed? How will managers and supervisors be affected by these changes in technology? How can a career development effort avert major problems?)

3. Higher productivity and capital investment will be difficult to generate, despite increasing demands to do so. These demands will create conflict with rising expectations and existing entitlements.
   (Discussion Example: Some organizations are experimenting with wage and benefit programs that are tied to productivity rates. What could be the effects of such a policy on highly labor-intensive organizations? On high-technology organizations? What new skills would be required of managers and supervisors under such a plan? How would movement along career paths be affected?)

4. There will be a slowdown in real economic growth, possibly involving recession and/or depression. These developments will be exacerbated by persistently high rates of inflation, which will continue to erode our standard of living.

5. World competition for shrinking resources will result in heightened economic nationalism and international tensions, possibly leading to war.

6. The work force will undergo important demographic changes, such as a shortage of young employees, a pronounced middle age bulge (53% of the labor force will be 25 to 44 years old by 1990), and a growing percentage of older workers (7.6% increase per year).

7. The expanding role of women will have a profound impact upon the work place (60% of new jobs are likely to be filled by women), the home (70% of employable women will be working by 1990), and society in general (fertility rates have decreased from 3.8 to 1.8 children per woman of childbearing age over the last thirty years). For these and other reasons traditional role identities will continue to change and blur.

8. A basic shift in values from the traditional work ethic to a focus on self-actualization and leisure will require an enhanced quality of work life, greater participation in decision making, and alternatives to established work patterns to overcome growing alienation from work.

9. Competition for jobs, particularly among an increasingly overeducated and aware workforce, will lead to social and generational conflict, a backlash against affirmative action, and possibly a job lottery/draft system.

10. A larger percentage of the population will adopt the new entitlement mentality, which transforms personal needs into social rights, and may well expect expansion of this domain to create a zero-risk society. Continued growth of this mentality will certainly intensify expectations that organizations be socially responsible, ethical, fair to employees, and responsive to other stakeholders.

11. Bilingualism, polarization, and racial conflict will arise as immigration from underdeveloped nations continues to grow and third world people increase as a percentage of the population and the workforce.

12. The revolt against high taxation and uncontrolled government growth will continue, posing potentially grave problems for those dependent upon social programs and raising the specter of serious class conflict, as well as a crisis of confidence in our system of government.

13. All pervasive government will become immobilized, as its fear of alienating special interest groups, dependent upon the status quo, prevents it from solving critical national issues. This could deepen the present trend toward political conservatism into a desire for strong, authoritarian leadership to solve

pressing problems and increased conflict. On the other hand, it may encourage the development of loose-knit organizations that believe in shared control.

14. Continued existence/evolution may require world view transformations of the basic premises upon which modern industrial society, third world status, and present perceptions of reality are based. The development of new age paradigms (such as holograms and heterarchy) will accompany these basic belief system transformations.

15. Situations that are complex, multicausal, and holographic in character will frustrate our attempts to apply linear mechanistic approaches to problem identification and solution in the future.

16. New age values and a growing awareness of factors related to health will result in greater emphasis upon nutrition, exercise, stress reduction, and holistic health philosophies and practice.[1]

Though discussing the issues just mentioned could seem somewhat remote from the career development process, the need for more complete long-range planning is becoming more and more apparent.

Even economists, who have often been accused of operating with one foot in the present and the other in the past, are beginning to have concerns about the capabilities of managers and organizations to meet future needs. Robert J. Samuelson, in his column in the *Los Angeles Times,* says that one of the primary causes of the United States's slippage in the area of technology, which occurred during the 1970s, was management's overconcern with the short-term situation at the expense of providing for the future. He feels that managers and organizations have needs for increased competence in the technical area and a greater awareness of future trends and problems.[2]

Practitioners who can design and implement career development programs that address long-term organizational needs, therefore, will not only be making contributions to the personnel goals of organizations but could very well be providing management with tools with which to forecast and prepare for conditions ten, twenty, or thirty years hence, and, at the same time, selling top management on the need for such a program.

A Need in Deed. If career development programs and practitioners are to be effective adjuncts to the organizational effort, future trends and philosophies must be considered. However, the future is not the only area of concern. The feelings, attitudes, and personal "hang-ups" of those in the organization who are actually concerned with career development must also be taken into account.

Message Analysis is one process that the practitioner may use to assist individuals and groups to uncover and discuss these factors. It may be used to identify how those working together feel about the need for a career development program or, on a larger scale, how division, group, or department heads see the need for (or may support) the effort. The purpose is the same—determining where the starting place is that has the most probability of program success.

Exhibit 2-2 is an example of a Message Analysis worksheet that could have been completed by members of an organization that decided to start a career development effort with a particular target group, and that used the process to assess each group's attitudes toward that effort.

Questions which can be used by the practitioner include

1. If a spokesman for each of the groups identified were to send you a clear, uncensored, unfiltered message regarding the career development effort, what would it be? Penetrate for the underlying meaning or underlying message.
2. Is the message real (true)? That is, do you like it? Do you agree with it? What in the organization maintains it as such? What can be done to turn the message more in support of the career development effort?
3. Is the message a myth (false)? If so, what in the system perpetuates it? What can be done to end or to debunk this myth?
4. Where does this analysis suggest we begin? Which group might be most supportive? Where would we be likely to succeed?

The need for career development—and other human resource development programs that are linked to it—relates directly to the need for more effective employees. Profitability and performance are often seen as the bottom line, and career development is viewed as a means to that end. Career development can materially enhance the abilities, commitment, and appropriate skill utilization necessary to motivate and activate employees to increased effectiveness. In this way it offers a return on investment based on higher personal and organizational productivity.

Determining the sources of need for career development can help in setting relevant program goals, in designing appropriate activities and, not insignificantly, in justifying or selling the program to others in the

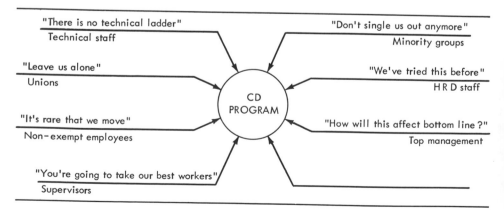

Exhibit 2-2 A Technique for Finding a Starting Place

organization. Organizational analysis and diagnosis is therefore the first vital step in the Preparation Stage.

To Begin, You Begin

Once practitioners have established that a career development program is actually needed and desired by the organization, the next step is to fully prepare for the long and arduous task of designing the most effective program possible.

Chance and Change. Of primary importance in this personal preparation is the recognition that career development is going to introduce change into the organization. It would be nice if change could be accomplished with no accompanying disruption, but because it is what it is, change disturbs, or totally alters, the status quo and often causes conflict. As a result practitioners must be prepared to deal with a variety of action, reactions, and counteractions once the program is introduced.

Why do organizations and the people within them resist change? A great deal has been written on this subject, most of which can be summed up as follows:

- Change is resisted because it is not understood.
- Change is resisted because it transfers control of the situation from the one who is exercising it to others who are imposing the change.
- Change is resisted because people do not feel that they possess the skills to deal with the new situation.
- Change is resisted because those who are subjected to it feel that excessive demands are going to be placed upon their time and energy.[3]

Practitioners, in order to ensure the success of the career development effort, must be, or become, expert agents of change. They must recognize ways in which organizations will resist change.

- *Ignoring the change* by simply refusing to recognize that it has or is about to occur.
- *Compartmentalizing the change* by allowing it to take place in only a limited area or to a limited degree, for example, tokenism.
- *Limiting the change* to the least acceptable amount that will be allowed by the powers that be, for example, paying lip service to the change by showcasing only the most obvious part of it.
- *Co-opting the change* so that it serves the ends of the organization or individual rather than those intended, for example, distorting a change in order to allow the group or person to continue as before.[4]

How can this resistance be avoided?

Structure vs. People.   Change can be effected by altering the structure in which people operate or by attempting to modify the behavior of the individuals themselves. Individual habits and behaviors are extremely resistant to change because they are ingrained and personalized. Normally, therefore, the most effective way in which change can be introduced is through the structure or organizational policies themselves. When the structure within which individuals operate is altered, they will, by necessity, change themselves in order to adapt.

Though the most effective way to introduce change is through the structure, anyone who has ever attempted to modify a procedure or alter an existing reporting arrangement (or—heaven forbid—a performance appraisal program) knows that organizations will strongly resist any tampering whatsoever, regardless of its intentions or probability for increasing effectiveness. Therefore, most career development programs have followed the path of least resistance and aimed their efforts solely at individual behavioral change through workshops or counseling programs. This is not to say that such an approach is wrong or undesirable. The contention here, however, is that to ensure success and to effect lasting change *both* the structure and the individual will have to be addressed.

In either case, practitioners must often be prepared to deal with hard-core resistance to change. They will be called upon to show why the change is needed and to get others involved in the problem-solving process. They will have to gain the active support of not only top management but also of the formal and informal opinion leaders of the organization, and the practitioners would do well to find someone with influence to sponsor the change process.

It will be necessary to realistically consider all of the possible consequences of the proposed changes and provide options or trade-offs in order to make the changes and their ramifications more palatable. Practitioner agents of change may also find it necessary to help the organization's leadership realize the risks involved in the effort and develop reward systems for those willing to take those risks. They may find themselves in the forefront of dramatic structural or technological changes and be called upon to demonstrate how the changes will benefit those involved. In extreme cases it may be necessary to provide means for the organization to coerce those who are most reluctant into accepting the change.[5]

One of the most effective ways to head off many of the problems associated with change is to set a tone of candor and realism at the very beginning about what a career development effort can and cannot do. This can also help defuse the "Yes, but…." responses from defenders of the organizational status quo and can steer program participants and others to a realistic level of expectations. As the word about career development spreads, it is important to emphasize that career development does not deal with vertical mobility alone—"up is *not* the only way." This message should be reinforced throughout all program phases, as it will reduce those unrealistic expectations. Supervisors and employees must realize that upward mobility is only one possibility in the career development realm— albeit often the most accepted and seductive direction for today's organizational man or woman. They must recognize that career development can also mean movement laterally, downward, out of the organization, or toward enrichment within the current job. The employee may take on new challenges or different tasks that are personally meaningful and rewarding but that do not necessarily require a move to the next higher rung on the corporate ladder.

It is also important to clarify (over and over) that career development is not a panacea for all mobility problems. In all organizations there are a limited number of job openings, and movement into them can be slow. Furthermore, if career development equaled only upward mobility, the ultimate value to the organization would be slow to materialize and difficult to identify. Nothing about a career development effort is quick or easy. Clearly its greatest potential may take longer to realize than many managers and rank-and-file employees would prefer.

"Small Is Beautiful." All too often programs fail before actually getting off the ground because they are too massive in their approach and attempt too much too soon—before the organization is ready to accept the concept of career development. This can be avoided by beginning "small," only after a thorough understanding of organizational and individual needs and supports has been established. This may mean that some practitioners will have to deal with pressures to "make a showing" or "just do something." Handling the pressure to begin something big may be difficult, but those who persevere will be rewarded in the long run.

Rather than beginning with an organization-wide effort, practitioners may find it advantageous to begin with a focused effort in one particular portion of the organization, where support for career development has already been established. A close analysis of attitudes displayed in the Message Analysis conducted earlier may show one manager, one unit, one division, or one target group of the organization that is ready for career development. Beginning in a place where support is strong can accomplish a great deal toward ensuring success. In such case beginning "small" may mean beginning with a guarantee.

Another aspect of the "start small" admonition is that it is not necessary to "re-invent the wheel" in order to begin a successful career development program. Certain departments or divisions may have built-in structural supports that are already providing a basis upon which to build. Massive change of the organization may not be necessary. The first step, then, is to investigate and analyze the sources of support and help that are already available.

Who Can Help?   Clearly involvement and commitment from all three "players" identified in Chapter 1 is crucial at this stage, as they are throughout the remaining five stages. Top management should be closely involved, in order to provide resource allocation information, problem-solving advice, contextual limitations, and long-range goal directions. It is crucial to obtain full "sponsorship"—not just lip service—of key managers for two reasons: (1) if uncommited, they can easily sabotage the program by discouraging (or failing to encourage) employee involvement and revoking resources, and (2) if committed, they can substantially promote program visibility, which signals others to assist in making it succeed. If top management is involved at early stages, and if they can see clear benefits for themselves and for the organization, the success potential for the career development effort at later stages is greatly enhanced.

The involvement of select human resource development (HRD) professionals (in addition to the practitioner) is also vital. If the personnel or human resource staff is not committed as a staff, the program will lose data necessary to its success. Often members of a personnel/HRD staff do not see the relevance of their own units to the career development effort. Attempts by the practitioner to assist colleagues in recognizing their special contributions to career development will result in substantial payoff.

One way to assist personnel staff in visualizing their input is to develop a "contribution matrix" and invite managers of specific personnel functions to brainstorm and contribute ideas at each career development stage. A workshop or retreat setting is ideal for generating this data and for formally and effectively launching the Preparation Stage. Exhibit 2-3 is an example.

In addition to involving top management and HRD professionals, the wise career development practitioner will also involve line managers as representatives of the user department(s) to be addressed in the program, or if one has not been defined, representatives of various levels and functions in the work force. Such representation would complete the necessary cast of players discussed in the preceding chapter.

At the earliest time possible all of these representatives should be organized into an advisory body to act as a guiding and reference task force throughout the program. The payoff for forming this group will be great. Such a task force will provide the practitioner charged with the overall "get it off the ground" responsibility assistance in the form of sounding boards, channels to the "outside," stimulation, and challenge. The task force participants are sure to gain new skills in program design, interpersonal awareness, and sensitivity to organizational needs. For many, participation in a task force of this type will be in itself a kind of job enrichment. The organization also benefits when this effort becomes, not just one more program designed in some dark corner by a practitioner, but a collective effort that requires active involvement from disparate parts of the organization.

Contributions	Training and Development Staff	Wage and Compensation Staff	Human Resource Planning Staff
To Profiling	Sponsoring workshops and administering tests to identify employee skills		
To Targeting			Providing information about jobs that will be needed and jobs that will be deleted in the organization's future
To Strategizing		Assisting development of career paths	
To Execution	Providing skill training and seminars		
To Integration		Determining new reward systems	

Exhibit 2-3   A Contribution Matrix

CAREER DEVELOPMENT TASK FORCE: PROSPECTIVE PARTICIPANTS

Top Management	HRD Professionals	Employee Representatives
Who will best articulate the feelings and insights of the top? Who can most easily carry back information?	Who has information and expertise to contribute?	Whose area will be affected? Which line managers can make important contributions?

Use this chart to jot down names of potential task force members as they occur to you.

Exhibit 2-4   Career Development Task Force Planner

The analysis phase of the Preparation Stage is aimed at giving management and the career development practitioner a clear picture of how the organization's current needs, opportunities, and activities relate or may eventually become related to career development. This can substantially aid the organization in clarifying rationale and goals of career development, in determining the necessary components of preparation, and in developing criteria by which the eventual success of the program can be measured. The endproducts of serious analysis are clear program intentions and objectives. The activities undertaken during this phase are not necessarily chronological steps and, therefore, many of them may be undertaken simultaneously.

Now is the time to dust off corporate goal statements, internal reports and reviews, growth and human resource plans, and issue papers. These can provide a wealth of information for analyzing why and how the organization might benefit from a career development program; they can aid in making the goals of the program consistent with overall plans and needs.

Linking HRD Activities: The Structural Supports

During this stage the practitioner will also want to fully review existing human resource activities to determine which ones represent necessary links to the career development effort. Typically, these have already been established through a variety of efforts that fall under the aegis of human resource development, but they may not have been integrated into a system that is recognized as a coordinated career development approach. Also, it is likely that some programs of activities that are needed to support career development are either incomplete or missing, and it may be necessary to get them in place before the effort is formally announced to employees.

It is during this analysis that prior inclusion of other HRD staff on the career development task force will prove to be valuable. With these professionals taking part in the review and analysis of programs there will be less possibility that they will see the career development effort as competing with their own programs. Rather, they will probably appreciate how ongoing human resource events can actually complement and mutually support the career development effort.

The HRD links described here are those activities which can both reinforce and be reinforced by an integrated organizational career development effort. They affect the various stages and in turn are affected by them. They provide information vital to the career development program and assure its interaction with organizational principles and policies. Establishment of the six-stage career development framework suggested here benefits these other programs by providing an integrative and coordinating element and encouraging employees to be more responsible in using the programs. There are several generic human resource links suggested here that provide input to various stages of the career development process. Although these links may differ from one organization to another, they are discussed more to suggest ways in which practitioners might look at their own unique systems to select appropriate activities than to be seen as *the* HRD activities vital to a successful program.

At the Preparation Stage, for example, the practitioner must know the basic direction of the organization, its *human resource plans* and *future trend forecasts,* as well as its *affirmative action* goals and timetables (career development contributes substantially toward meeting affirmative action guidelines). Appropriate supervisory training must also be available if supervisors are to have a central role as career coaches. Such training must occur prior to the program's inception.

Skills identified during the Profiling Stage are useless unless they are tested against reality. The *performance appraisal* is a perfect vehicle for this in-depth assessment. Moreover, skills identified and tested against reality must be documented and catalogued if the organization is to benefit substantially—a *skill inventory* can store such information.

At the Targeting Stage not only do individuals and their managers need to once more make use of organizational *forecasting information;* they also need to know the *succession plans* that have been outlined so that employee goals can be set in light of these organizational plans. It will further help in

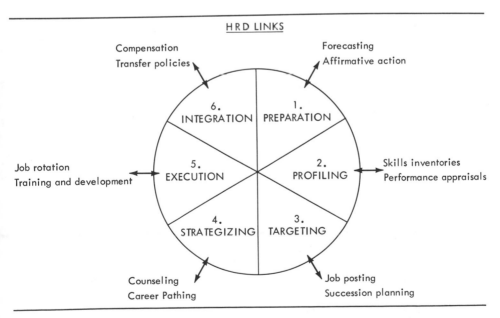

Exhibit 2-5   The Career Development Process and Human Resource Development Links

determining of realistic goals if the employees can make use of a *job posting system* (anything from a simple bulletin board display to an elaborate computerized system) to see if they have the skills required for particular positions and to determine the scope of job opportunities available.

Similarly at the Strategizing Stage, employees will have an easier time developing an action plan if they can be apprised of the *career paths* followed by others in similar jobs, to determine if the action plan they are pursuing makes sense. When strategies indicate unexpected directions, employees may wish to avail themselves of specific *counseling*, such as preretirement or outplacement counseling.

During the Execution Stage the employee is expected to follow through on an action plan. This may mean taking advantage of certain *training and development* opportunities or gaining skills through an assortment of *on-the-job training* programs. Although rewards come throughout the six-stage process, it is at the Integration Stage that the organization witnesses movement and responds with fair *compensation, promotion, and transfer policies* that meet the needs of a diverse employee population.

Minimally the concerned practitioner could respond to the career development call by organizing a few specialized activities, such as a workshop which covers or alludes to most of the stages in the model. Clearly a workshop could present appropriate and meaningful profiling, targeting, and strategizing techniques. It could even introduce the Execution Stage by describing the availability of in-house resources or by distributing a catalogue of courses and tuition reimbursement policies.

However, *a workshop is seldom sufficient.* If the practitioner sincerely wants to see maximum career growth and change for the organization, structural supports must be introduced. Structural supports are those human resource activities that can be institutionalized and adopted system wide. They exist as a clear statement of the organization's commitment to individual growth and development. The human resource development links just described are examples of structural elements. They must be *identified, studied,* and, if necessary, *upgraded* so that they truly support each career development stage.

The beauty of such a system is that the benefits are twofold. Each of the human resource development activities reinforces a particular career development program stage and is, in turn, reinforced by that stage. The information available through job posting, for example, adds valuable supplemental data to the process of targeting career goals. In turn, employees' awareness of and ability to intelligently use the job posting system is reinforced by knowledge gained during the activities of the Targeting Stage—more employees are apt to make appropriate use of job posting, if only to gain more information for use in formulating their career goals. In this manner one clear benefit of career development will be more active use of current human resource development systems by employees. (Granted, this may be frightening to some practitioners and some organizations!)

In practice, however, the links are not usually as clear as might be suggested. Typically there is a great deal of overlap between the stages and their supporting HRD activities, with many of the HRD activities affiliated with more than one stage. Performance appraisal is a good example of an HRD link that, if well done, is actually affiliated with—reinforces and is reinforced by—all of the career development stages. Visually it could be drawn as shown in Exhibit 2-6.

Performance appraisal begins with (1) the manager and the employee *preparing* for the process. It assists the employee and manager in (2) *profiling* the strengths and weaknesses of the employee in connection with current job responsibilities and gives feedback about the employee's own self-assessment. It provides a means by which they can (3) *target* future career paths or areas toward which the employee might aspire while establishing specific objectives for continued growth on the present job. Together manager and employee (4) *strategize* ways in which the employee might pursue his or her objectives and determine (5) a developmental plan and activities for *executing* the plan, which encourages the employee to add certain skills to his or her repertoire. At the conclusion of the process,

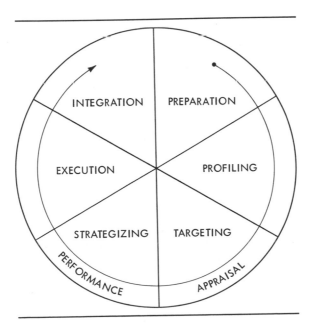

Exhibit 2-6 The Performance Appraisal Process as an HRD Link

(6) the *Integration* Stage, the employee is rewarded (merit increases) for his or her work, and the process begins again.

Each of the succeeding chapters will discuss these links as they apply to the stage that seems most relevant. Readers are advised to determine those links that are familiar in their own organizations and to affiliate them with stages that they consider significant. All human resource activities must be investigated and considered to determine how they will support or influence the career development stages. The following are suggested questions which may serve to help practitioners further analyze those activities currently in place.

At Preparation:

Forecasting

Forecasting is an integral component of human resource planning. It requires collecting and analyzing information about future human resource needs, including a continual examination of relevant factors within the organization (such as talent resources and expected structural and personnel changes) and in the outside environment (such as potential technical, social, and economic changes). This information is vital to the career development cycle. Without it goals are set in a vacuum.

- Do we have a formal system for forecasting future manpower requirements throughout the organization?
- Is the data in this system regularly updated or challenged as to accuracy?
- Are we clear on our human resource needs for the next five years? Ten years?
- Is this system visible to and used by management for decision-making purposes?
- Do employees know of and understand this system?
- Do employees have access to relevant outputs of this system?
- What steps must we take to create a forecasting system that will adequately support the career development program?
- How can data generated by the program help us inventory our current manpower supply?

(Forecasting is one of the human resource functions which will normally have applicability during a number of stages, for example, during the Preparation Stage, the Targeting Stage, and the Strategizing Stage.

Affirmative Action Requirements

Organizations which have successfully recruited women and minorities must now deal with their training and development. An integrated career development program has a direct affirmative action payoff at every stage.

Career development practitioners interested in the greatest payoff from their career development effort should consider the following:

- Are we satisfied with the state of the art of this organization's affirmative action activity?
- How will each career development stage make our organization more accountable for its affirmative action policies?
- Are we using the skill identification information developed at the Profiling Stage to give us a better picture of needs of women and minorities set at the Targeting Stage realistic?
- Is the organization doing all it can to support these goals?

Supervisory Training

If immediate supervisors are the primary contact for each employee's career development, they must be prepared to act as a catalyst and an advisor. Through an assessment survey (written questionnaire or oral interviews), the organization can determine what supervisory skills are already available and which are needed to function in this capacity. Supervisory training can be provided to supplement existing skills. Questions include:

- Do supervisors have basic skills in counseling and coaching, employees, providing performance feedback, setting mutual goals, and assessing training needs?
- Do supervisors have full awareness and understanding of the organization's existing human resource development programs and of the need for career development?
- What training is needed to prepare supervisors for the career development program?
- What information needs to be developed before we can conduct this training?

At Profiling:

Performance Appraisal

Typically performance appraisal is one of the few existing opportunities for dialogue concerning present skills, career futures, and developmental needs. Often, however, it is implemented simply as an annual checklist of employee characteristics, with few persons taking advantage of its potential for communication and testing against reality. Ideally performance appraisal should include face-to-face interchange between manager and employee and should involve setting mutual objectives, establishing methods to monitor performance, discussing past performance success and deficiencies, examining career aspirations and opportunities, and discussing career development needs. The following questions might be asked about the organization:

- Do our performance appraisals aid supervisor-subordinate communication about current performance and future plans?
- Are managers, skilled and willing to give frank, honest performance feedback regarding employees' personal, technical, and conceptual skills?
- Do employees view performance appraisal as an opportunity to test their self-perceptions against reality? Are they assisted in preparing for this dialogue?
- What steps should we take to improve our performance appraisal vehicle so that it supports the career development effort?

Skill Inventories

Skill inventories are information storage, update, and retrieval systems (often computerized) that monitor employee backgrounds, training, experience, and skills. If it is to be used as a resource data bank for replacement and advancement, the inventory must be continually updated, easy to assess (tabular, graphic formats), and readily available for use. Skill inventories store and catalogue the precious skill identification data that is generated during the Profiling Stage.

The following questions are helpful in assessing skill inventories:

- Is information fed into the skill inventory in a timely, consistent manner?
- Are employees consistent about updating their own inventories?
- Do managers adequately use the inventory—or do they bypass it when they have staffing needs?
- Do all employees understand the purpose of the inventory?
- What steps must we take to create an inventory that will document information generated by a career development effort?

At Targeting:

Job Posting

Announcing vacancies visibly throughout the organization enables potential candidates to learn about the kinds of positions that become open and to apply for those that fit their qualifications and career aspirations. The existence of a comprehensive and visible job posting process can help set a favorable organizational climate, provide the organization with the benefit of a broad applicant pool, and assist employees in identifying career goals. Ideally posted jobs should include information about possible career progression stemming from them, as well as the necessary job description and qualifications. They are especially helpful during the Targeting Stage, because they provide an idea about the range of opportunities which might be goal alternatives. Questions useful in assessing job posting policies include the following:

- Do employees sometimes feel that jobs are filled before they even hear about the vacancies?
- Do employees frequently complain that they can't find out about the kinds of jobs they could qualify for in other parts of the organization?
- Does management resist openly advertising vacancies because they feel it will hinder their ability to select who they really want?
- When jobs are posted, are interested applicants given enough information to understand how those jobs fit with their past experience and training and their future career goals?

Succession Planning

Succession planning requires formally charting replacement needs and time frames and looking internally for those who may be ready to move into upcoming vacancies. These individuals may be groomed for succession when titles such as assistant, deputy, or associate carry with them appropriate responsibility and exposure. Recruitment and selection should also take into account succession possibilities. Succession plans can be integrated with goals developed by employees during the Targeting Stage.

- Do we have adequate plans for succession into key positions?
- Do we too often have to search outside our own organization for candidates for key positions?
- Do our recruitment, selection, placement, and training practices reflect future succession needs?
- Are managers involved in and aware of the organization's succession plans?
- What steps must we take to improve our succession planning, so that it reinforces actions taken in the career development effort?

At Strategizing:

Career Pathing

This method of planned job progression generally involves delineating on-the-job experiences and training that can lead to appropriate movement in the organizational hierarchy. Establishing career paths may also entail plans for lateral movement. Since the timing and availability of vacancies is subject to constant change, establishing career paths can also be a series of short-term (one- to two-year) plans that are continually revised, supplemented by a more general, longer-range plan. Information about career paths can provide valuable assistance to employees in developing realistic action plans during the Strategizing Stage.

Career development practitioners might ask

- What are our formal mechanisms for creating career paths?
- When was our career path information last updated?

- Do managers have access to career path data?
- Are managers able to explain career path data to their employees?
- Do employees have access to career path data?
- Do employees have any informal mechanisms that can help them develop insight into their own individual paths?
- In the environment in which we operate, is it realistic to develop specific career paths (with specific job slots in mind), or do we need to develop more generalized lines of career progression?
- What steps do we need to take to create a career path system that will provide valuable input to the career development effort?

Counseling

More and more organizations are making specializing counseling service available to employees. Two such specialized services include preretirement counseling, which would prepare mature employees for plans and decisions they need to make regarding their nonfull-time work years, and outplacement counseling for employees who are, for whatever reason, being asked to leave the organization after rendering years of service. These counseling services are performed by individual specialists or external consultants, who serve employees on a full- or part-time basis. Needs for these services may be evidenced during the Strategizing Stage. Some questions the practitioner might ask regarding the viability of these services are

- Have we established services to meet special employee needs?
- Have we framed adequate policies to allow employees to seek the help they need outside the organization?
- Are we cognizant of the areas that need development, as suggested by the number of employees seeking special services?
- Are we aware of the quality of counseling services available through our own organization?
- Do we have a statistical summary of the increasing or decreasing number of employees seeking services and the implications of those numbers?
- Have we kept up to date with trends in the counseling field and services that other organizations are performing?
- Are our counseling practices supportive of the career development program?

At Execution:

Training and Development

Training and development involves sending employees to special workshops and seminars, generally outside their immediate work setting. To be most effective, such training must relate to immediate or realistic future work needs, and it must be linked to employees' own expectations and desires about their career development. If training and development is linked to both organizational needs and employee career development goals, it will be more cost-effective. Training and development experiences can include, among others, tuition reimbursement programs, one-time workshops, or seminars for entire groups of employees. They may involve going out to specialized programs, or they may include programs conducted by internal resource persons who have adequate experience in the subject matter being taught and have skills in designing and conducting training. During the Execution Stage employees will select those training and development programs which will aid them in achieving their goals. The practitioner might ask

- What training and development experiences are now available?
- Is training and development available to all employees who can show a need and desire, or is it more often used selectively as a reward (or punishment) process for certain levels of employees?
- Are employees selecting training and development opportunities that are in line with their career goals? (If so, are we measuring the results of those efforts in helping them meet their goals?)
- Have we conducted any formal assessment of the organization's training and development offerings? Selection procedures?
- Are supervisors able to identify training and development needs and suggest ways in which they might be met?
- Are supervisors able to counsel their employees regarding the training that should be selected?
- Is there top level commitment to training and development as an appropriate way to help assure organizational health and maximum return on investment in human resources?
- What steps must we take to create training and development that is tied to the variety of career goals selected by employees?

On-the-Job Training

OJT is one of the best means by which employees can gain or update skills. Often, however, the system is so ad hoc that employees are just plain lucky if they get to work with someone able to give them necessary training and willing to expose them to new experiences. On-the-job training may include formal orientation and training sessions conducted by experienced employees, deliberate efforts to pair employees with resource individuals responsible for their learning, or job rotation for exposure to a variety of experiences. OJT may be another developmental resource for employees during the Execution Stage. The practitioner might consider the following:

- What efforts are now going on that could be characterized as deliberate (not ad hoc) OJT?

- Does OJT occur throughout the organization or only in isolated departments?
- Do supervisors feel they have a responsibility for assuring that OJT occurs?
- Are employees encouraged to actively pursue OJT opportunities?
- Have we conducted any formal assessments of our OJT needs or of the abilities among supervisors to develop OJT experiences?
- What steps must we take to create OJT opportunities that prepare employees to move toward the goals identified in the career development program?

At Integration:

Compensation Practices

Compensation is a complex network of processes directed toward remunerating people for services performed and motivating them to attain desired goals of performance. Among the intermediate components of this process are wage and salary payment; the awarding of insurance and vacations; and the provision of essentially noncost rewards such as recognition, privileges, and symbols of status. A wide variety of systems and policies are used to facilitate the administration of the process. Organizations also supply a wide variety of fringe benefits. Careful attention must be given to the planning and installation of fringe benefits if they are to be useful incentives for the development of organizational careers. Compensation policies have a profound effect on the recruitment, retention, satisfaction, and motivation of employees. Some questions that can be asked are

- Do our compensation policies support movement other than vertical?
- Do our employees have a sound understanding of our compensation system?
- Are we aware of all the possible benefit plans that can be used to support various kinds of career mobility?
- Is there a way for us to reward managers who do an excellent job in the career development of their subordinates?
- Are we aware of the ways in which our present practices may hinder the motivation of individuals in the career development effort?

Transfer and Promotion Policies

It is important to clarify transfer and promotion policies and communicate them throughout the organization. Transfers within an organization are usually those moves made from one job to another, one unit to another, one shift to another, or one geographical location to another. They are often initiated by the organization, but can also be initiated by the employee, with the approval of the organization. Transfers have many purposes: they move employees to positions where there is a higher organizational need for that individual, they fill vacancies, and they place employees in positions that are more appropriate to their interest and abilities. Many organizations have intricate lateral transfer programs, which give employees the opportunity to work in another area of the organization, but in jobs equal in status to the one they left.

A promotion is a type of transfer involving reassignment of an employee to a position having higher pay, increased responsibilities, more privileges, increased benefits, greater potential, or all of the above. Promotions are used to staff vacancies which in general are worth more to the organization than the incumbent's present position. Promotion policies and lateral transfer systems need to be studied if they are to support a variety of career moves that may have been selected earlier in the career development cycle. Some questions to be considered are

- Are our current policies concerning promotions and transfers understood by managers? By employees?
- Have we developed an appropriate system for transferring an employee into a position which is appropriate for his or her qualifications?
- Are we able to relate present salary to a different salary structure of another unit within our organization if a transfer is made?
- Is career development limited by geographical constraints?
- Are our employees involved in geographical transfer decisions?
- Are our promotion policies and procedures reasonably acceptable to the unsuccessful candidate?
- Do we have our employees' confidence about the fairness and thoroughness of our selection procedures?
- Would employees agree that we have a promote from within policy, or do they think otherwise?

Warning. In analyzing these links, it is *not* essential to find that they are all in perfect harmony with the career development effort before starting the program. In some cases action may be taken immediately to provide more effective program integration; in other cases action may be initiated but not completed until later. An organization that waits until it finds that all supporting human resource links are letter perfect is probably stalling for other reasons on the installation of the career development effort. At this point the emphasis should be on becoming aware of the potential weaknesses in the current structural systems and considering some action to strengthen them.

Career Development Program Approaches: The People Supports

In addition to structural supports, the practitioner must also be ready to develop mechanisms that directly affect people and influence their behavior. In other words, if change is to be effective, it will also affect those who make up the target audience of the career development effort. The practitioner will have an easier time gaining commitment and assistance from the organization in this area since the organization itself can become involved to some extent. The range of that potential involvement can be shown by the model which follows:

This involvement can be translated into four major categories of activity that can be used to deliver some of the important steps of the career development process. Each has its array of benefits and drawbacks, strengths and deficiencies. Practitioners who are familiar with each of these types of activities can more effectively pick and choose in deciding which approaches will be most effective, given the organization's degree of involvement and its basic style, culture, norms, and ideology. The choices include:

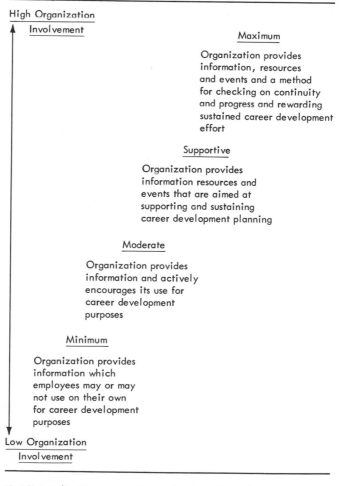

High Organization
Involvement

Maximum

Organization provides
information, resources
and events and a method
for checking on continuity
and progress and rewarding
sustained career development
effort

Supportive

Organization provides
information resources and
events that are aimed at
supporting and sustaining
career development planning

Moderate

Organization provides
information and actively
encourages its use for
career development
purposes

Minimum

Organization provides
information which
employees may or may
not use on their own
for career development
purposes

Low Organization
Involvement

Exhibit 2-7   Range of Organizational Involvement

- Self-directed activities
- Counselor guided activities
- Group supported activities
- Combinations of the above

Self-Directed Activities. Self-directed activities rely heavily on the employees' desires and abilities to map out career development strategies for themselves. Organizations using this approach generally support individual efforts by providing programmed workbooks that can help employees conduct personal assessments. The workbooks may be the off-the-shelf variety, published nationally and widely applicable to various organizational settings, or they may be especially designed by and for the organization at hand. Obviously the latter allow greater opportunity for specifying issues that relate directly to the individual's career potential within the given organizational setting.

Workbooks usually are highly diagnostic in approach, offering exercises and questionnaires which require the individual to assess personal values, career preferences, life satisfactions, and career-related strengths and weaknesses. They may include self-scored tests to pin-point individual styles and priorities, and they may contain instructions for sharing and validating the information with others. Generally they conclude with goal setting and planning exercises and an admonishment to set firm timetables, periodically review progress, and revise as necessary. Sometimes these workbooks have companion versions for counselors or supervisors, so they can assist employees in the development process.

Richway Department Stores in Atlanta, Georgia utilize a Career Development Workbook to help employees assess their skills in light of their work preferences and desired lifestyle. They feel that this is a good approach because a person in retailing spends a tremendous amount of time at the work place. The career workbook lets employees see if their work preferences and desired lifestyle are congruent with the working world of retail. For example, if an employee prefers a 9:00 A.M. to 5:00 P.M. job, then that desire would not be congruent with the real world of work at Richway. The employee would need to re-examine his/her lifestyle preference or the desire to pursue retailing.

The workbook is self-administered and therefore can be done at the employee's own pace. A career chart is the culmination of the workbook. This chart is a summary of the previous pages and gives the employee a chance to outline two possible career paths which he/she may want to pursue at Richway. The employee then discusses the chart with his/her supervisor, who provides some reality counseling. If the employee feels uncomfortable discussing the career path with a supervisor, then he/she may talk with the Personnel Manager, their bosses' boss or the Store Manager. All are trained in career counseling.[6]

Workbooks are most useful when supported by a good deal of written communication to employees about HRD activities, such as job openings, possible career paths within the organization, and other developmental opportunities. In this way the employee can incorporate both personal knowledge and organizational knowledge to realistically pursue plans for career development.

Another self-directed approach in a number of organizations has been the establishment of career information centers. Such centers are usually staffed by full- or part-time specialists who can guide employees to the particular information necessary. Centers are sometimes seen as libraries, and sometimes as storehouses where employees can come to read, review, and search for particular information related to career concerns or questions. Career information centers contain books, cassettes, and information on specific careers within and outside of the organization. Some also possess computer terminals that provide access to a local computerized career information system.

The drawbacks encountered in the self-directed career development approach often stem from the level of individual self-motivation required to make this approach operative. It is extremely difficult for most people to maintain the impetus for career development when it appears that nobody but themselves is either knowledgeable about or interested in their plans, and when they have little opportunity for dialogue with others. In addition self-directed activity is an operation in a vacuum. Employees are almost totally reliant on the resources and information provided them, with nowhere to turn if additional assistance or information is needed.

However, self-directed activities do allow those who are highly dedicated to career development to voluntarily pursue a course of self-assessment, to design career plans to individual specifications, and to exercise total personal involvement and responsibility. And this generally can be done at a relatively low cost to the organization.

Counselor Guided Activities. Counselor guided approaches entail one-on-one discussions with someone especially trained to help guide an individual's perceptions of his or her career future. This approach may involve professional counselors (often psychologists) from outside the organization, specialized staff within the organization (generally employee counselors in the personnel department), or supervisors who initiate career conversations with subordinates. Counseling may range from the formal administration and analysis of aptitude and personality tests to the informal rap session.

Through this approach the employee receives highly individualized advice and support, as well as substantial motivation stemming from the notion of shared responsibility for career planning. Counseling personnel from outside the organization can contribute a sense of anonymity, objectivity, and some specialized professional capabilities. However, they also contribute a hefty price tag and, occasionally, a sense of reluctance among employees who feel they would be visiting "the company shrink."

Individual counseling is available from specially trained managers at Lawrence Livermore Labs in California for any employee who requests this service. Employees seek counseling for a variety of reasons. These reasons range from request for simple factual information on available educational courses or for assistance in developing education and occupational goals, to request for feedback on the reality of career goals. Employees are given whatever assistance and information is available. When appropriate, they are referred to specific sources of factual information in a selected career. The major focus in the career counseling sessions is on assisting employees in the process of decision-making around careers by providing them with the tools and techniques that they can use to gather appropriate information and data and to make informed decisions for themselves. Over two hundred laboratory employees receive career counseling each year.[7]

Ideally counseling by the boss should be available to the subordinate in some form, even before the decision to prepare for a career development program is made. In reality, however, this is rarely the case. Instead, the annual performance appraisal is often the only occasion where such discussion takes place. And often, it is an occasion of mutual discomfort where both parties are happy to just put check marks in boxes or move through the routine. There is little offering or seeking of any real counseling. This is particularly unfortunate in the area of career development, since supervisors are often in the best position to provide realistic information about the organization and possible career paths, as well as to understand the capabilities and needs of their subordinates.

To take advantage of the potential benefits of manager-employee counseling, an organization will need to commit resources and time to training supervisors in basic counseling techniques. It will also need to establish systems of reward and accountability for the counseling function as an ongoing required supervisory responsibility. At a minimum the supervisor will need skill in listening, questioning, and providing feedback, and a capacity for knowing and explaining career-related resources and options within the organization.

Group Supported Activities. Group supported activities generally take the form of workshops aimed at generating collective discussion and mutual support for career development.

A typical career planning workshop is one to five days in length and is often used to kick off a larger, more integrated effort. A well-designed and conducted workshop will give participants an opportunity to at least

Hughes Aircraft Company, as a part of its ongoing Management Action Workshop (M.A.W.), has spent a greal deal of time and effort developing the counseling skills of managers and upper-level executives. Phase III of the coaching, counseling, communicating, and helping skills. The high point of this experience is a twelve-hour exercise in which participants take the roles of workers, supervisors, and managers. The workers solve a problem as a "problem owner" and "helper." Each of these role players then is evaluated in his/her performance by individual supervisors who are, in turn, given an appraisal by a management board. By the end of the workshop, performance evaluation, a theretofore dreaded task, is seen as an exciting and valuable experience.[8]

partially work their way through the career development cycle in a highly supportive low-risk environment. Using a variety of instruments and appraisals, participants help each other to *profile* their personal traits and career preferences. Career goals and objectives are *targeted* as participants discuss with one another the opportunities and paths available within their organizations. Action plans are *strategized* and tested on one another for realism and practicality. Mutual support is often pledged and provided after the workshop, as participants return to the workplace to *execute* their individual plans.

The "we're in it together" aspect of the workshop setting can make this approach a powerful strategy for initiating career plans that have maximum potential for follow-through. The workshop strategy can be used to initiate career decision making and to inform participants of available options and relevant organizational directions. In this manner each individual is provided with a support system of others who are having similar experiences and who can contribute assistance after the formal workshop is completed. Though workshops can provide a great deal of organizational

The Education staff members at Polaroid designed a Career Development Workshop Series which has since been regularly offered to employees at all Polaroid locations.

The Career Development Series consists of a group orientation session and four formal career workshops. During the group orientation, employees share their expectations with the career staff and learn about what the Series can do for them. Interested employees can then enroll in the formal career workshops. The first of these is the Career Awareness Workshop, which involves participants in basic career and life planning exercises. This is followed by workshops in Resume Organization and Interview Skills, which give participants practice in organizing their skills and experience and presenting them to a hiring supervisor. The final Career Search Workshop then teaches employees how to gather information about Company job opportunities and how to best use the Job Posting System.[9]

information, they have their greatest impact and return on investment when follow-up activities, specifically designed to keep the process active, are provided.

Integrative Combinations. Many very comprehensive career development programs incorporate self-directed, counselor guided, and group supported activities at various stages of program implementation. For example, self-directed activities may initiate personal diagnosis, counseling may help individuals understand and apply that diagnostic information, and workshops may generate goals for future action. Then the program can be sustained with further available counseling, group activities, and tools to facilitate individual reflection.

A typical integrative approach might ask employees to complete a workbook or some career preference tests before attending a career workshop, or it might provide a workbook at the close of a workshop, so that individuals may delve further into special career considerations after the workshop has concluded. During and after the workshop one-on-one counseling is available to provide further assistance on an individual basis.

> The U.S. General Accounting Office Counseling and Career Development Branch (CCD) has developed a unique and comprehensive program of services that combines both counseling and career development. It provides confidential individual and group assistance to all GAO employees on personal, performance, or career related matters. Specifically the CCD guidance and counseling services offered are (1) CCD orientations and developmental workshops, (2) the CCD Career Resource Center, (3) individual counseling appointments with the CCD psychologists, and (4) consultation to supervisors and managers in the areas of problem identification, the referral process, performance counseling, and career development.[10]

While these approaches and their differences are important for the practitioner to know, it is extremely important to recognize that none of these activities alone is enough to produce an effective career development effort. A workbook, workshop, or counseling session may stimulate planning but will usually not in and of itself provide all that is necessary to insure organizational mobility. Each must be carefully linked with the other human resource development activities discussed earlier, in order to provide the true supportive structure for carrying out a successful career development effort.

Come One, Come All? No matter what approach is introduced, deciding on the level of participation in the career development program will be crucial. There are four general arrangements for dealing with the issue:

111375

- Everyone in the organization participates—all levels and all divisions.
- Volunteers are solicited from throughout the organization on a first-come-first-served basis, with a ceiling on the total number that can be accommodated by the program.
- Special groups of employees (such as, women, minorities, fast trackers, midmanagers, or preretirees) are offered the program.
- Employees in certain divisions or units of the organization are offered the program.

Clearly anything less than full organization-wide coverage requires grouping employees for selection. This may be done by using place of work (unit or division), personal/professional characteristics (level attained, future potential, or minority status), or managers selecting certain subordinates based on certain criteria.

Groupings by division or unit can provide an opportunity to selectively install a pilot program, in order to work out kinks and test various strategies. Additionally careful selection of units where commitment and enthusiasm is greatest can give the program the impetus of early success and favorable word of mouth. In fact organizations which set out to fully implement career development throughout all units often find a substantial differential among how various offices put the program into practice—ranging from some that embrace all phases on a comprehensive basis to others that simply undertake certain discrete events without installing a truly systematic approach.

The possible drawbacks in selecting only certain organizational units arise from the difficulty of making appropriate choices. The unit(s) selected should provide a good pilot example of how the program will be received and what problems might occur; but it should also be assured (as much as possible) of initial success and the opportunity for transference to other units.

Organizations which select special groups of employees most often choose to conduct career development for management trainees or fast track management candidates. This executive development approach, often referred to as the "crown prince" strategy, allows for succession planning at the highest levels, but it may limit career development opportunities to those who would be likely to take the effort into their own hands even if no organizational assistance were available.

Organizations may also single out women and minority employees, mid-career employees, pre-retirees, or others. Whatever the group, the stages of the career development process remain essentially the same, so that this approach may also be considered a limited experiment to be expanded to other employees at later dates.

The question of grouping participants will always be one that stimulates a great deal of discussion. Should participants be from one homogeneous work group, or should they be representative of the organization at large in a cross-sectional heterogeneous group? There are pros and cons of both approaches.

Homogeneous work groups tend to know each other, have common problems, and can deal with each other openly and frankly. However, they tend to be parochial in their view and to have common well-defined biases, prejudices, and opinions. They are often cliquish and tend to be somewhat closed to new ideas and approaches.

Heterogeneous groups have a broader organizational view, represent a wide variety of backgrounds, and can stimulate each other with new ideas, new material, and different options. However, heterogeneous groups tend to be somewhat closed at the beginning and are sometimes difficult to "open up" in order to begin the sharing of data. Representing, as they do, a wide diversity of backgrounds and attainment levels, they bring to the group a diverse set of prejudices, biases, and opinions, and these must be dealt with before the larger task can be addressed.

Time, resources, and practitioner skill must all be considered before deciding whether to work with homogeneous or heterogeneous groupings. If time is not a factor, if resources are relatively unlimited, and if the practitioner is experienced and highly skilled, the approach that is more difficult in the practitioner's view may be undertaken. If the opposite factors are present, the practitioner's view may be undertaken. If the opposite factors are present, the practitioner may wish to work with an easier arrangement.

It is important to recognize that not all employees will be interested in career development. And it is unlikely that mandatory participation will provide them with an incentive to wholeheartedly implement career plans. While employees may need strong encouragement to participate in the program, those who feel that the final decision has been voluntary are most likely to realize the full benefits of the career effort. The organization can offer information, opportunities, and assistance, but the primary responsibility for career development still remains with each employee.

THE PLANNING PROCESS

The second essential component of the Preparation Stage is planning —— mapping the specific strategy and methods of the career development effort. It involves the setting of objectives, designing an evaluation scheme, assigning responsibilities for the entire effort, and determining methodologies, resources, and support.

The Setting of Objectives

Most objectives are defined in terms of what activities will be undertaken and who will be responsible for them. These are the *inputs* of the career development effort, and though they are important, they do not provide a means by which a program's effect can be measured. For this reason the concept of writing objectives in terms of *outputs, impacts,* or *results* is emphasized here. There are the projected accomplishments of the proposed effort and the effect of those accomplishments on the organization and program participants.

Results can be measured; they can be seen, touched, heard, smelled, and tasted; they are real. An *input* objective might call for establishing a series of workshops and training programs for secretaries. Once these efforts have begun, the objective has been accomplished, but to what organizational benefit? A much more effective *output* objective, addressing the same end, might call for creating a qualified in-house secretarial applicant pool and reducing the turn-over within secretarial ranks. When this objective has been reached, something measurable has been accomplished, and the organization can see what has happened. Instead of merely monitoring the progress of the establishment of a program, the organization has a benefit that is real.

As indicated earlier, objectives of career development efforts in most organizations relate to increased organizational productivity and individual efficiency. They include such factors as improved performance, reduced turnover, and decreased "dead wood." While internal pressures to quickly and measurably demonstrate the program's material benefits will tempt the organization to state objectives only related to more productive performance, it may be valuable to reach beyond these to include more pragmatic and measurable factors, such as improved performance, skills, abilities, and productivity; increased adaptability; improved attitudes; and a greater feeling of personal identity and job involvement.

It is unlikely that a single objective statement will adequately account for such a great variety of desired outcomes. Objectives should take into consideration intrinsic payoffs to employees, as well as dollars and cents benefits to the organization.

The following chart is designed to serve as a checklist for human resource problems, which could generate specific outcome objectives. Before moving ahead practitioners may want to consider whether their organization is facing any of these problems and whether solutions to the problems should be included among the objectives for the career developing effort.

Approaching Evaluation

Developing an evaluation approach at this early stage provides a guide for further specifying objectives in terms of outputs, for setting in motion systems to monitor progress of the effort, and for measuring its success.

The time has now come to make certain that program objectives are stated in terms that are clearly measurable. What is each objective specifically intended to accomplish? How can this be stated in terms of measura-

Check below those statements which apply to your organization.

_____ The rate of turnover requires us to continually train and retrain employees.

_____ Absenteeism, grievances, and other counterproductive employee activities are creating problems.

_____ Some jobs leave employees with little opportunity to advance, other than by leaving the organization.

_____ A lot of people seem to be just "coasting along" until retirement.

_____ We hear some grumbling about low morale, but we're not really sure what causes it.

_____ Through our affirmative action efforts we have been able to recruit women and minorities, but they tend to stay clustered in certain jobs, job categories, or classes.

_____ We have problems effecting lateral transfers when employees reach a plateau in their current positions.

_____ We don't have a complete picture of in-house talent and skills that might be resources for future needs.

_____ Our supervisors are not generally able to counsel employees about their career development.

_____ Performance appraisals are more a necessary formality than an opportunity for real information exchange between superior and subordinate.

_____ Many managers have unrealistic aspirations toward advancement.

_____ People tend to know very little about the organization and its direction, beyond their immediate work place.

_____ Many people seem to be unaware of how accomplishment of their jobs fit into larger organizational goals.

_____ We do a lot of things that could be called career development, but they are isolated and vary among departments and levels of employees.

_____ Many employees don't really know their mobility options within the organization.

_____ People don't seem to know how to go about preparing for advancement.

(If you checked 5 or more, you probably need to devote greater attention to human resource development. A career development effort with specific outcome objectives can assist in addressing these problems.)

Exhibit 2-8 Human Resource Problems

ble results? Many repetitions of this step, with review, critique, and inputs by others in the organization, may be necessary. For example, one of the objectives may now read, "to increase first-line supervisors' understanding of their human resource development function." Restated in more measurable terms, this may become, "to increase the number of first-line supervisors who use counseling, coaching, and on-the-job training as means to develop employees' potential. Before this objective is completely acceptable, several further iterations of this statement may be necessary. Developing performance criteria, which can function as measures of program outcomes as they relate to objectives, will bring even more clarity. In the above example, performance criteria may include a specific increase in the number of reported counseling instances, a precise increase in hours spent in on-the-job training, or a targeted decrease in the number of employee complaints related to insufficient understanding of tasks.

Establishing performance criteria at this point will often uncover a need to collect base-line data about current activities, to be used later as comparisons. If increases or decreases are to be used as indicators, they will only be useful for comparison if there is a clear understanding of what existed before implementation. In this way change can be measured and analyzed for its significance and program relevance. Clear performance criteria also enables timely determination of the data collection and analysis methods to be used in the career development program. Data collection may entail looking at numbers on staffing reports, constructing tests of performance, and designing attitude surveys. Often, to increase the validity of eventual evaluation results, data will need to be collected and analyzed before the program begins and at various points during its implementation. As practitioners will discover, if they have not already done so, establishing an effective program will require a great deal of dexterity in moving from one stage to another and in carrying on several functions simultaneously.

Depending on the rigor with which evaluation is undertaken, practitioners may find the assistance of statisticians and other numbers wizards useful. However, much valuable information can also derive from less formal and rigorous methodologies, as long as care is taken early on to define objectives and indicators in measurable, outcome-oriented terms.

Success Indicators.   One helpful step in preparing for evaluation is articulating what specifically will constitute success. A description of the essential program components that contribute to a successful career development effort will help to further determine evaluation criteria. These components relate to both the process—how the program will be carried out—and the product—what will happen—and vary greatly from one organization to the next, depending on needs, objectives, and activities already in place. One way of actively involving the planning task force (described earlier in this chapter) is to engage them in selecting the success indicators that would be relevant to the career development effort of the organization. Success indicators describe an effective program and its impact on all individuals involved. Success indicators and ideas for their measurement can be collected from top management, supervisors of prospective participants, various levels of employees throughout the organization, and even human resource development staff personnel. The planning group could determine those indicators which are most vital as a demonstration of program success and those which, in addition, are most easily measured. The data collection process will stimulate interest in the program and build commitment from others not yet involved.

What constitutes success varies with one's point of view. Participants might measure program success in terms of personal learning, discoveries, and accomplishments. The managers of participants might determine success of the program by looking at employee performance, productivity, and reduced conflict. Top management might measure success by examining participants' contributions to organizational effectiveness and reduced turnover. The following lists of success indicators and means of measuring them are designed to serve as suggestions or stimulants for practitioners wishing to establish success indicators for their own organizations.

Success Indicators (I am able to...)	Potential Measures
Learn what I want to do.	Identified three potential career options.
Get feedback on where I need to improve.	Requested performance appraisal input from supervisor and completed exercises in workshop, which proved to be valid.
Identify my strongest skill(s).	Was able to list and discuss these skills and receive reinforcing feedback.
Identify jobs for which my skills are transferable.	Listed four other jobs that fit my present skills.

Exhibit 2-9   Success Indicators for Program Participants

Success Indicators (My employees are/have:)	Potential Measures
Fewer complaints; more satisfied with their status and appraisals.	Check for decrease in number of EEO complaints.
More productive.	Ascertain quality/quantity measurements. Less turnover over fiscal year.
Less dependence on me for guidance—taken more initiative on career matters.	Record number of individuals who ask for time to discuss career plan with me and come in with a plan in hand!
More realism regarding their strengths and weaknesses.	Better preparation by employees for performance appraisal, and more realistic self-assessment during appraisal.
Retained longer—that is, effective job enrichment.	Less turnover due to lack of job challenge, as ascertained from exit interview data.
More opportunities for transfers.	Increased number of lateral transfers into my department and from my department to others. Greater cooperation from my peers.

Exhibit 2-10   Success Indicators for Managers of Participants

Success Indicators (I witness the following:)	Potential Measures
Reduced turnover.	Statistics at end of fiscal year.
Improved productivity.	MBO goals met, improved performance appraisal reviews.
Succession planning.	Identification of backup personnel for key positions.
Improved morale.	Pre/postattitude surveys show substantial changes.
Change in use of human resource activities.	Active use of present systems. More knowledge about company present HRD activities.
Loyalty to company.	Less dollars spent on recruitment. Length of stay with company improved.

Exhibit 2-11   Success Indicators for Top Management

Success indicators can be used to form program objectives and to design evaluation procedures that each group sees as valid and acceptable proof that the career development program does actually bring a return on their investment.

Following are several questions concerning the areas of Activities, Processes, and Results, which can be additionally helpful in drawing up meaningful success indicators:

Activities

- Have we undertaken necessary structural adjustments to link career development to other human resource development programs?
- Have orientation activities been conducted for management?
- Have career development assessment and planning activities been conducted by and with employees?
- Has a forum for discussion/counseling been made available?
- Are educational and training and developmental experiences (on and off the job) available?
- Is there evidence that employees are pursuing their plans toward career goals?
- Have we established a system for monitoring and updating the career development program?

Processes

- Is open dialogue among and between levels of employees being used as a mechanism to facilitate the program?
- Are information sharing and personal guidance being undertaken to help individuals understand career opportunities and options?

- Is participation being sought and used as a means of helping employees be involved in undertaking career development that is specifically relevant to individual needs and goals?
- Do we use feedback among and between levels of employees as a means of helping employees to set realistic goals and monitor progress on career plans?

Results

- Do employees, supervisors, and other report changes in attitude or morale?
- Do employees, supervisors, and other report improvements in utilization of skills?
- Do employees, supervisors, and others report changes in career directions or expectations?
- Has manpower planning and forecasting been made more effective?
- Have we reduced turnover, absenteeism, and grievances?
- Have we improved our ability to meet the needs and requirements of affirmative action?
- Do we have more effective means of manager-employee communication, including performance appraisal?
- Do various units report more effective means of having the right people in the right places at the right times?
- Do our tracking systems show we are making progress toward meeting the impact-oriented objectives we stated for ourselves at the outset?

As a final impetus to the list of success indicators, practitioners might consider whether the program encompasses the following five essential features:

- *Dialogue* between individuals and their managers, which is essential for successful career development and should serve to generate openness and trust among the parties involved.
- *Guidance,* which is the means by which management provides individuals with an understanding of the career milieu in which they operate—including information about organizational goals, opportunities, and options.
- *Involvement* of individuals in their own career development processes, which is required to enable employees to set goals and timetables that are personally meaningful and to undertake activities that reflect personal needs and aspirations.
- *Feedback* to individuals, often in the form of manager-employee discussions, which enables employees to assess their learning and to plan appropriate changes as they go through the career development process.
- *Process mechanisms,* the techniques and methods (such as workshops, counseling, on-the-job training, and performance appraisals) by which career development is brought about and which must interface with one another as a systematic developmental approach.[11]

These important process elements can further help in identifying the components of a successful program.

Putting the Plan on Paper

Formulating a plan of action that will clearly state anticipated activities is a vital task of almost any preparatory activity. Organizations have different ways of formulating project plans (task matrices, PERT charts, time lines, or GANTT charts); any of these may be used to help specify plans for the career development program, as long as the final scheme can be readily understood by the key persons involved and can accommodate all essential action planning components.

Who's in Charge? One of the first tasks, then, is to decide exactly where responsibility for each career development task will lie.

The practitioner, the individual, and the organization will each have a distinct and vital role. These might be outlined in a planning matrix like the one which follows.

Specific tasks to be fulfilled by each of three crucial players at each of the stages are defined and placed on the matrix. Human resource development activities that link with specific stages, and those tasks affiliated with readying these links may also be identified and placed on the planning guide.

The major question which the practitioner must now address is

	Practitioner	Individual	Organization
Preparation			
Profiling			
Targeting			
Strategizing			
Execution			
Integration			

Exhibit 2-12   Task Planning Matrix

Who should have major responsibility for administering the various tasks that comprise the program?

Most often career development efforts are the responsibility of the personnel or industrial relations function. However, they may also lie with individuals in other staff functions—such as organizational planning, manpower planning, or affirmative action. The important point is that responsibility should rest with someone who is capable, dedicated to the task at hand, trusted by employees, and heard by top management. If the personnel office is a place nobody thinks of after their recruitment and orientation, it may not be visible enough to successfully carry out a career development effort of the magnitude described here. (The personnel office can, however, assume responsibility for one particular component of the effort.) If employees have a historical sense of distance about the executives on the top floor, the program may be better lodged elsewhere.

Additionally responsibility for coordinating the effort must reside with someone who has—or can be given—staff resources to accomplish the necessary work, and authority to make wide-ranging decisions. The practitioner will need to be an effective manager of programs and an effective leader of people. In at least some cases the organization's first opportunity to implement career development will be to identify and develop such an individual! It will then be up to that individual to manage the variety of specific tasks and projects affiliated with the effort.

A useful tool for mapping responsibilities of key personnel is the "Management Responsibility Guide" (MRG), developed by Robert D. Melcher, and adapted from the Linear Responsibility Chart developed by Ernest Hijams and Serge A. Bern. The MRG utilizes a matrix and "responsibility language" to display roles and relationships.[12] Specifically the MRG language deals with who is accountable to whom for what—

A. *General Responsibility:* Individual who oversees and guides the program function through the person with operating responsibility.

B. *Operating Responsibility:* Individual who is directly responsible for execution of the program function.

C. *Specific Responsibility:* Individual who is responsible for execution of a specific or limited part of the function.

D. *Must be Consulted:* Individual who must be called upon for advice or information before a decision is made, but who does not make the decision or grant approval.

E. *May be Consulted:* Individual who may be called upon for advice or information before a decision is made.

F. *Must be Notified:* Individual who must be informed of action that has been taken.

G. *Must Approve:* Individual (other than those with general and operating responsibility) who must approve of disapprove of action.

In developing a matrix using these categories, positions are listed horizontally across the top, and task descriptions are listed vertically down the left side. The letters corresponding to the above responsibilities and relationships are used to fill in the matrix squares and show what function each individual will undertake during each task. The MRG approach is a vital step in the preparation process—it assigns accountability and keeps important functions from falling between the cracks.

The chart that follows give an example of how the MRG approach can be used to chart some of the key tasks during career development (form supplied courtesy of MRG Associates).

The first task in the MRG matrix suggests that the Director of Personnel would have the major operating responsibility (B) for developing goals and objectives related to the career program, whil the Vice-President for Human Resource Development would hold major overall accountability (A). The Director of Personnel would need specific input in terms of suggestions, ideas, and conceptual frameworks from the Manager of Manpower Training and Development (C), input on how the pay and classification system is affected from the Manager of that area (C), and specific suggestions about needs in the work force (C) from the Manager of Recruitment and Orientation. The Director of Personnel would consult with the Manager of Training as needed (E), and the Manager of Special Projects (E), but would be sure to keep the Vice-President of Administration informed after the goals and objectives were formally written.

The second task suggests that the Manager of Special Projects would be responsible (B) for reviewing current human resource programs, with consultative help (D) from Managers of Employee Training, Manpower Planning and Development, and Pay and Classification. Vice-presidents would be notified of the results of the review (F), and before anything was published, the Director of Personnel would approve (A) of the report.

The MRG matrix, or other responsibility charting system, can be introduced at an early meeting of the planning task force and can serve to instigate important discussions regarding responsibility and accountability for the career development effort.

Again it must be emphasized that some means designing the time sequences and events of the plan must be included. Planning without the time factors involved can lead to looseness and slipping off target. Not only must end times be included, but milestones will also have to be determined, so that progress can be monitored and event sequencing can be conducted smoothly. A great many sources are available for this type of planning, and further discussion is included in Chapters 4 and 5.

MANAGEMENT RESPONSIBILITY GUIDE

NUMBER	TASK DESCRIPTOR	VP Human Resource Dev	VP Administration	Personnel Director	Mgr, Training & Dev	Mgr, Mnpwr Plng & Dev	Mgr, Pay & Classif	Mgr, Spec Projects	Mgr, Recruit & Orien	Mgr, Financial Ser	Career Dev Task Force
1.	Develop goals & objectives for Career Development Program.	A CG	DF	(B)	E	–	C	E	C		
2.	Review existing human resources.	AF	F	CD	CD	CD	CD	(B)	E	CE	
3.	Identify success indicators.	ADF		CD	E	E	E	CD			(B)
4.	Develop plan for structural revisions & new program activities.	AF	F	(B)	C	C	E	C	F	E	
5.	Develop PERT chart of activities & time frames.	AF	G	(B)	DF	DF	F	C	F		
6.	Develop budget for Career Development Program.	ADG	(B)	CG	E	E	D	C	E	C	
7.	Schedule & conduct orientation meetings with department heads.	F	(AB)	CF	E	E	E	EF			

POSITION/ORGANIZATION

RELATIONSHIP CODE: **A** GENERAL RESPONSIBILITY — **B** OPERATING RESPONSIBILITY — **C** SPECIFIC RESPONSIBILITY — **D** MUST BE CONSULTED — **E** MAY BE CONSULTED — **F** MUST BE NOTIFIED — **G** MUST APPROVE

IDENTIFICATION | MANAGEMENT RESPONSIBILITY GUIDE © MRG CORPORATION 1976 | DATE | PAGE 1 NO. OF

APPROVAL:

Exhibit 2-13 The MRG Matrix

Another essential task in the planning phase involves clarification of management and supervisory roles in the career development process. The key question that will pop into most managers' minds when they hear that a career development program is in the works is: "What will I have to do?" In many cases, they are really asking, "Will it mean more work and responsibility replacing employees?" or "I will have to conduct a bunch of soul-searching discussions with my employees."

The options for management responsibility are numerous, and the degree to which managers take an active role in carrying out those options depends on the preference of the organizations, their assessment of the current managerial capacity, and their willingness to provide managers with the time and resources (possibly including training) that may be required. Some roles in which managers may be involved include that of

- Role model: Managers demonstrate interest and activity in their own career development.
- Information source: Managers provide information to employees about career development and career opportunities.
- Motivator: Managers encourage employees to undertake career development and reward these activities.
- Counselor/Coach: Managers conduct counseling interviews with employees to help guide and monitor their career plans.
- Diagnostician: Managers assess strengths and weaknesses of employees on the job and give feedback about how these apply to career opportunities.
- Training specialist: Managers create on-the-job training opportunities and guide employees to other, off-site opportunities.

The role model, information source, and motivator roles may require only that the organization clearly state to managers that these responsibilities are expected of them and provide some basic orientation information to aid them in carrying out these responsibilities.

The informality of the Tektronix work environment fosters frequent discussions between managers and their employees. While many of these discussions may center around a specific job task or rescheduling of work hours, it is common for employees to initiate general talks with their managers about their future career directions. As a rule, Tektronix managers are highly supportive of career development and career change options for their employees. Most managers have made several job changes in the course of their own careers at Tektronix and tend to view this employee desire for change in work content and setting as a natural phenomenon. Some managers will actively facilitate such changes by making contacts with other managers in areas of the company which interest their employees. This kind of cooperation usually exists whenever there is rapport between a given employee and his or her manager.[13]

The counselor, diagnostician, and training specialist roles, on the other hand, may necessitate specialized training that begins well in advance of the program. Although career development is ultimately an individual respor - sibility, the process is usually strengthened when immediate supervisors and managers lend their support to the effort. Managers are often the most available resources to employees for feedback on strengths and weaknesses and for information about opportunities within the organiza- tion. With adequate training and coaching skills they can often offer the assistance that employees need in order to formulate adequate self- assessments, goal statements, and action plans. If managers are also encouraged in this effort by their own superiors, the impetus to offer this service will be even greater.

Recognizing that supervisors at NASA's Goddard Space Flight Center may need to acquire skills to carry out their career development responsibilities, a workshop series was designed. The objective of the workshop is to help utilize employees productively. The workshop is based on a collaborative career planning approach, emphasizing the critical link that line managers must play to insure the success of the organization career development program. Specific objectives include:

- identifying work requirements;
- identifying employee skills, abilities and motivations;
- matching employees to work; and
- communicating with employees.

To demonstrate management support and commitment to this process, the Director of Goddard Space Flight Center meets with participants of the workshop. The purpose of the meeting is to review supervisor action plans constructed during the workshop and to identify organizational obstacles which may impede implementation of the plans.[14]

Often practitioners find that their roles and tasks intermingle with those of managers. In systems where the manager is to be clearly involved, yet not carry the major responsibility for the program design and implementa- tion, the roles and tasks *may* look something like those suggested on the chart that follows. This delineation may help in further outlining respon- sibilities or in just clearly articulating the sometimes subtle differences between practitioner and manager.

What Have We Got To Lose?

The final step of the planning phase is to realistically account for the possibility of snags, snafus, and other undesired circumstances or con- sequences. While there is no need to be pessimistic to the point of creating

Career Development Stages	Practitioners	Managers
Preparation	Review existing programs and plan for their linkage to C.D. Gain commitment/understanding of others Set program objectives Determine delivery vehicles Design evaluation Assign staff roles	Allocate resources Demonstrate commitment Collaborate on program objectives Provide information
Profiling	Provide surveys/questionnaires for self-assessment Administer workshops Assure linking programs (that is, skill inventories, performance appraisals)	Provide encouragement Counsel employees Allow time for employee profiling efforts
Targeting	Encourage top management to share organizational information Catalogue information for employees Instruct in career alternatives Instruct in goal setting	Share organizational information Give feedback on goals Refine support programs as necessary Provide guidance/counseling
Strategizing	Arrange workshops Instruct in analyzing the system Assess and refine linking programs as necessary Encourage management support Execute Examine and refine existing educational programs Development additional programs for education and training, on-the-job experiences, professional support Provide information about developmental resources Monitor progress Document activities	Encourage employees Provide information Provide guidance developmental plans Provide information Allow time necessry for employee development activities Establish means for utilizing new employee abilities Provide recognition and reward
Integration	Develop formal reward and recognition systems Design tracking system Evaluate program progress Analyze needs for program revision Demonstrate to top management return on investment of program	Provide feedback and rewards Provide information that contributes to program valuation Continue utilization of new employee abilities

Exhibit 2-14   Roles of Practitioners and Managers

a self-fulfilling prophecy, it is only good sense to prepare for constraints and problems that might occur.

Organizational Risks.   Risks for the organization are varied and vital for the practitioner to consider before launching a program. They include

- Inability to meet increased demand for career mobility.
- Loss of some valuable employees who find a better career fit elsewhere.
- Excessive internal mobility.
- Need to commit greater resources than anticipated to training, job restructuring, incentives, and new personnel practices.
- Newly surfaced employee dissatisfactions with organizational practices.
- Inability to demonstrate a quick payoff of developmental efforts.
- Employee desires for more human resource development activities than the organization is prepared to deliver.

Individual Risks.   Risks for the individual differ in many respects but are just as important to consider. These factors include

- Unmet expectations about career alternatives within the organization.
- Dissatisfaction on discovering that career desires may not mesh with personal strengths and weaknesses.
- Frustration of personal inability to follow through on career plans.
- Uncertainty or anxiety among those who are satisfied with current job and responsibilities and do not desire career development or change.
- Competition among employees for scarce career opportunities.
- Surfacing fears of change, personal inadequacy, loss of job security.

All of this is not to say that every career development effort is going to meet with an endless mass of problems. Some, in fact, meet with very few problems; they are conceived as necessary by top management and welcomed by people at every level of the organization. Others, for a variety of reasons, are resisted or misinterpreted from the beginning.

Practitioners who are aware of the possible problems and make allowances for them are those who conduct successful programs. They plan in advance and are rarely surprised.

Rewards for the Weary

Oddly enough one of the major problems, and one which should be addressed during the Preparation Stage, deals with the rewards and incentives that can do much to make the program successful after it has been launched. Though this will be dealt with in more detail in the Integration Stage chapter, it is essential that it also be mentioned here.

Traditionally career programs reward only upward movement within the organization. The theme of this book, "up is not the only way," means, as will be shown, that all sorts of mobility should be encouraged (by necessity)—upward, lateral, and even downward. Unless the organization is prepared to recognize and reward these other directions of movement, practitioners will find their programs falling flat—individuals will discover that upward mobility is the only kind that is rewarded, and other career goals set at the Targeting Stage will become meaningless. Therefore, during the Preparation Stage, *before* the effort is ever launched, these reward systems must be addressed and provided.

Secondly, managers do not like to lose good people—many do not like to lose even their marginal performers. A successful career development program should make good performers out of the marginal people and outstanding performers out of the good ones. Employees want to move in all directions. Unless managers and supervisors are rewarded for encouraging employee mobility in a variety of directions, they will witness only problems—that is, the loss of good people. The organization must also provide a reward system to compensate (monetarily or otherwise) managers and supervisors for their developmental efforts and encouragement of subordinates. Simultaneously they must reward employees who opt for other than vertical mobility. Practitioners, in consort with their colleagues in compensation, must address these problems early on if the effort is to succeed. Creativity and imagination are the tickets to success.

On Your Mark, Get Set

Clearly one could go on preparing forever! But that would not launch a career development program, nor motivate employees in career paths, nor provide much return on investment for the organization. The Preparation Stage comes to a close when the practitioners, to the very best of their ability, feel that the necessary groundwork has been laid and that both the people and the structural interventions have been determined and comfortably established.

The chart that follows emphasizes some typical errors that seem to snag human resource practitioners when they get ready to launch a new program. Any of these can snag YOU. So beware!

In delivering effective career developing efforts, the practitioner has to be aware of two very specific killers—underdoing, beginning before the program is well thought out and before organizational support functions are ready; and overdoing, readying resources to such a degree of perfection that managers and employees alike lose impetus and commitment and feel that all the career development talk was just that—talk!

Either extreme can adversely affect the remaining five stages, which will be described in the ensuing chapters.

ACTING WITHOUT DIRECTION
- Moving away from something, rather than toward something
- Not knowing what you want, but acting anyway

SPURNING HALF A LOAF
- Rejecting partial success
- Refusing to attempt minor achievements

DECIDING THE TASK IS TOO BIG
- Not starting on a small part of the job, because the whole job looks too enormous

LEAVING THE BACKYARD UNATTENDED
- Ignoring the people whose support you will need

BUILDING FOUNDATIONS ON SAND DUNES
- Acting on what you want, even though you know others don't agree

NOT KNOWING WHAT YOU'VE GOT WHEN YOU'VE GOT IT
- Failing to determine what constitutes success, and not stopping to look for it.[15]

Exhibit 2-15   Errors of a Grievous Kind

TAPPING TALENT
the profiling stage

"If we knew what talent we had, we'd be glad to promote from within."

There is an adage in sailing that says the most important navigation skill is being able to determine the vessel's position. When a ship begins a trip, the point of departure and the destination are known. Once the voyage is underway, however, the vessel becomes subject to wind, tide, drift, and minor errors in steering. The original course can hardly ever be maintained throughout the trip, and determining the current position becomes important, in order to correct the course.

The employee's career is similar to a sailing voyage. Initially the departure point is known, and a destination, or goal, has been established. As time passes the employee experiences buffeting by the winds of organizational necessity, drifting as priorities and circumstances change, setbacks or accelerations from the changing tides of organizational fortunes, and erroneous steering directions from well-meaning, but often incorrect, advisors and friends. Often, after starting toward one goal, employees find themselves seeking new destinations as their priorities and desires change. For this reason many not only lose sight of where they are going, but do not know for certain where they have been.

This chapter will address the problem of determining the employee's present position.

The Profiling Stage is a self-discovery process for employees whose assessments of self and career may have previously been limited to a wistful view of uncertain upward opportunities within the organization. The essence of this stage is to assist the employee in answering the question,

"Who Am I?" ... Since that question is often taxing to answer fully and honestly, employees need strong encouragement throughout their efforts to identify existing skills and to recognize their potential for transferring present skills to future career settings. During the Profiling Stage, the employee is responsible for identifying skills and interests, but the practitioner must support the effort by providing opportunities and guidelines.

THE COMPONENTS

The Profiling Stage occurs in two distinct phases: *identification* and *reality-testing*. During the identification phase employees are assisted in using a variety of methods to uncover their range of skills, knowledge areas, values, and work context preferences. This enables them to develop a personal skill inventory that provides direction for selecting appropriate goals at the Targeting Stage, which follows.

During the reality-testing phase, employees test these self-perceptions by soliciting feedback from other individuals and by cross-checking with existing organizational resources, such as past performance appraisals and job descriptions. Skill identification without reality-testing would encourage the individual to select goals based on skills that are only *self-perceptions*. Reality-testing forces a system of checks and balances on the individual. While skill identification usually begins the Profiling Stage, one need not wait until all skills are identified to begin testing them against reality. There is much oscillation between the phases throughout the Profiling Stage. It is also possible to invert the two phases, that is for the employee to receive data about an area of expertise from a colleague or boss and then proceed to identify more specific skills involved or to identify other situations in which that skill was used. What is important to remember is that each skill identified must be verified—before the Profiling Stage concludes and the individual begins to determine career goals at the Targeting Stage.

A Bevy of Benefits

Although profiling is largely an individual activity that results in information for the employee, its output extends to the organization as a whole. Typically, organizations have only scant knowledge of the depth of human resources in their work force. Even companies that have developed formal skill inventories have often catalogued only the abilities now being used on the job and have not assessed additional skills or current ones that may be available to fill future needs. Employee profiling activities can provide useful information to the organization, suggesting strategies for further employee training and human resource planning. Individual managers can also gain a wealth of information for more effectively structuring job tasks and guiding employees in appropriate directions.

The value of profiling for employees lies in their increased ability to articulate their skills and abilities, thereby enabling them to more intelligently choose career alternatives. Even if employees stopped the cycle after having done only this self-assessment process, they would have gained a great deal. Most would have learned that their skills are much more extensive and transferable to a wider variety of job settings than previously imagined. For example, an individual who may have identified "bookkeeping" as a major skill, now discovers other skills, which might include fact-finding, organizing, and negotiating. Such discovery builds self-confidence, with benefits extending beyond the job setting. The profiling process also encourages employees to discuss self-perceptions with supervisors and to formulate a wider base for defining career goals and performance standards. Such an understanding of personal abilities and preferences increases productivity on current jobs and helps in projecting career futures. The Profiling Stage is a crucial step with immediate payoff, but only a first step in the total career development cycle.

Now, for the Hard Part

Unfortunately skill identification is no simple task. Individuals are often prevented from verbalizing their skills by a cultural norm which gives high priority to personal modesty. It is, therefore, often difficult for employees to sell someone on their skills, even when it is appropriate to do so. Complicating matters is the fact that jobs are often identified by vague labels rather than by specific activities or skills. The question asked is, "What do you do?" not, "What are your skills?" And the reply is, "I'm a personnel analyst," not, "I organize, write, interview, and analyze." The ability to articulate specific skills used on the job is often the most difficult to master. And many individuals take their abilities for granted, failing to recognize the multitude of skills they use in accomplishing even routine tasks. For many it is easier to define skill deficiencies, since negative feedback from supervisors may be more common than positive. Even when skills are well defined, most people contribute to this negativism by putting themselves down in order to appear "humble" and "worthy." Furthermore, employees often fail to consider skills used less frequently, on prior jobs, or in personal endeavors.

The challenge for practitioners at the Profiling Stage, therefore, is to assist employees in exploring their wide array of personal capacities. This requires that practitioners work with employees, either directly or through managers, career advisors, or trainers, to increase awareness of how present work activities encompass specific skills that can become future building blocks. The areas of inquiry which practitioners can help employees explore include

- What do you do particularly well on your current job?
- What specific skills have you used well in the past or outside the work setting?
- Which of your skills and talents do you feel are most highly valued by the organization?
- What factors in the work setting (that is, congenial colleagues, competent supervision, pleasant surroundings) are most important to you?
- What values do you have (close friendships, sense of power, autonomy, continued learning) that are most important to work context?

Additionally practitioners will need to establish among employees, their supervisors, and their colleagues an appreciation of candid communication and feedback as mechanisms to support the reality-testing of identified skills and work values.

THE IDENTIFICATION COMPONENT

The identification phase of profiling entails examination of three major attributes that can influence the selection of future career goals: skills, values, and work contexts. Employees will need to embark on thoughtful self-exploration in each of these three areas before gaining the clear composite picture needed for the Targeting Stage.

The Skill of It All

Before undertaking skill identification activities, the practitioner needs to understand the nature of skills and their use at different levels of the organization.

A skill may be defined as specific behavior that results in effective performance. During the Profiling Stage, it is important to remember that a skill must be demonstrated in performance, not merely in potential.

Skills can be learned in three specific ways: theoretically, through simulation and by on-the-job experience. In the first approach an individual is exposed to knowledge by reading or listening to a lecture. In simulated learning the individuals actually practice a skill in an artificial situation and receive feedback on their performance. Skills are learned through on-the-job training when individuals perform a skill as a natural component of their work. Skills are most effectively learned when individuals can actually perform the skill in a realistic situation and then explicitly analyze their performance.[1]

A great many systems have been advanced for categorizing work skills. These include classifying them by people, data, and things; by personal, technical, and management; or by discovering, analyzing, and synthesizing skills.

Perhaps one of the most common means of classifying work-related skills is to categorize them as those which are technical in nature, those which deal with human relations, and those which pertain to the conceptualization of problems and situations.[2] Because of its many applications, this classification system has been selected for use in this book. (At this and subsequent stages reference will be made to these three skill areas.)

Nearly every job can be broken down into requirements for skills in technical, human, and conceptual areas. All employees possess skills in these categories, and success in almost any career field will require proficiency in them. Analyzing the relative importance of these skills will show what areas are potential sources of strength.

Technical Skills. Technical skills are the most concrete and most easily identifiable of the three types. They are represented by proficiency in a particular activity or process related directly to the job. These skills are acquired through training and experience in using whatever tools, processes, or techniques apply to a specific function. Work specialization has put a high priority on technical skills—ranging from surgery to accounting to pipe fitting—and they are typically emphasized in most professional, vocational, and on-the-job training programs.

While they may be easily identifiable, technical skills are probably the least transferable of the three—they are the type of skill that an individual would be most likely to change or leave behind as one moves through the organization.

Viewed in terms of the four classic levels of organizations—nonsupervisory, first-line supervisory, managerial, and executive—technical skills tend to change greatly according to level, as shown in Exhibit 3-1.

Level	Nature of Technical Skill
Executive	*Directive*—Ability to guide, coordinate, and administer suborganizational efforts so as to accomplish organizational mission; *and* ability to determine, from a variety of inputs, the technological directions and trends that will necessitate organizational responses to maintain or improve market position.
Managerial	*Administrative*—Ability to guide, coordinate, and administer the several group functions that make up the suborganizational effort.
First-Line Supervisory	*Task Coordination*—Ability to understand and coordinate those specific functions that make up the group function.
Nonsupervisory	*Task Specific*—Ability to work with tools of the trade to accomplish the routine job functions.

Exhibit 3-1 Technical Skills

Human Skills. Human skills are primarily related to working with people. While they can be developed through conscientious effort, these skills require a strong natural inclination and must be consistently demonstrated if they are to be successful. An asset at all job levels, these skills are reflected in the way an individual understands, communicates with, and motivates others. They facilitate cooperative efforts, from effective delegation to teamwork to negotiation; they are marked by productive relationships with colleagues, subordinates, and supervisors. An individual skilled in this area is sensitive to the personal needs and capacities of others, as well as to the functional needs of accomplishing a task. These skills permit one to develop and maintain a network of contacts, in order to do favors for one another and pass along information; to motivate, train, counsel, and guide a staff; and to mediate conflicts between individuals.

The nature of human skills changes as one moves up through the organizational hierarchy. These changes may be depicted as shown in Exhibit 3-2.

Conceptual Skills. Conceptual skills are the most complex to identify because they involve a mental coordinating and integrating ability that embodies both technical and human skills. They include the ability to visualize various components of an enterprise, problem, or decision as a whole, to recognize the overall functional relationships of those components; and to sense what action is appropriate in terms of the total situation. This skill enables individuals to base decisions on creative

Level	Nature of Human Skill
Executive	*Interpersonal/Intraorganizational/Interorganizational*—Ability to conduct effective one-on-one relationships within the organization, and in the organization as it interfaces with other organizations. (Inspiring)
Managerial	*Interpersonal/Intragroup/Intergroup*—Ability to conduct one-on-one relationships in all directions; to maintain harmonious relationships within a large group, and between one's own group and those with which it interfaces. (Negotiation)
Supervisory	*Interpersonal/Intragroup*—Ability to conduct one-on-one or supervisor-to-subordinate relationships *and* to keep group relationships harmoniously directed toward group goals and missions. (Leading)
Nonsupervisory	*Interpersonal*—Ability to conduct one-on-one and small group peer or worker-to-supervisory relationships. (Communicating)

Exhibit 3-2   Human Skills

thinking about the past, present, and future, by being able to visualize a mental model of the organization as a whole unit. Broken down by organizational levels, conceptual skills may be depicted as follows:

Although all three types of skills are valuable at every level of the organization, they vary in relative importance at different places in the hierarchy. Those employees operating in the professional/technical area have the highest need for technical skills, while also requiring some degree of human and conceptual skills. With an increase in supervisory and administrative responsibility the demand for technical skills decreases, while that for interpersonal and conceptual skills sharply rises. At the top levels of the organization, especially in policy-making positions, the need for conceptual skills is highest. The chief executive officer may be able to draw upon technical and interpersonal skills that exist at lower levels, but it is critical that the leader's conceptual skills provide the overall coordination and integration needed to meet the firm's objective.[3]

The relationship of skills to organizational levels are depicted as follows in Exhibit 3-4.[4]

For any particular organization and the hierarchies within it, the functions and specific skills required at each level will vary. Practitioners will find it necessary to assist employees in identifying their specific technical, human, and conceptual skills and in matching what they see as their current abilities against those required for their future work. It may be necessary to gain managerial support in defining and specifying skills in order to accurately determine them.

Level	Nature of Conceptual Skill
Executive	*Entrepreneurial Creativity*—Unfocused creative emphasis on the "big picture" of how the organization interfaces with the world around it. Strategic planning and long-range problem identification, as well as the ability to determine trends in the environment.
Managerial	*Organizational Creativity*—Focused on the problems, goals, and missions of the organization; the determination of needs to accomplish goals; and the bringing together of resources to create generalized purposes.
Supervisory	*Areal Synthesis*—Focused on the problems, needs, and resources involved in an area and the bringing together of effort to accomplish a series of tasks which relate to an overall objective.
Nonsupervisory	*Local Convergence*—Focused or the individual task as it relates to the surrounding function.

Exhibit 3-3   Conceptual Skills

SKILLS NEEDED

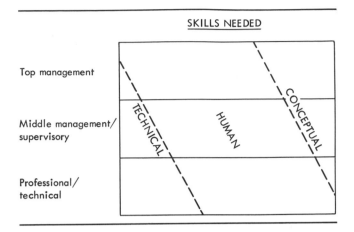

Exhibit 3-4   The Skills Necessary at Various Levels of an Organization

Prudential Insurance Company's mid-America home office (Merrillville, Inc.) has developed a career planning program for its more promising clerical employees. The program is based on a job family concept that makes the tasks people actually do and the key skills inherent in doing them more comprehensible to employees.

During the sessions participants analyze key job duties and skills required for successful performance and listen to a series of audiotaped interviews with present jobholders from the various job families. On their own, employees fill out a self-assessment of job interest and abilities and undertake an 86-item personal job analysis survey and fill out a set of scoring keys for each of the four job families that enables them to relate their interest patterns as shown by the job analysis survey to each of the job families.

Transferability of Skills

One outcome of the identification phase is the ability to determine which skills are potentially transferable to other locations within or outside the organization. Without transferable skills individuals would not move at all from one position to another within an organization. The more the practitioner can assist individuals to become more aware, not only of the specific skills relevant to their particular job, but of those skills which are transferable to other jobs, the broader the range of goal options that can be opened to them.

A transferable skill means that an individual has gained particular knowledge that is necessary to move from one area of an organization or one kind of work to another. If an individual can see that a particular skill is transferable, abilities acquired elsewhere and at other times in that individual's life can be considered acceptable background for a particular position.

Transferability can occur in one of three ways: (1) A specific skill—such as typing, budgeting, programming, or organizing—can be transferred from one job to another. (2) A knowledge area—such as accounting, consumer credit, sales, or data processing—can be transferred. (3) An entire activity or array of skills—such as supervising operations procedures, analyzing customer needs, or interviewing prospective candidates—can also be transferred. Each of these can be used in many parts of any one organization. Each can also be transferred from organization to organization.

The practitioner can use a variety of approaches to help employees describe their transferable skills, identify alternative uses for those skills, and determine how those alternatives relate to other jobs within the organization. Exercises could include determining skills and then naming other places in the organization where those skills would be used, whether or not one wanted to move in that direction.

Verifying Values

While it is essential that an individual base career choices on appropriate skills, it is equally important to mesh career considerations with the personal values that shape life preferences. Values are those esteemed ideals and concepts which are expressed in our everyday behavior and our long-term priorities. Because of their influence on behavior and priority-setting, values affect satisfaction and determine effectiveness on the job. For a person to be productive and happy, a fit must exist between the job and the employee's personal values.

An individual who places high value on personal freedom, for example, may need to work independently, unhampered by restrictions imposed by others. Those who value a sense of accomplishment require strong feedback in response to their endeavors. Security is a high priority for some people, who may feel the work doesn't have to be exciting or challenging as long as there is little fear of losing the job.

Practitioners need to build a repertoire of exercises to help employees identify values. Most values assessments suggest various values and ask respondents to prioritize or rate their importance. Typically work values that can affect career decisions include

Achievement	Continued learning
Security	Prestige
Authority	Social contribution
Autonomy	Monetary rewards
Social contact	Pleasant surroundings
Variety	Opportunity for advancement
Creativity	Chance to demonstrate abilities
Esteem of others	Self-esteem

These work values are clearly related to general life values, such as a stable and loving family life, rewarding friendships, time for leisure activities, good health, and a secure future. Individuals must establish a fit between their values for working and their overall life values, in order that each contributes to and builds upon the other. Career decisions that take values into account are more likely to result in satisfying and rewarding job achievement.

The Right Context

The context of the job is the psychological and physical setting in which work is performed. Context preferences closely reflect personal values. A job that requires a great deal of travel, for example, might be considered desirable or undesirable, depending on individual values and lifestyle. Comfort with work requiring selling, persuading, or directing interaction with other people reflects other values. The degree of stress involved in a job is part of its context. Even the nature of an organization, or an entire industry—conservative, progressive, or in-between—sets the tone of the work context and helps determine how individuals will fit with it. Product lines and the primary customers are also important in considering individual value systems. For instance, a person who highly values peace and nonviolence could hardly be happy working in a defense- or nuclear-related industry, the products of which were aimed at armaments.

Often it is these job characteristics that are responsible for an employee's sense of job satisfaction. If the profiling process is intended to lead to setting realistic goals, it is important that an employee's profile include an examination of the contextual factors which contribute to their sense of job satisfaction, as well as those factors leading to stress or dissatisfaction.

Practitioners can design exercises to assist in bringing these preferences into the open and to make them a vital part of the career profile. Some job factors which may be considered include

1. Its environmental context:
   - The "look" of physical surroundings (such as furniture and lighting)
   - Mobility (ability to move about to perform tasks)
   - Location (such as urban/suburban or indoor/outdoor)
   - Privacy (space from or closeness to others)
   - Communication (face-to-face, written, telephone)

2. Its interactional context:
   - Degree of supervision
   - Degree of contact with peers
   - Degree of contact with clients
   - Degree of friendliness in relations with others
   - Degree of and frequency of feedback about performance

3. Its functional context:
    *   Degree of challenge in work
    *   Degree of certainty about scheduling and duties
    *   Opportunities for learning
    *   Type of work (technical, supervisory, policy-making)
    *   Work hours
    *   Degree of control (formal procedures, rules)
    *   Pay and benefits

Employees can be guided through a review of these factors, asking themselves, "What do I feel I need in each of these areas?" Those who go through this process will be better equipped to select career opportunities that have the greatest personal fit and are most likely to lead to satisfaction.

RESOURCES FOR IDENTIFICATION

Very few individuals are capable of conducting the in-depth self-exploration necessary for effective profiling. Therefore, the practitioner needs to provide guidance at this point. The charge for career development practitioner is (1) to provide this broad-based support for a number of people in a manner that recognizes their unique individual needs and (2) to determine who in the system is most appropriate to deliver these services to employees.

A variety of proven tools and techniques exist, which can be drawn upon to guide employees through the identification process. They can be delivered by the practitioner, or administered (with proper training) by managers, career counselors/advisors, or members of the training staff. Two categories of instruments that can facilitate profiling are self-assessment exercises and scored surveys.

Self-assessment exercises generally call for individual creativity and internal brainstorming. They ask open-ended questions that give respondents the latitude to develop answers out of their own experience and self-knowledge. Such inventories may ask a respondent to create a composite of the ideal work setting, to prioritize a list of value statements, or to select key words from a list of personal adjectives. The results are examined by the participant and may be discussed with others in order to add to the composite developed at the Profiling Stage.

Scored surveys are pen and paper tests geared to previously determined measures, which indicate vocational interests, aptitudes, motivations, values, and other personal characteristics. Generally, they ask a number of closed-ended questions (answers limited to yes/no, true/false) and lead to scores which connote different degrees of skills or preferences for different jobs or job characteristics. For example, individuals can determine if their strengths lie in working with concepts or working with numbers, or if their preferences are for leading the team or following the lead of others. Often practitioners have these surveys available on the shelf but overlook their usefulness at the identification phase of the Profiling Stage.

Each of these aids may be delivered individually, by using self-scored tests in workbooks that contain scoring interpretations or through group activities, such as workshops in which participants share results and assist one another in interpretation. The current trend is to combine both methods, by first administering individual exercises and then using the results as a basis for group workshop activities. Participants can thus gain information that relates to their unique characteristics, but they can be motivated and assisted by others in analyzing that information in relation to the career development process.

Clearly workshops should be led by skilled facilitators who can draw from individuals the information and interpretations that may not readily come to mind. A group setting adds to the profiling process because of the motivational impact of peer assistance. Individuals discover that they are not alone as they move into the more difficult aspects of profiling. Additionally the power of group interaction during a workshop can lead participants to more in-depth discussion about their skills and job preferences than might be possible when they work alone.

Both kinds of interventions, self-assessment exercises and scored surveys, stimulate the identification process. The selection of activities best suited to a particular group depends upon the nature of the group and the skill level of the professionals administering the activity. To assist practitioners in making the most informed choices, a detailed description of the two categories of instruments follows.

Self-Assessment Exercises

Because they are designed to maximize creative thinking and internal brainstorming, self-assessment exercises leave substantial latitude for individual interpretation (unlike scored tests in which interpretation is predetermined for various numerical results). This interpretive latitude places particular emphasis on *how* the exercise is used by the individual administering it as well as several other factors that contribute to interpretation such as

- Setting—individual, small group, or large group
- Opportunities for sharing individual results
- Opportunities for peer-to-peer feedback and advice
- Probing questions by the facilitator
- Interpretive assistance by the facilitator

Self-assessment exercises rarely end with the respondent completing a form and putting down the pen. Generally additional prodding is necessary to generate ideas that do not readily come to mind. Quite often some discussion of responses is useful to inspire in-depth interpretation of results. While the design of the exercise itself is important, the format in which it is used is often the key to its success as a profiling tool. Books containing self-assessment exercises proliferate the market place. They contain many exercises that help individuals define their skills. Generally these approaches start with a design for listing skills or related personal qualities and continue through a format for further probing and interpretation. Practitioners may want to familiarize themselves with the wide variety of exercises available before selecting those to be offered to employees. Although the examples that follow only scratch the surface of possible self-assessment techniques, they demonstrate the variety of designs and formats that may be used.

- Search
- Success Stories
- Career History
- Typical Day
- Values Card Sort
- Work Preference Profile
- Work Benefits/Pleasures

Identifying Skills. The *Search* technique helps participants define a wide range of skills, by naming a primary technical or conceptual skill used on the job and then brainstorming related subskills that it entails. The primary skill is written in the center of a piece of paper, with subskills placed, like branches, on arrows leading into it, giving participants a visual aid to prod their thinking. The technical skill of "copy editing" may actually involve a great range of subskills that may be difficult for the individual to think of (such as "interviewing," "organizing," "researching," "rewriting," "decision making," "creating," "planning,") or that the individual may well take for granted. An example of a "search" appears in Exhibit 3-5.

The practitioner can facilitate this process by verbally probing what other skills one would use to accomplish the central skill, by sharing new ideas that come to mind, and by providing lists of other skills to which participants may refer when they run out of ideas. "Search" can be done by a manager or career advisor in a personalized setting, or in a workshop setting where participants are encouraged to assist one another and learn, from the searches done by their colleagues, more about their own unacknowledged skills. The payoff of this technique lies in participants' realizations that their skills far exceed frequent characterizations such as, "I'm only a secretary," or "All I do is edit copy."

Success Stories, one of the oldest and most widely used profiling techniques helps individuals recognize the personal skills that they may have demonstrated in the past, may not be using on their current jobs, may

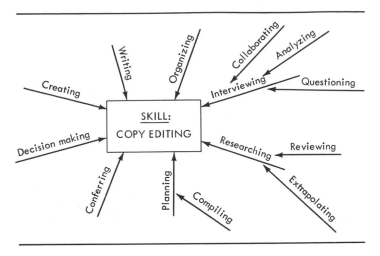

Exhibit 3-5 The Skill "Search"

take for granted, or may have completely forgotten about. If a workshop setting is selected, each person in a small group would relate a past experience in which he or she felt successful. Group members then assist each other in developing a list of the skills demonstrated in the story. This exercise can also be used in a one-to-one discussion between manager and subordinate or between career advisor and employee.

The excitement generated by this exercise can break through old mental blocks such as "I don't have any particular skills," or "I can't think of anything I'm good at." Employees find that past achievements, such as managing a class president's campaign or organizing the local celebration of Earth Day, demonstrate abilities in planning, organizing, public speaking, negotiating, fund raising, delegating, and so on. These may be skills that can be reactivated and used toward achieving specific career goals.

Another way to use success stories is to center on a person's accomplishments over the past twelve to eighteen months on the job. Employees are asked to think of examples of success stories that characterize such things as decision making, problem solving, or interpersonal style. Employees find themselves becoming more specific about their current skills as a result of this exercise. It can be especially useful when the success stories being told relate to specific behavior to be evaluated in performance appraisals. Individuals can use the information gleaned from this exercise to more effectively prepare for an employee-initiated dialogue during the performance appraisal.

A similar exercise, *Career History,* asks employees to describe the progression of their work life. Group members listen for skills that have been demonstrated, particularly those that have reappeared time and time again. Individual values and work context preferences may also be revealed. This exercise serves as an excellent warm-up activity and can easily be done in either a one-to-one or group setting.

The *Typical Day* exercise seeks to identify currently used skills that may be overlooked or taken for granted. A facilitator uses guided imagery to move the individual through a typical work day. Prodding the memory for exactly what happens hour-by-hour helps individuals to elaborate about daily activities, so that they can begin to note the variety of skills practiced each day.

A great many books on the market contain exercises useful in eliciting skills from participants. The problem is not so much in finding exercises or designing them as in determining which ones offer the right combinations for a particular group of employees. Practitioners are encouraged to search out the materials available and weigh them against program needs in a manner such as the one shown in Exhibit 3-6.

Identifying Personal Needs. Other inventory techniques can help individuals analyze their values and work contexts which, along with skills,

Technique	Objective	Format	Use
Search	Determine numerous skills emanating from one central skill.	Individuals brainstorm their associated skills with help of others.	Going beyond using immediate descriptor of job at hand as only skill definition.
Success Story	Understand how past achievements contribute to personal skills inventory and identify preference patterns leading to successful feelings.	Individuals relate past successes to others who draw out skill definitions.	Discovering skills which may be forgotten or taken for granted.
Career History	Develop a complete list of skills indicated by job experiences, and identify preference patterns for types of work and contexts.	Individuals relate career history to others who suggest skills that have been used.	Naming a wide variety of skills that have been evidenced throughout an array of work experiences.
Typical Day	Determine variety of skills that are used on current job.	Individuals are asked to relate typical day and skills used throughout.	Discovering skills which are frequently used, but may be taken for granted as routine.

Exhibit 3-6   Skill Identification Techniques

provide a solid base for the self-understanding so vital to profiling. A useful self-assessment inventory designed specifically to elicit personal values is the *Values Card Sort.*[6] In this exercise participants are given stacks of cards, each card listing a brief description of a value. The cards are prioritized according to personal preference: "always valued," "often valued," "sometimes valued," "seldom valued," and "never valued." Participants then prioritize and list on a worksheet their most highly prized values (approximately seven in all) and write out a career decision they expect to confront in the near future. These anticipated career decisions are weighed against the prioritized values, and areas of conflict are identified. Including information about values in one's profile helps complete the composite picture and assists in delimiting career goals.

A great many values clarification exercises are available, which practitioners can adapt to the needs of particular populations.

Work Preference Profile, an exercise developed to help respondents analyze their feelings about certain job factors and skills, provides lists of items which can be rated "prefer," "dislike," or "no preference."[7] Respondents rate their preference for such job characteristics as

- Types of work (selling services, providing services, problem solving)
- Types of supervision received (the less the better, frequent guidance)
- Types of supervision exercised (none, few people, many people)
- Types of work content (words, numbers, concepts, policies, interaction)
- Types of contact with others (with higher levels, peers, lower levels)
- Types of feedback (prompt, within a year, written, spoken)

Additionally preference ratings are determined for a list of twenty-one transferable skills, ranging from "analyze" and "evaluate" to "supervise" and "sell." Job context is further defined through an exercise that asks employees to identify "Preferred Job Settings/Job Traits" in order to determine how they feel about various work contexts. The exercise offers a list of job context factors and asks respondents to determine their preference for them on a scale of one (strong preference) to five (strong aversion). Among the factors listed are

- Establish procedures/controls
- Travel frequently
- Work with frequent guidance from supervisor
- Supervise large numbers of people
- Work alone
- Work with many people in the work place
- Receive prompt performance feedback
- Interact frequently with public
- Communicate in writing
- Communicate verbally

Completion of such lists is a solo activity, but following up with a group discussion can make it even more meaningful. These discussions might be used as forums for asking

- Why are these your preferences?
- How did you arrive at this decision?
- Which preferred skills are you now using?
- How could you use them in the future?

Yet another way to use these rating lists is to ask participants to formulate sentences about themselves which incorporate words from their high-preference job factors and skills. This requires individuals to define more specifically why their preferences are meaningful to them and to build toward the succeeding stage of targeting.

These self-assessment exercises help determine and evaluate work preferences and personal values. They also provide participants with a context in which they can begin to seriously think about their past work experiences and apply personal and professional meaning to their careers to date.

Scored Surveys

The objectives of scored surveys are similar to those of self-assessment exercises—to aid individuals in discovering abilities, job interests, values, and other factors that can help shape an appropriate match between the individual and the job. Scored surveys, however, accomplish this through a tangible bottom line, the score; which indicates exactly how test results are to be interpreted.

For many individuals these concrete results are preferable to self-assessment information, which is really left to the vagaries of individual interpretation. Others, however, feel constrained by the narrow categories into which test results may fall, and question the validity of test construction. It is valuable to offer a mix of self-assessment exercises and scored surveys, so that varied profiling methods appropriate to different individuals can be presented. Variety also offers a cross-check on results.

Scored surveys can also be used as the basis for interaction in group settings, significantly enriching the potential use of these instruments at the Profiling Stage. As with self-assessment exercises, a workshop setting can encourage the sharing of conclusions and the discussion of general questions pertaining to each individual's results.

Tested and validated survey instruments are available from numerous sources, including universities, training and consulting firms, and publishing companies. Generally they are aimed at extracting information about interests, styles, and work/life values.

These surveys can assist individuals in acquiring self-knowledge in different areas of their personal and professional lives. However, it is still up to the individual, with guidance and encouragement from the practitioner, to pull the pieces together into a single, coherent view. The following section describes some of the survey instruments that can be used to further the phases of the Profiling Stage. This list is by no means exhaustive, and practitioners may find that other materials, not listed, fill their particular needs better.

Occupational Interests Scored Surveys

Kuder Occupational Interest Survey
Strong Campbell Interest Inventory
Self-Directed Search

Personal Styles/Values Scored Surveys

LIFO
FIRO-B
Personal Profile System
Androgyny Scale
Strength Deployment Inventory

Occupational Interests. Interest inventories are designed to help individuals translate their likes and dislikes into specific work preferences. They can provide information that helps in determining occupational choices, as well as in identifying sources of job dissatisfaction. However, in administering these surveys, practitioners must emphasize that they are *not* tests of aptitudes, but rather of interests in and possible satisfaction with a range of occupations. (The more familiar practitioners are with these surveys, the more they will be able to selectively choose among them.)

Working with interest inventories is best done by career counselors or by advisors or by trained facilitators within a workshop setting. Line managers may not be as effective in using these, unless they have had a great deal of experience and find themselves sincerely interested in the inventory.

One of the best-known and most widely used interest tests is the *Kuder Occupational Interest Survey.* The survey lists a wide variety of interest areas, asking respondents to select their most preferred and least preferred activity in each group. The scores from the test result in an interest profile, demonstrating how the respondent's preferences compare with those of other people in various occupations. Occupations for which the respondent receives the highest scores are those that indicate highest inclination and preference.

Group exercises might be developed around the results of this survey by simply asking employees to discuss their surprise or lack of surprise at the way the interest inventory displayed their preferences. It is probably important to discuss results of the inventory as soon as possible after it is taken. Individuals can reality-test their inventory results by discussing whether or not the results meet with their own self-perceptions. (For further information on the Kuder Occupational Interest Surveys, practitioners should contact Science Research Associates, Inc., 259 East Erie Street, Chicago, IL 60611.)

Likewise, the *Strong-Campbell Interest Inventory,* one of the oldest and most reliable career assessment devices available, identifies similiarities in a respondent's interests to those of individuals in a variety of occupations and helps indicate those occupations that are likely to bring the greatest personal satisfaction. An Occupational Scale shows high and low scores, relating to similarity of interest with people in given lines of work. Six General Occupational Themes (based on the work of J.L. Holland, 1973) provides interpretive analysis for different types of work environment preferences:

1. Realistic (outdoors, technical, mechanical interests)
2. Investigative (scientific, inquiring, analytical interests)
3. Artistic (dramatic, musical, self-expressive interests)
4. Social (helping, guiding, group-oriented interests)
5. Enterprising (entrepreneurial, persuasive, political interests)
6. Conventional (methodical, organized, clerical interests)

Specific scales are used to demonstrate degrees of sociability (introversion/extroversion) and to show inclination for work in an academic environment (Academic Orientation Scale), both of which can be helpful factors in making occupational choices. (For further information, practitioners can contact Consulting Psychologists Press, 577 College Avenue, Palo Alto, CA 94306)

The Holland *Self-Directed Search* helps identify occupational choices by asking respondents to explore four major areas:

1. Activities: Respondents reply "like" or "dislike" to sixty-six activities, such as, "give talks," "solve math or chess problems," and "read fiction."
2. Skills: Respondents reply "yes" or "no" to a list of sixty-six skills, such as, "I can make pottery," "I can supervise the work of others," and "I am a good salesperson."
3. Occupations: Respondents answer "yes" or "no" to indicate which occupations from a list of eighty-four appeal to them.
4. Self-estimates: Respondents rate themselves on a scale of one to seven—low to high—in twelve categories of ability, such as "musical," "teaching," "managerial," and "sales."

Answers in these areas are organized according to Holland's six occupational themes, and an "Occupations Finder" booklet helps respondents locate specific occupations that match their results. (For further information, practitioners can contact Consulting Psychologists Press, 577 College Avenue, Palo Alto, CA 94306).

When the Social Security Administration determined that existing interest inventories were not adequately related to job areas in that organization, it developed its own Career Interest Profile (CIP). This tested and validated instrument was designed to relate specifically to 12 SSA occupational areas (i.e., public contact claims, disability examining, social insurance policy and procedures, and supervision). The activities within these areas became the basis for questioning personal interests. Employees are presented with 240 statements corresponding to job activities and asked whether they would like to perform these activities on a regular basis. Responses are scored for comparison with those of satisfied employees in the 12 SSA occupation areas used as the basis for test design. Employees receive a profile of the results and are invited to contact a career counselor for follow-up discussions. Thus, the CIP goes beyond general occupational interest exploration to specifically indicate interests—and potential satisfaction—in job areas existing within the immediate organization.

Personal Styles. Surveys aimed at helping people become aware of their personalities and styles of interpersonal behavior can provide useful information for the profile and additional insight toward helping the individual work more effectively with others, a key to career success.

Such surveys generally ask respondents to build a self-portrait by choosing from a variety of descriptive adjectives, or by answering questions about how they behave in a number of different situations.

The Life Orientations Survey (LIFO) helps individuals understand how they use personal strengths and styles under both productive and defensive (stressful) conditions. This awareness is helpful in improving self-management and personal interactions. Designed to be administered by a specially trained facilitator, LIFO asks multiple-choice questions about interactions with others in a variety of settings. The scoring and interpretation helps individuals recognize their preferred, back-up, and least preferred styles in four categories of interaction types: conserving-holding, supporting-giving, controlling-taking, and adapting-dealing. Preferred styles in each of these categories can be used productively or used to excess.

LIFO also serves as a profiling instrument, when various adjectives that describe the four categories of interacting styles are formed into sentences that describe the way a person uses that particular characteristic on the job. Adjectives such as "self-starter" and "persuasive" can help individuals describe, for example, that they are "self-starters" when it comes to seeing that customer complaints and letters are answered effectively: that they are "persuasive" in dealing with clients who are upset about lack of service. Individuals can be also asked to select those adjectives they need to work on or to elicit feedback from other people about—for example, if I consider myself controlling, I wonder if my boss or my colleagues also see me that way? In this way the LIFO questionnaire can be used as a reality-testing mechanism. (Practitioners may gain further information from LIFO Associates, Division of Stuart Atkins, Inc., 8383 Wilshire Blvd., Beverly Hills, CA 90211)

Honeywell, Inc., conducts two separate career development workshops as a part of the organization's overall program. Both the Career Development for Women (CDW) and Career Exploration Workshop (CEW) use the Strong-Campbell, LIFO, and Myers-Briggs instruments as a mirror, reflecting and organizing each participant's self-perception about the various facets of personality which are presented. Career blocks are also discussed. Later, all results from the surveys used are placed on one information sheet and used as an observation guide to individual behavior during a simulation. The insights garnered are then used when career goals and action plans are established.

The Fundamental Interpersonal Relations Orientation—Behavior *(FIRO-B)* is another popular questionnaire, which asks questions about how the respondent behaves and feels in various types of interpersonal situations. The scored results indicate the behavior individuals express toward others and how they want others to behave toward them. This behavior is categorized in three dimensions:

1. Inclusion: The desire to be accepted, understood, listened to; to join; to be well known; to be social (or conversely, the lack of desire for inclusion).
2. Control: The desire to have order or structure, to control others, to be in charge, to make decisions (or, the other end of the scale, no desire for control).
3. Affection: The desire to have close, personal relations with others; to initiate relationships; to love and be loved. The giving of oneself.

Each dimension is measured on a zero to nine range; the higher the number, the more strongly a person feels about inclusion, control, or affection. Scores in each of these areas can add to the identification process, by indicating types of work situations that are likely to fulfill personal needs and to give the greatest degree of satisfaction.

The results of the FIRO inventory can also be used to suggest additional means of self-description. Using the inclusion scores, for example, a high score on "expressed inclusion" could assist the person in adding the following statements to a profile: "I make an effort to include my staff in meetings," "I initiate contacts with colleagues and people around me," or, "I have a need for prestige and recognition in this organization." In the case of a low expressed need for inclusion the individual might state, "I like my staff to work on their own and feel responsible for projects," "I do not need to be included in their decision making," or, "I consider myself fairly independent and am happy in that kind of a work context."

Similar descriptions can be developed for high and low control and affection scores. As with other inventories, the FIRO-B can be used to foster additional identification statements during the Profiling Stage in both identification and reality-testing. (Practitioners may order FIRO-B instruments from University Associates, 8517 Production Avenue, San Diego, CA 92126.)

One of the newer instruments on the market, The Personal Profile System (PERFORMAX), presents a plan to assist individuals to understand themselves and others in the work environment. Four behavioral styles are presented: dominance, influencing of others, steadiness, and compliance. The inventory heightens understanding of these styles and identifies the environments most conducive to their success. Action ideas are also offered to help individuals recognize the styles of others that would be most harmonious with their own.

The DISC (Dominance, Influencing of others, Steadiness, Compliance) profile information can be used in a workshop setting to build understanding of self and others, or used in personal counseling to help employees develop the increased sense of personal worth necessary in pursuing career development goals. (Practitioners may gain further information from Performax Systems International, Inc., Minneapolis, MN.)

The *Androgyny Scale* creates a personal style profile by examining the degree to which respondents display characteristics typically labelled "masculine" or "feminine." Among typical masculine traits are those which indicate aggressiveness, independence, and entrepreneurship; while feminine traits connote nurturing, compassion, and sensitivity to others. Respondents rate each of sixty characteristics (for example, loyal, forceful, unsystematic, dominant) on a scale of one to seven, depending on how accurately they feel those characteristics describe them. The results demonstrate a personal leaning toward typical masculine, feminine, or androgynous behavior.

Adjectives from the androgyny scale can also be used to prepare a more detailed self-profile. Adjectives from the scale can be placed in context, so that individuals who see something as describing their own behavior could use this information further. For example, if individuals noted that "sensitivity" was a characteristic that was typical of them, they might further identify this "sensitivity" as it relates to clients, subordinates, or colleagues on a particular issue or problem. Practitioners will find that adjectives taken from this scale, and from others such as the LIFO, may be helpful to individuals who have difficulty describing themselves. These adjectives also become excellent self-descriptions in readying employees for the performance appraisal process. The more employees can describe their skills and abilities to their supervisors, the more the performance appraisal process can become an interactive adult-to-adult interchange. (Further information is available from University Associates, 8517 Production Avenue, San Diego, CA 92126.)

The *Strength Deployment Inventory* (SDI) provides an excellent means for investigating the behavior, values, and motivations underlying certain career choices. The SDI is based on the assumption that people behave toward others in ways which will lead to and result in the greatest degree of personal gratification. People react to and behave with others in different ways at different times. If, for example, a certain person is perceived as wanting help and nurturing, others who desire compatability with that individual will provide as much help and nurturing as they can offer. Since all people are a blend of three motivational modes—power and control, helping and nurturing, and organizing and structuring—the SDI helps individuals understand their own combination of those modes and to develop tolerance and understanding for those of others. Such information can provide an increased understanding of those factors in the job context that will provide personal gratification. (Further information available from Personal Strength Assessment Service, 571 Muskingum Avenue, P.O. Drawer 397, Pacific Palisades, CA 90272.)

These surveys and inventories represent only a few of those available to practitioners. The primary value from any identification inventory lies in the self-insight provided to employees embarking on a career development program. Whether they deal with job contexts and the expectations that individuals seek to fulfill in the work environment, or with behavior and motivations one takes into that context, surveys and inventories provide basic information that has to be validated in other contexts and with other individuals before it can be used in setting goals.

REALITY-TESTING: TAKING A SECOND LOOK

To acquire serious personal validity, identification information needs to be supported by additional data available from immediate experience. Such information provides the basis for the second phase of profiling. Reality-testing can be generated from two major sources: (1) the perceptions of individuals who can be called upon to supply candid impressions of the employee's strengths and weaknesses, and (2) the existing programs and policies in the organization that serve as additional support for career development at this stage. The reality-testing process, then, can be viewed as a means of tapping external information sources, in order to verify the new information that has been developed, mostly by individuals themselves.

People Perceptions

Reality-testing must include discussions with individuals who have some knowledge of the employee developing a profile. This is the most informal, but generally most difficult, aspect of the profiling process, and it is often difficult for both the giver and the receiver of feedback. The likelihood of discomfort can be decreased, and the possibility of honest interchange can be increased, if certain norms or principles are followed. Practitioners should familiarize employees with these before they engage in reality-testing.

The first concerns the notion of respect. Individuals must respect the views, knowledge, and capabilities of the person offering assessment. If the individual does not value and trust the other person's opinion, reality-testing input will have little effect. Trust partly develops from the feeling that the other person's input will be sincere and helpful. Employees receiving feedback must also be convinced that assessments offered are intended to be in their best interests.

The second norm is privacy. Employees should have a feeling of safety with those selected for this process. They must be convinced that anything revealed will remain confidential and will not be misused.

Openness is the third norm, and this involves a willingness on the part of the assessor to be frank. Openness is two sided—the employee must also be willing to hear frank statements and must not become defensive when information is provided. The employee must be willing to listen closely, but must also be encouraged to reflect on what has been said. The idea is not merely to hear the feedback, but also to put it to use.

Those providing reality-testing information should recognize that they are merely providing feedback and not trying to make another individual more like themselves. The assessor is concerned with providing perceptive information, not with correcting faults or the shaping personalities and behavior into that more compatible with their own beliefs.[10]

The career development practitioner will need to develop ways to create an environment where these principles prevail and where effective reality-testing can occur. For example, part of a workshop can include a reality-testing exchange between pairs of people who know each other well. An assignment to be completed before a workshop, or in the time between two workshops, can be to discuss with friends and colleagues a set of questions such as, "What do you see as my strengths/weaknesses on the job?" or, "Here is a list of skills I have identified—what do you think?"

Employees can go beyond the immediate job setting for reality-testing information. While peers, supervisors, and subordinates can give important feedback about task performance and interaction on the job, family and friends can assist in exploring essential information priorities. Furthermore, sharing profiling information with family and friends at this stage in the career development process enables employees to generate personal support and understanding that will be valuable as career changes are being contemplated or implemented later on.

Reality-Testing in Real Time. In addition to gaining feedback from others as a means of reality-testing the profiles developed, a number of organizations have found that these new self-perceptions can be tested in the work place through work experience programs. A work experience reality-test allows participants to rotate through several jobs on a short-time basis, so that they can determine the validity of their perceived preferences. While it is relatively easy to *assume* that one would like the work associated with a particular field or interest area, seeing the function performed is often the acid test.

Carefully planned and executed preparation with managers and top-level executives can overcome organizational resistance to work experience reality-testing. Practitioners might offer assurance that a short-term test is more cost-effective than a long-term misplacement due to a false assumption. Furthermore, such a test helps to retain those who might leave the organization if they make a career mistake.

> Many career development programs emphasize the evaluation of employee skills and abilities, interests and values, but few provide a mechanism for testing the work environment. The Career Development Work Experience at NASA's Goddard Space Flight Center provides that unique mechanism. Through participation in the program, midlevel employees can assess the appropriateness of certain career options by actually working in short-term job assignments outside their normal working area.[11]

Structural Supports

It is important for practioners to remember that every organization has ongoing systems and procedures which, if fully used and linked with the career development program, can enrich individual career development activities and contribute to organizational objectives. When taken into account during the planning of career development efforts, they provide valuable structural support for its activities.

Several of these structural support programs are particularly relevant to the Profiling Stage, because of their ability to aid in identification and in providing information for reality-testing. Three programs that can make major contributions are job descriptions (often including job analysis and performance standards), performance appraisals, and skill inventories.

A Job Well Defined.   Employees who are encouraged to review their written job descriptions, or to elicit verbal descriptions from supervisors, often find supporting information to supplement the personal profile they have developed. Often review of a job description will remind employees of skills that have become so routine and intuitive that they have forgotten them. For instance, many jobs require organizational and analysis skills that employees perform so routinely that they forget these are valuable talents to be included in a profile.

Obviously, the more specific and current the job description is, the more complete the information it provides. Because job descriptions are often outdated documents no longer relevant to the actual activities performed on the job, updates are frequently necessary.

A complete and updated job description contains job duties, accountabilities, and specifications. Profiling activities can lead employees to revise their own job descriptions. Employees can use the job description to see whether or not the skills identified earlier in this phase are required of them on the job.

Job descriptions are sometimes supplemented by written performance standards related to goals to be accomplished over a set period of time. Performance standards state what is to be done, as well as how much and how well it is to be done. Generally performance standards need review and revision at least annually and should be arrived at through mutual agreement between employee and supervisor. Job descriptions support not only employee profiling activities, but also human resource planning, orientation, recruiting and screening, training and development, hiring and placement, and the development of organizational career ladders.

Performance Appraisal. As described in the preceding chapter, performance appraisal systems and techniques are closely linked to all stages of a career development program. During the Profiling Stage, however, performance appraisals help supply employees with an opportunity to candidly reality-test their skills with supervisors. And if it is to enhance the profiling process, a performance appraisal system must be more than a signed list of check-marked ratings slipped surreptitiously on employees' desks by their managers while the employees are on a lunch break. It should involve face-to-face discussion that affords opportunities for

- Description of performance strengths and suggestions for capitalizing on them.
- Description of performance deficiencies and suggestions for correcting them.
- Establishment of performance standards for the upcoming year in light of these strengths and weaknesses.
- Exchange of mutual expectations and needs for interaction between supervisor and subordinates.

Performance appraisals are commonly given only at prescribed times and, even then, under conditions of formality and discomfort. However, feedback given regularly, appropriately, and soon after significant events helps the employees do a better job, provides valuable information for their profiles, and makes the supervisor-subordinate interface easier.

In order to be effective, reality-testing feedback from supervisors should meet three criteria:

1. The employee should understand what the supervisor is saying.
2. The employee should be willing and able to accept what is being said as constructive.
3. The employee should be able to use the feedback as a basis for action or change.

Feedback that is focused on behavior rather than on the personality, that is based on observations rather than opinions, that is descriptive rather than judgmental, that involves the sharing of ideas and information, that is specific about situations, and that is given at the appropriate time will be effective as a reality-test of the employee's own perceptions.

Thus, adequate performance appraisal is not just a rating activity to provide data for personnel files. It is one of the best means of providing employees and supervisors with in-depth information about their work skills and abilities. If both parties prepare for the process and are conscious of their common need for this information, it can add to the self-awareness of the Profiling Stage. These conditions can make performance appraisals a WIN/WIN situation to be anticipated, rather than a drudgery to be feared. All but the most cursory written appraisals are generally difficult and undesirable tasks for supervisors. Special training, close accountability, and attractive incentives will probably be required to motivate more meaningful appraisals. Attempts have been made to provide this training through workshops, counseling sessions, and workbooks. Active identification of skills at the Profiling Stage is one of the best ways to prepare employees to effectively use the appraisal process.

The Broadway Department Store chain has initiated an approach to performance appraisal training for both manager and subordinate. They utilize a set of workbooks, which are customized to their industry and provide exercises and instruments to assist both parties to prepare for the appraisal process. Exercises for managers assist in helping them to carefully consider the strengths and weaknesses of employees and exercises also help employees develop strength profiles which can be used as the basis of exchanges with the manager during the performance appraisal process.[12]

Assessment Centers. Another structure which can contribute to profiling is the assessment center, either in-house or at an outside location. By providing evaluation in a variety of group and individual settings, assessment centers offer objective off-the-job evaluation of abilities, potential, strengths, weaknesses, and motivation. Most organizations currently using assessment centers do so to identify and evaluate potential for advancement or even initial selection, usually at supervisory and managerial levels, rather than to provide profiling information. However, when individual results are provided to employees at the end of an assessment center session, participants are exposed to vital information they can readily apply to their self-profiles.

The assessment center, which has grown increasingly popular in recent years, is generally two days to one week in duration, with six to twelve participants observed by a team of assessors. Participants are evaluated in a variety of group role-playing sessions, which simulate leadership and leaderless situations in decision-making settings. The sessions also generally include individual interviews and may require one or more pen-and-paper tests. It is important that the assessing organization determine beforehand the skills and characteristics being evaluated, which typically include

leadership	motivation
oral communication	decisiveness
planning	personal impact on others
work under pressure	teamwork
response to stress	organization
energy	analysis

Self-awareness in the above skill areas contributes much to the identification process and, because those skills are witnessed by an impartial observer, the assessment contributes to reality-testing.

When used as a selection tool, the results of the assessment center's feedback would normally be sent to a manager several levels above the participant in the participant's organization. The material may, of course, be sent to the assessee's direct supervisor. When the feedback is employed as a profiling tool, the report would go to participants themselves, giving them the opportunity to ask questions and to choose whether or not to share the data with anyone else.

Assessment Centers have been used at InterNorth in Omaha, Nebraska for some selection decisions, but the majority have been for developmental purposes. The first line field supervisory positions within the company have major administrative requirements but are filled most often by people of proven technical competence who may be unfamiliar with supervisory tasks. The Assessment Center provides the employee the chance to experience, through simulation, some of the administrative problems of the job. Because the employee gets feedback on their assessment center performance they can make an informed decision on how best to develop their career. At the same time the company identifies a pool of employees with the required level of administrative skill for consideration when vacancies occur.[13]

Organizations who have assessment center technology available to them are beginning to recognize its usefulness as a profiling vehicle and as a selection and developmental tool.

Skills Inventories. The skills inventory serves the vital purpose of documenting the profile developed, so that the organization can utilize that information further. The ability to have skills inventories available in most firms of any size allows better use of employee skills. Talents are also more easily identified, which benefits both the organization and the employee. Overall efficiency can be increased, and general employee morale can be improved.[14]

Skills inventories, once completed, are rarely updated. Employees seldom see the importance of maintaining their own data banks. A clear benefit to be derived from work done during the profiling stage is that employees might recognize the need to update their skill bank and would have a large array of information to draw from.

A skills inventory data bank might include these items about individuals:

- Title
- Department
- Grade/job classification
- Salary
- Current work experience
- Past work experience
- Foreign language proficiency
- Willingness to relocate/geographic preference
- Career interests
- Education
- Professional designations, certificates, licenses
- Training courses completed
- Professional organization memberships

This information should be updated at least annually; and, depending on the capabilities of the personnel data system, it should be revised as often as is necessary to reflect new training, new professional memberships, or other changes.

Annual updates could be completed by supervisor and employees jointly agreeing on new information before it is submitted to the system and, in this way, providing valuable face-to-face feedback for profile development.

Skills inventories, especially those that are computerized and cover thousands of employees, have been particularly valuable to organizations committed to employee development and recruitment from within. Not only do they make it possible to locate individuals with existing skills, they also identify deficiencies (which can be addressed at later stages in the career development cycle). As selection devices they quickly narrow the

A simplified but highly effective inventory system has been developed by Citibank for matching job vacancies with candidates inside the organization. The computerized "Jobmatch" system relies on two major sets of information: 1) a profile of tasks required on the job (and frequency with which they will be performed) and 2) a profile of tasks and performance frequency which the employee has perfromed satisfactorily.

The tasks related to the job are determined by the supervisor, who selects from a list of 74 task descriptions and ascribes frequencies to them. The employee specifies tasks satisfactorily performed from the same list of 74 and verifies this with a personnel interviewer. Additionally, Jobmatch allows employees to indicate on a preference scale the degree to which they desire to perform the various tasks on their next job. The system can be initiated by a request to find a candidate who can fit an available position or to find a position that fits a candidate seeking a change. A match is run prior to attempting outside recruitment to assure that no qualified internal candidates have been overlooked.[15]

field to a manageable number of candidates. Many managers are surprised to find qualified individuals within their own organizations who can fill vacancies without expensive recruitment campaigns. A negative attitude not only denies employees visibility and possible advancement, but also denies the organization the benefit of using human resources to their fullest potential. It is important that managers be required to use the skills inventory.

Union Oil developed a skills inventory which became a data base of vital organizational information. Its structure permitted immediate retrieval of almost any desired item or combination of items of employee-related information. Nicknamed IRIS, for Industrial Relations Information System, the data base is quite different from many so-called skills inventories; yet all of the information needed only amounts to two sides of one page for each employee.

IRIS can be thought of as a giant honeycomb containing over 600,000 individual items of factual, cross-referenced information about employees, information such as "John Doe has a bachelor's degree in chemical engineering," or "Fred Roe was manager or corporate accounting in 1959." IRIS also contains some information about employees' skills, career interests, and activities not related to their jobs, but the emphasis is on demonstrable fact versus what employees say about themselves.

Each employee annually corrects and updates his IRIS profile, thus enabling Union Oil to fulfill one of the basic requirements of governmental "right-to-privacy" legislation, namely, that the data are correct. Operation of the data base meets other regulatory requirements as well.[16]

Profiling, then, is not just a matter of arranging a series of workshops or using an array of instruments. To be effective, profiling must be supported by ongoing policies and procedures that shape it and ensure that the assessment and validation processes continue, even if the workshops and counseling sessions do not.

Responsibilities for Everyone

The Profiling Stage is primarily the responsibility of the employees who are creating their own profiles. It is each employee's responsibility to review the past, draw inferences from the present, and project a mental picture of the future. Profiling requires employees to undertake exercises in self-insight that may seem laborious and tedious and to exhibit a great deal of motivation to complete the process. Career development practitioners and managers throughout the organization also have responsibility for the profiling process.

The Practitioner of Many Hats. During the Profiling Stage, the practitioners are called upon to play a number of roles stemming from their unique position as liaison between employees, their managers, and the organization. Roles of practitioner may be summarized as

1. *Innovator.* Knowing that different profiling techniques are necessary for different people, the practitioner must creatively seek out and experiment with a multitude of formats for use in a variety of settings. While many tools and techniques already exist for profiling uses, the practitioner must be innovative in adapting these to immediate needs, as well as in designing others as required.
2. *Support generator.* It is essential that the practitioner generate support, especially from managers, career advisors, or trainers, before the profiling process begins. Generally this means making the process visible and introducing the rationale, benefits, approach, and technology of the process. Building commitment will help facilitate support for the entire career development effort.
3. *Information channel.* The practitioner must work toward ensuring that the information generated during profiling is fully used by the individuals and the organization. This entails clarifying the link between profiling and setting goals. It means ensuring that, where possible, profiling results are used in skills inventories and performance appraisals, and that managers seek ways to use employees' profiling information as a guide in making decisions about personnel.
4. *Support giver.* The practitioner must give support to employees and their managers during profiling. This can include verbally encouraging them, scheduling workshops, administering batteries of tests, and accommodating special needs.

The Supportive Manager. During the Profiling Stage, as elsewhere during the career development effort, the manager plays a never-ending role of providing encouragement and guidance. The manager, if actively involved in the process, should personally discuss profiles with employees and assist them in translating profiling information to on-the-job concerns. The manager must also be willing to allow the employee the time necessary (often taken out of working hours) to pursue the exercises vital to this stage.

Even managers with the best of intentions often do not realize the dramatic impact they can exert by being a role model or by providing guidance to employees seeking new paths to career satisfaction. Managers can sabotage the career development process by doing nothing when the supporting and advancing the process requires only a little effort.

Practitioners, then, must build a partnership between employees, managers, and themselves, if the Profiling Stage is to be a success. They must make each of the players understand the benefits of profiling and the successes that can be attained if all participate.

Though this effort may seem monumental, it is essential that it be accomplished at this point to set the stage for the continued sharing of responsibility during the Targeting Stage.

OPTIMIZING OPTIONS
the targeting stage

" . . . but won't we be setting a bunch of tigers loose?"

In his essay, "To Reach Port," Oliver Wendell Holmes (1809-1894) said, "I find the great thing in this world is not so much where we stand, as it is what direction we are moving." Dr. Holmes seems to have had the career planning process in mind.

Profiling, determining where the employee stands, is an important part of the career development effort, but perhaps the most significant effort takes place at the Targeting Stage.

For employees targeting means *exploring* possibilities and *specifying goals.* For organizations targeting involves making available to employees the means for exploration and providing the guidance that will keep employees' efforts pointed in a direction in consonance with the organization. For practitioners the Targeting Stage will be filled with challenges and opportunities to make the exploration an opening of possibilities and the goal-setting a realistic and profitable exercise.

This stage often makes managers nervous. Perhaps what management most fears about a career development effort is that it will raise unrealistic expectations, that employees will believe they are more mobile in the organization than they ever can be. In line with this concern is the fear that the career development effort will cause rapid promotion or transfer of master performers, leaving the supervisor to continually train new staff members. Because of these concerns many managers are reluctant to encourage their subordinates to participate in workshops or seek counseling.

But, if well executed, the process of targeting can prevent employees from setting unrealistic goals, and it often encourages them to look closer to their present work environments in seeking job satisfaction. Setting effective career goals helps ensure that employees undertake appropriate action toward achieving desired overall ends, and it helps minimize the aimless groping that does not benefit the individual or the organization.

Exploration and Focus

There is no single way for a person to move as a result of a career development effort. Targeting will often show that a current job can be enriched to provide satisfaction that a lateral move, either within one's own group or to another related one, may be the ideal direction for a worker, or that a move downward can be the first step toward accomplishing a long-term goal.

In the typical organizational environment, it is easy to lose sight of the whys and wherefores of the tasks, problems, crises, and routines of the working day. More long-term goals get lost among day-to-day activities. Refocusing on the original goals, in retrospect, often shows that all concerned have been failing to progress toward the outcomes they have desired.

During the Targeting Stage the employee formulates workable career goals, the foundation for all remaining career development steps. The career development practitioner and concerned managers can help employees lay this foundation, remembering that individuals must still be the architect of their own career goals.

An architect does not simply look at a construction site and insert a window here and a door there. There is a well-designed plan for the building process. Similarly employees need an organized method for approaching the goal-setting process. And just as the builder does not start with the roof, the person selecting and specifying career goals must not begin with "the job." Yet, unfortunately, this is just the place where most begin—by singling out a job title or functional area that sounds appealing, without ever getting a feel for the realities of the organization and larger environment in which they operate. Without the careful analysis, planning, and examination of options that comprise the targeting process, the career goal is not likely to be built—or, if built, it is not likely to withstand the passage of time.

Partners in Planning. The process of targeting requires ongoing interaction between the individual and the organization. The employee needs assistance in translating skill profiles into desirable and realistic objectives. Without the knowledge of skills, personal values, and contextual preferences defined during the Profiling Stage, individuals have neither the self-insight nor the self-confidence to select appropriate goals. Similarly, without knowledge of company business plans, individuals do not have the necessary information to set personal career goals that link with organizational realities.

There is a great deal of data that the employee must know before beginning a targeting effort. Information about the organization's human resource plans, performance requirements, career paths, projected openings, and current job titles and tasks are all necessary. Most employees do not have access to this information or know how to find it. The practitioner can provide employees with access to the appropriate information channels and to the technology that enables evaluation and choice among several alternative goals. Managers can provide invaluable assistance by discussing organizational long-range plans and staffing requirements. Peers also play a major role by providing support and information about the organization to one another through sharing their personal experiences.

Attempting to build a successful career development goal without access to organizational data is similar to attempting to paint a picture in a dark room. Certain things—the canvas, the palette, the brushes, and the paint tubes—can be identified by feel, but even a skilled artist must be able to see in order to develop the colors, composition, and image. The employee who has limited information may have some feel for what must be done in career planning, but the light can only be provided by the organization. Although the employee may be able to create something in the dark, the result may not be in the best interests of either the individual or the organization.

The organization can reap substantial benefits from encouraging employees commitment to well-defined career goals. Setting goals encourages the motivation to pursue purposeful personal development and job achievement, rather than aimless movement from job to job. Jobs have less meaning for individuals and the organization if they are not perceived as a step in a particular direction. The Targeting Stage is, therefore, a vital link to using human resource productively. Job satisfaction results from employees feeling that they are a part of the team. If the organization translates its perspective for its own plans and goals in a top-down fashion to employees, they can then weigh their own desires and directions against those of the organization in order to determine the degree to which they support one another. With information about where and how the organization is changing, employees can more effectively voice their own ideas regarding that fit, thereby minimizing surprises on both sides. The process can be summarized as shown in Exhibit 4-1.

Aiming for Action. The major phases of the Targeting Stage are directed at (1) assisting employees to explore a number of goal options and to use them in (2) specifying action-oriented objectives. While goal exploration, and particularly the selection of multiple goals, is critical to the

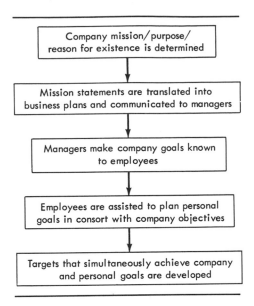

```
┌─────────────────────────────────┐
│   Company mission/purpose/       │
│   reason for existence is determined │
└─────────────────────────────────┘
              │
              ▼
┌─────────────────────────────────┐
│ Mission statements are translated into │
│ business plans and communicated to managers │
└─────────────────────────────────┘
              │
              ▼
┌─────────────────────────────────┐
│ Managers make company goals known │
│           to employees           │
└─────────────────────────────────┘
              │
              ▼
┌─────────────────────────────────┐
│ Employees are assisted to plan personal │
│ goals in consort with company objectives │
└─────────────────────────────────┘
              │
              ▼
┌─────────────────────────────────┐
│ Targets that simultaneously achieve company │
│   and personal goals are developed │
└─────────────────────────────────┘
```

Exhibit 4-1   A Targeting Model

targeting process, it will not by itself instigate change. There is little motivation to act upon a goal until it has been clearly articulated, committed to paper, and, ideally, shared with others. Thus, there is a need to proceed from selecting goals to formulating them. Goal formulation is the process of translating them into precise statements that clearly specify anticipated results.

During the first phase of targeting, which involves exploring alternatives, employees are assisted in understanding that career development goals may relate to a wide range of options beyond the usual notion of upward advancement as the only route to follow. The practitioner will need to help individuals explore possible career paths that include

- Vertical mobility
- Lateral mobility
- Realignment (downward mobility)
- Relocation
- Job enrichment
- Exploratory research

It is important that the practitioner help employees understand the value of considering goals in each of these areas. The concept of selecting multiple career goals is particularly relevant in today's rapidly evolving job market. In the twenty-year period between 1955 and 1975, 28 million jobs were added to the American work force. More than one million jobs were added each year between 1975 and 1980. A great many of the jobs opening each year are brand new, the result of changes in technology, new products, and altered priorities.

Futurists tell us that more than half the jobs that people will hold within the next twenty years do not even exist today. Both economic and technological change make it virtually imperative that today's worker keep open as many options as possible. Ideally, individuals should not only select goals that reflect the range of possible career paths; they should, in fact, begin to work toward each of them simultaneously.

Everyone is familiar with the horror stories of workers who could not make a transition to another field when their particular trade was phased out or cut back. The transition from coal to diesel-electric power on America's railroads caused thousands of firemen, or stokers, to suddenly begin searching for new careers. Although some were able to make the shift, a great many had never done anything else, had no secondary skills, and were too locked in to their jobs as fire stokers to change.

How many of today's jobs will be eliminated in the next twenty years? How many jobs will require new skills because of changes in technology or organizational structure? These are realities to be considered during the Targeting Stage.

The second step in targeting engages employees in specifying goals. This is the point at which goals evolve from general options to precise statements of objective. But how many employees know how to make the transition from the general to the specific? How many employees know how to effectively develop step-by-step procedures that will make goals attainable? The practitioner can provide instruction in how to write and test goal statements that will ensure clear action. Failure to complete this component of the Targeting Stage results in goals that can be easily and conveniently overlooked in the hurly-burly of one's daily routine. Vague goals do not act as a reminder of plans that have not been executed. They do not generate an imperative to act.

Goals committed to paper help motivate individuals to assess their efforts toward attaining them, while there is still time to act. Individuals with their goals clearly in mind are much more alert to opportunities to move toward them and are much more likely to act on those opportunities.

Targeting information can be delivered through workshops and counseling activities, which help employees learn the essential steps for specifying goals and provide a means of *sharing* and *reality-testing* goal statements. Much of the organizational data employees will need can also be provided through these activities, often through specially designed handouts and workbooks. The practitioner provides opportunities for learning the art of targeting.

Clearly targeting is a structured experience, and effectively implementing it requires a great deal of training. Designing an approach to teach this procedure is one of the practitioner's most important tasks. The process must be demonstrated to employees, and skills in its application can be developed through exercises and simulations. The practitioner, through staff members or supervisors, must guide employees through the process at least once, and employees must internalize the approach, so that it can be called upon again and again throughout ensuing career changes.

EXPLORATION: NO STONE UNTURNED

The Age of Discovery in world history began when Christopher Columbus sailed westward in 1492 to discover what lay beyond the horizon that limited the world of Western Civilization. Though he sought a new route to China and the East Indies, he found a new world to be explored, charted, and settled.

The employee's Age of Discovery can begin in the same manner. What lies beyond the horizon of the employee's current job? What exciting new worlds lie out there to be explored and charted? How can employees' jobs and lives be expanded and enriched by their discoveries?

Exploration is more than just searching for new territories and options. It also consists of using the information gained during Profiling. Career goals cannot be selected without a reality-tested inventory of skills to be meshed with information acquired about organizational plans and needs; neither can goals be selected without knowledge of typical options that are available. This creates an important role for the practitioner. It will help if the practitioner is familiar with various types of career options and is prepared to describe them to employees who can then select from among them.

Again, up is not the only way. While vertical mobility is the most traditional career goal, practitioners who also encourage the consideration of lateral and downward transfers, relocation, job enrichment, and exploratory research will greatly increase the options available to employees. The first four paths involve actual movement to different jobs, while the latter two involve career development actions within the existing jobs.

Practitioners should encourage employees to select at least one possible goal in each category and to pursue multiple and simultaneous goals. This multi-faceted approach allows the employee to remain ready for and open to any changes that may occur within the system, whether they reflect the opening of new opportunities or the foreclosure of existing ones. Multiple goals allow employees to perceive themselves as more in control of their future and less at the mercy of outside forces. Should the desired direction become blocked, one has at least begun to think in terms of other options. The following discussion of career path possibilities may help the practitioner show employees the range of alternatives.

Up, Up, and Away—Vertical Mobility

Assistant Director of Personnel

↑

Personnel Analyst

Traditionally vertical mobility was considered the only acceptable and rewarding way to develop in a career. Vertical mobility meant that one climbed the hierarchical ladder, gaining more status, responsibility, remuneration, and authority along the way. Movement up meant success; all other movement did not count—or counted against the individual. Much of the literature on career mobility of the last two decades concerned itself with moving vertically within the organization. Indeed, much of the current literature, both scientific and popular, still touts the idea that up is the best and only direction in which an individual should desire to move; for example, accountants are encouraged to become managers of the financial division; product designers are encouraged to become product managers; and machinists are encouraged to aim toward plant management.

Prompted by the limited opportunities in most organizations today and by shifts in cultural values vis-a-vis the work ethic, this belief is beginning to change. Both individuals and organizations are beginning to place a higher value on depth and breadth of experience than on the speed with which one can climb the corporate ladder. More and more workers are being encouraged to become generalists rather than specialists. Today some employees look to the present job for personal growth, evaluating new job opportunities (including vertical moves) in light of how they may conflict with personal values, and sometimes declining the new opportunities because of that conflict. Others still define personal success as upward career movement and remain interested in vertical goals. All employees often need assistance in determining what the next logical hierarchical move should be, as well as in assessing the abilities and experience required to make such a move.

Several major factors should be considered when setting a vertical career goal. The larger the organization, the greater will be the competition for the increasingly limited positions available as one moves upward in an organization. If everyone in the hierarchy wants to move upward, the competition for those limited jobs can be fierce. Too often employees see only the desirable status, authority, and money enjoyed by those at higher levels. They fail to realize that a price is attached to those benefits: stress. Some organizations have higher stress levels than others and some people have a higher tolerance for stress than others. Practitioners should help employees investigate this area of concern before a final decision to move upward is made.

Personal values are also important to consider before setting goals. The increased responsibility carried at upper levels in an organization often makes demands on family, leisure time, and ability to pursue nonjob-related interests. The practitioner must help employees investigate those demands and their own ability to make value adaptations *before* they begin exploring upward mobility goals.

Once the decision to move upward is made, the practitioner can assist individuals in identifying relevant higher-level positions by organizing resource materials and counseling support for them. This includes posting job opening and potential openings disseminating organizational charts, position descriptions, and job listings.

Dual Ladders. High technology organizations have a special problem in trying to provide vertical mobility for technical professionals, such as engineers and computer specialists. The most competent of these employees soon reach the top title and salary available in their technical specialty, and the only remaining advancement option is a switch to the management hierarchy. Yet, these individuals may not want to leave their laboratories and drawing boards, or may not be suited for the human relations skills and political maneuvering required of top executives. Still, they may desire an increase in status and pay, as well as greater influence over company policy-making.

Persons with high levels of technical expertise who excel at their jobs often find that to move upward they must give up their technical areas and go into the field of management. These high technical performers very often peak out, or reach their level of incompetence,[1] in their upward quest, and become organizational liabilities much sooner than they otherwise might.

Realizing that this is counterproductive and wastes human resources, many organizations have designed dual career promotion systems, which provide parallel hierarchies in the technical professions and administrative management. Technicians can advance to positions of technical decision making and policy input, while administrative executives retain general management of financial, personnel, and overall policy issues. Thus, technical professionals can continue to use their expertise while advancing to positions that afford them the benefits generally reserved for managerial functions. They are rewarded for their contributions to the organization through receiving status equal with managers, while the organization is not stripped of the benefits of their technical expertise.

The dual career ladder system can succeed spectacularly or fall miserably, depending on the organization's commitment to developing and rewarding technical personnel. If this system is merely temporary window dressing to placate technicians who are advanced in title but not authority, it will not meet the need. If the big decisions are still the purview of the executive suite and technical input receives only occasional nodding recognition, technical personnel will become disgruntled and will continue to vie for management posts for which they may be unprepared, and the organization may loose valuable technical expertise. Likewise, if the technical supervisory position become a dumping ground for people who have floundered on the managerial ladder, the entire system is jeopardized.

Project management is one method of advancing and using technical personnel. In this system individual projects—such as designing a new manufacturing system or developing an environmental waste disposal plan—are removed from the functional hierarchy. They are run by teams managed by individuals with appropriate technical skills who are responsible for the planning, monitoring, financial, and production aspects of the project. This allows individuals to gain greater autonomy and experience, while the organization benefits from the ability to draw talent from a variety of functional areas for teams that reflect the necessary mix of skills. Practitioners may be somewhat out of their element in this area, but they can provide valuable assistance to technical personnel by providing methodologies and mechanisms to help explore project management possibilities that may exist. Perhaps a matrix approach is required; maybe project management already exists under some other name. It may be necessary for technically oriented personnel to develop certain human relations and conceptual skills, as well as technical skills in different areas, such as financial management and information systems. Before providing aid to others, practitioners may have to do their own exploring.

Providing opportunities for vertical mobility in high technology organizations continues to be an issue that demands continued creativity from the practitioner.

Over and Out—Lateral Mobility

Supervisor, Planning Division ⟶ Supervisor, Marketing Division

Lateral moves involve a change in function and responsibility, but not necessarily a change in status or remuneration. Once considered a way of shelving "dead wood," lateral moves are fast becoming a way for employees to broaden existing skills, learn about other areas of the organization, develop new talents, demonstrate versatility, and prepare for future vertical moves. Such movement is also a method through which organizations with slow internal job markets can continue to challenge their highly motivated employees. In fact, in many organizations lateral movement is becoming a sign of recognized potential and promotability, as individuals are groomed for higher positions by broadening their base of knowledge across functional lines. Unfortunately the reverse is also sometimes true. A great many organizations have policies that forbid lateral movements. The feeling is that lateral movement encourages interdivisional pirating of promising personnel. Practitioners should thoroughly investigate organizational policy regarding this option.

Practitioners should stress the degree to which lateral moves reflect and demonstrate the concept of transferable skills and job knowledge. An employee who has a background in production and who has been successfully selling production proposals to top management may be qualified to consider a lateral move to a position in marketing, by virtue of that concept.

A lateral move in a retailing organization, for example, can involve moving from one store to another or from one department (furniture sales) to another (men's fashions) within the same store. Such a move can bring an increase in knowledge (learning a new commodity), a change in job pressures and expectations (new seasonal changes), a change in clientele (men instead of men and women), new colleagues, and a new supervisor. Employees should be encouraged to build skills and gain valuable expertise and self-confidence through lateral movement. Similarly a lateral move in a high technology organization may mean moving from one systems group to another—transferring a number of technical, functional, and personal skills to the new assignment and gaining new ones in the process. Human relations skills and conceptual skills may be added to existing technical skills.

One of the first steps the practitioner could undertake to present this as a viable option is to evaluate the attitudes within the organization toward such movement. In many companies lateral moves occur frequently and are seen as part of routine training and development. Job rotation programs are common and are designed to prevent overspecialization and to encourage understanding of the unique demands of each function within the organization. Where such movement is commonplace, it is possible to identify typical crossover points, to catalog logical crossfunctional moves that will provide the greatest depth of experience, to determine entry requirements into job rotation programs, and to otherwise identify information that employees may need in order to pursue lateral mobility. This information should be widely disseminated in order to encourage considering lateral movement when setting goals.

Where lateral movement is infrequent or seen as a sign of probable failure, the practitioner must determine whether and how lateral mobility can be legitimized. The practitioner may need only to review mobility patterns of the past six to twelve months and point out that the frequency of such moves is actually greater than generally perceived. Such a process is certainly made easier if a computerized personnel data system is available for retaining historical job classification data. However, a simplified version can be compiled by hand. For even greater impact some of this information can be compiled in internal publications that present the abbreviated work histories of several successful people who have benefited from lateral moves.

> Recognizing that financial considerations can be a major obstacle to employees who contemplate lateral moves, Connecticut General has instituted a lateral movement policy which removes the financial burden from this career option. If an employee wants to make a lateral move involving a job with a lower salary range, the Company will continue to treat the employee as though he or she was in the higher salary level for two years. The Company assumes that during this time period the employee will be able to move up within the new career ladder until he or she is earning as much or more than before the career move.[2]

A job posting/transfer system can encourage lateral moves, when jobs are publicized as providing opportunities to transfer skills to new work environments, and to learn about other parts of the organization. Job rotation programs encourage employees to experiment with transferring their present skills to jobs at similar levels in other functional areas.

Additionally an approach might be designed for making and processing transfer requests without unnecessary red tape. Primarily it is the practitioner's responsibility to ensure that the organization is open to lateral mobility and is doing all it can to make such opportunities available, and to help employees recognize the benefits of broadening their experiential base through lateral moves. Basic to such an approach is the necessity of convincing managers within the organization that lateral movements are beneficial to the whole organization, even though they may pose some hardships within its component parts. If Manager A loses a high performer to Manager B due to a lateral transfer, the organization still has that high potential person, even though Manager A will have to find a replacement. The loss and replacement can often be made easier if the employee being lost is available for the orientation and training of the replacement employee.

Down the Organization—Realignment

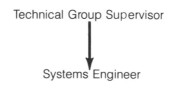

Technical Group Supervisor

Systems Engineer

Realignment moves involve downward shifts in the hierarchy, often from a managerial position back to one as an individual contributor. Although a downward transfer is not a common career development option, practitioners who recognize it as a viable alternative will be able to help employees expand their range of choices. It is not unusual that some employees find themselves selected for job levels that do not suit them and need assistance in making a career move back down the hierarchy. Other employees may simply decide that they can personally benefit from jobs that entail less pressure and responsibility, fewer overtime hours, and more day-to-day certainty than the ones they now hold.

An employee might choose to realign due to a desire to facilitate personal growth and development, or to change from one field of endeavor into another. Individuals who wish to change their routine and expand their knowledge of future options often find that their accrued salary and benefits have effectively priced them out of the market for learning opportunities or new starts. The organization, unwilling to pay the higher rate while waiting for the person to become productive in the new area, closes the door on personal growth involving such a major change. Only two choices remain open: stay on the present job and seek other ways of growing and developing; or trade income, benefits, and status for the opportunity presented by a realignment move.

> Connecticut General has attempted to remove the stigma usually attached to downward moves. Such moves are necessary when employees are not performing well on their current jobs, or when for health or other personal reasons employees desire less responsibility or pressure in their jobs. With the employee's permission such moves are announced in the same formal manner as are upward moves.[3]

Another type of realignment move involves returning to a previous position, in which an employee performed better or was more satisfied. An example of a realignment career move of this type can be seen when managers decide to return to their former positions as technical specialists, or when supervisors return to a clerical position they previously held. Realignment, if handled appropriately, can offer a satisfactory solution to the dilemma of having promoted the best worker, only to discover that the individual is not suited to managerial or supervisorial responsibilities. Similar situations occur when an employee in a promote-from-within training program moves into a supervisory position and finds that it is less attractive or more demanding than anticipated. By developing options for returning to a less demanding position without the stigma of demotion, organizations can retain their good employees in positions where they can be effective producers.

Developing plans and programs to handle realignments will challenge the creative and human relations skills of the practitioner. Several options and considerations follow, which may be useful in developing plans.

Some organizations have prepared in advance for this type of occurrence by creating fallback positions,[4] which reduce the risk involved in granting or accepting a promotion by guaranteeing each promoted employee the opportunity to return to a position equal in status and pay to the old job, if the new one does not work out as intended. This guarantee encourages an individual to accept the risk of moving into a different department or function, and benefits the organization by opening up blocked pathways for newer and possibly more talented employees.

Similar in many respects to the type of move just described, realignment is often chosen to relieve job-related stress. As the definition of compensable occupational injuries is evolving to include psychological damage induced by stress inherent in a job, companies are faced with a potential new financial burden, in terms of actual transfer payments made and days spent on medical leave. And individuals are beginning to believe that their personal health is more important than having a prestigious job. Accordingly the downward transfer is an important alternative. Employees could be encouraged to consider this type of career movement, even on a temporary basis, and the system could be encouraged to treat it as a viable career option, rather than a form of punishment.

Practitioners should recognize that realignment moves have been shown to have a positive effect on individuals at lower levels in the organization. When a more senior person chooses realignment, junior employees are afforded closer contact with an individual in an excellent position to coach and advise them as a mentor. In addition organizational communication is improved when individuals moving downward bring with them the information sources and communication channels they enjoyed in their previous organizational roles.[5]

Nevertheless, a strong norm still exists in many companies against moving downward. To encourage employees to seriously consider this option and to alleviate possible anxiety about downward transfers, practitioners could provide employees with information from the media about the increasing number of people who are choosing realignment rather than stressful positions. Internal publicity about individuals who have given up higher level jobs to learn other functions and who, perhaps, have now regained their former rank level can be an effective device. Practitioners could also review compensation policies to determine if fallback positions can be established, or if minimum salary guarantees or other job security measures can be enacted to foster effective realignment.

In addition counseling must be available to the individual who has decided to make a downward move. Counseling staff should be prepared to help individuals deal with the potential ostracism, discomfort, or alienation that they may encounter within the organization. Former coworkers may not know or believe that the move was voluntary, and they may feel that there is danger in being associated with one who has been downgraded. If it is clear that the move was for health reasons, coworkers wary of creating a new overload situation for the realigned individual may turn elsewhere for assistance or to assign work. If the realigned individuals happen to be women or members of minority groups who were, perhaps, promoted too quickly or placed above their level of capability, there will be a different pressure—one of having let down the rest of the group or of having justified the mistrust of those who did not want to see the person promoted in the first place. Even if the women or minority individuals functioned beautifully in the assignment, but simply found it not to their liking, choosing to realign carries with it the implied warning, "We gave you a chance and you let us down."

Practitioners might confront some of these cultural norms that support organizational resistance to downward transfers, so that such reactions are no longer typical, and realignment moves are legitimized as normal career options available to all individuals.

Outward Bound—Relocation

Trainer, XYZ Corp. ⟶ Consultant, Entrepreneur

The next option is one that practitioners will sometimes find necessary to pursue, but must do so with a great deal of tact and care. The primary job of the organizational career development practitioner is to help the organization and the people who work for it to grow and become more effective. However, there are times and situations in which the person-to-organization mismatch is so great that it would be to the decided advantage of both if the employee were to seek growth opportunities elsewhere. This option is most frequently invoked when retirement is imminent, when layoffs are frequent, when individuals feel they are at a dead end in the organization, when entrepreneural ventures attract employees, or when personal and organizational goals are in conflict.

While career development interventions in organizations should be aimed at keeping the employee satisfied, fulfilled, and challenged *within* the organization, it is naive to assume that this will always be possible. After serious introspection some individuals may find that their present occupation, industry, profession, or firm does not meet their needs and may opt to relocate. The practitioner needs to ensure that those whose needs *could* be satisfied by the company are able to recognize this fact, while others, better suited elsewhere, are not discouraged from leaving jobs in which they are only marginally productive or marginally satisfied.

Management is not always going to be happy when this option is recommended, and the practitioner must have the case carefully and completely documented. It must be shown that all other options were considered and explored before the relocation solution was decided upon. Even then it may take a great deal of diplomatic maneuvering before the hierarchy is convinced that this option is the best way. This is especially true in cases of high performers, whom managers believe can be brought around, or people with skills in high demand and of low availability, creating situations where replacement recruitment will be expensive and difficult.

Career development practitioners can assist employees by encouraging them to think through various alternatives and follow up on those that seem most appropriate. (The dilemma, though, lies in determining the degree to which relocation should be discussed as an option in career program literature.) The hope in some organizations is that employees will not think of relocation on their own, and the belief is that the organization should not encourage it. Other organizations go so far as to offer outplacement services to assist employees in obtaining positions with other firms, although this aid is generally used when the organization decides to terminate the employee.

These are two extremes. Somewhere in the middle are those firms which openly discuss this option in their career development approach. Employees of these organizations are encouraged to identify relocation as one of their potential goals, so that they are prepared for potential situations in which movement out of the organization is the best way to go. Organizations taking this approach soon find their credibility greatly enhanced and find that employees feel that the career development program is really geared to their personal needs, rather than being only intended to serve the expediency of the company. This approach encourages loyalty and commitment to the organization.

The practitioner can help the organization understand that employees who are mismatched with their present jobs or company are likely to be less productive than those whose needs are being satisfied by the job. Allowing an individual to leave, therefore, creates opportunities for others. In addition to potentially improved productivity and the increased promotion opportunities when relocation information is available, monies which might have been spent in trying to motivate, train, or develop the former employee can be redirected to those who have identified a desire for such work and development.

A relocation goal may involve changing fields or just changing organizations. Employees who have the desire to teach, for example, but cannot find the opportunity to do so within the present organization might find that returning to the formal education system or moving to a larger company, more oriented toward training, in the same industry will more directly meet their needs.

Relocation goals, particularly those that are motivated by the approach of retirement age, can be pursued simultaneously with intraorganizational goals and can be facilitated by one-on-one counseling, to prepare the individual for the lifestyle changes that may also occur.

Moving in Place—Job Enrichment

Secretary, Graphics Arts Dept..............Secretary and Preliminary Layout
Designer, Graphics Arts Dept.

While the four career path options discussed on the preceding pages involve actual movement to new positions, it is essential that practitioners remind employees that career goals do not always mean moving to a greener pasture, but also involve growth in current jobs. Indeed, the actions that are often easiest to enact and quickest to show results are those directed at an employee's present environment.

Many employees who recognize opportunities available in their current jobs decide to remain in them for some time. The job enrichment option, clearly presented as a viable option, can win over supervisors who fear that career development means *losing* valuable employees.

The accomplishment of an individual action plan in the Career Planning and Development process at State Farm Insurance does not necessarily mean that the best career option for an individual will be promotion or movement to another job.

A change in job is clearly a possible result of Career Planning and Development. But other more likely results are adding additional dimensions to current job duties or even undergoing further training and development to stay effective in the present job.

Career Planning and Development is seen as a tool that can stimulate employees to grow within their job interests and capabilities, and maximize their contribution to the organization.

Job enrichment is a way of increasing the challenge and meaningfulness of a job by changing the job and its responsibilities. It means recognizing the job tasks or functions that the employee finds personally stimulating and rewarding, and working to discover a way to more strongly build those tasks or functions into the job. This does not mean simply adding more tasks in the hope that greater variety will lead to greater meaningfulness. Job enrichment provides developmental opportunities without employees leaving their present positions.

One way to distinguish between job enrichment and job enlargement is to think of how responsibilities would be expanded. Additional responsibilities that are piled on vertically and simply increase the time and pressure required to carry them out cause job enlargement. However, the addition of duties and responsibilities that expand the scope, visibility, attractiveness, and learning potential of the job result in job enrichment. Often a job can be enriched by giving the employee the authority to sign or approve certain items that had previously required approval by another. Similarly a job enlargement might occur if an additional responsibility is given to an employee, but the authority to carry out that responsibility is withheld.

Examples of job enrichment goals include developing and implementing a particular procedure, task, or project on the job; learning computer programming, in order to be able to respond to internal software needs; becoming a member of a special task force; and achieving greater responsibility and autonomy on the job.

Accountants who take on responsibility for orienting others to a new accounting system are enriching their jobs. Similarly job enrichment occurs when a secretary not only types, but also drafts, letters in response to inquiries, or when a management trainee is given full authority over management of a new project.

The practitioner's role is to stimulate employees to consider their present jobs as potential candidates for job enrichment before, or while, looking elsewhere, and to encourage support for such efforts from supervisors and the system as a whole.

It is important that practitioners understand the concepts underlying job enrichment. Three critical psychological states are conducive to motivation and job satisfaction.[6] They are

1. *The experience of meaningfulness:* The work is perceived as being meaningful;
2. *The experience of responsibility:* Individuals believe that they are responsible for the outcome of the job; and
3. *The experience of knowing results:* Individuals are able to determine whether or not the outcome is satisfactory.

Certain job characteristics can contribute to the creation of these three psychological states. These characteristics include job enrichment achieved in one of the following ways:

*   *Skill Variety*—Increasing the number and variety of skills and talents used in carrying out a job.
*   *Task Completion*—being assigned an identifiable unit of work to complete (doing a job from beginning to end).
*   *Task Significance*—understanding the type and degree of impact a particular job has on the lives and work of other people in the organization or the organization as a whole.
*   *Autonomy*—increasing responsibility, independence, and discretion in determining work procedures.
*   *Feedback*—establishing opportunities for feedback intrinsic in the job itself, as well as for feedback from coworkers and supervisors.

Other factors that have good potential for creating enrichment opportunities are

- *Interpersonal Relationships*—providing employees with opportunities to work more closely with clients, or with people in other parts of the organization, in addition to other members of the work unit.
- *Training*—providing opportunities for growth through on-the-job training, special seminars, and courses.

Employees can often develop ideas for enriching their own jobs, but typically need assistance in beginning the process. The practitioner can help employees recognize a variety of starting points to aid them in building job enrichment goals, which encompass the characteristics mentioned above. One way in which this might be done is to suggest that employees select short-term projects that meet these job enrichment criteria. Projects could involve designing new systems for the organization, or the department, or the division of which the employee is a member. Projects could be designed to encourage taking on personal assignments which, during their course, cause employees to be recognized in the organization as having skills. (A description of a program using the notion of project assignment is described in the next chapter.) A rating form such as the one in Exhibit 4-2 could be used by the practitioner as a check for job enrichment capacity:

Rate the project's potential job enrichment on the following factors: (H) = High (M) = Medium (L) = Low

1. *Skill Variety:*   H   M   L
   Will the project increase the number and variety of skills and talents used in carrying out the job?
2. *Task Completion:*   H   M   L
   Will the project provide an opportunity to complete a particular task from beginning to end?
3. *Task Significance:*   H   M   L
   Will the project help the individual to understand the degree of impact that the project has on the lives and work of other people in the organization?
4. *Autonomy:*   H   M   L
   Will the project assist the individual in exploring ways to increase independence and discretion in determining work procedures?
5. *Feedback:*   H   M   L
   Does the project provide opportunities for feedback from the project itself, as well as from coworkers and supervisors?
6. *Interpersonal Relationships:*   H   M   L
   Does the project provide opportunities to work more closely with clients, or with people in other parts of the organization, in addition to other members of the work unit?
7. *Training:*   H   M   L
   Does the project provide an opportunity for growth through on-the-job training, especially seminars?

Exhibit 4-2   A Form for Rating Job Enrichment Potential

Another exercise individuals might use to identify the potential for job enrichment in their present positions is to list their job duties on a typical day. Working from the list of job enrichment possibilities, employees write out and discuss how each duty could be modified to use a variety of skills, to complete a task in its entirety, to provide more autonomy, or to provide more feedback from or contact with others. The list can also be used for employees to explore the importance of a particular task to others. The resulting data provides an excellent starting point for individuals to apply their own problem solving skills to discovering job enrichment opportunities. The employee could, for example, rank the possibilities on the list in order of importance and ease of attainability. Those changes that would be easiest to implement and that are of greatest import would represent the first job enrichment efforts.

If successful, implementation of job enrichment offers rewards that are twofold. First, employees will have created one psychological success upon which future successes may be built. Second, the odds are high that a supervisor, who may have previously been reluctant to support the individual's hopes for growth or change, will become a supporter. Thus, efforts on the present job can enhance opportunities for attaining other career goals.

For those whose present position is unchanged, job enrichment still offers the opportunity to encourage the supervisor to become a supporter and salesperson for the individual, especially with regard to future moves. In addition, employees who learn to look upon their present jobs as an opportunity to showcase their present skills and to help develop new ones will be rewarded with increased job satisfaction.

It is essential that practitioners gain managers' commitment to employees' job enrichment goals. This may include setting up orientation sessions, so that managers understand the potential organizational benefits, and providing staff who can meet individually with resistant managers. Those managers who see development of subordinates as one of their responsibilities or who feel rewarded for developing subordinates should become immediate and enthusiastic supporters. Others may have to be encouraged to support job enrichment on the basis of the improved job commitment it provides. When the morale of employees is high, turnover and absenteeism can be reduced, and productivity can be increased.

Casting About—Exploratory Research Projects

Librarian............Research about personnel division

Often employees feel vaguely discontent with their present jobs but have difficulty selecting alternative career paths. It is important that they be shown how to undertake an experimentation process that involves researching, interviewing, and testing ideas and opportunities within or outside the organization, so they can eventually decide about another field of interest. By encouraging employees to set research goals, practitioners can help them overcome the frustration of feeling they have no choices. The practitioner uses this option most effectively by encouraging employees to select one area of interest and to research researching possibilities associated with it. Research goals should include a detailed statement about areas of possible interest and a structured plan for researching those areas. As a result, employees should gather enough information to enable themselves to make a sound decision about whether or not moving into another area would be desirable.

Employers in the accounting department, for example, might research a variety of jobs within the personnel division in order to understand more about why they might wish to move into a particular area of personnel, rather than simply claiming that they "like people." A research goal of this type could involve interviewing various department members to learn about the scope and variety of jobs within the department; investigating job availability; attending meetings of affiliated professional societies; and reading selected journals, books, or articles. At the end of a predetermined research period, the employee might elect to continue exploring in one particular area of personnel (for example, training and development); decide that the personnel function is, in fact, no longer appealing; or reframe the goal to a specific lateral or vertical move to the area of personnel that is of interest.

Practitioners can help employees recognize that vertical and lateral goals may be based on unfounded assumptions made as a result of work experience in other areas. Research goals replace fantasizing with structured, goal-oriented behavior and ensure that potential goals are tested against reality. Research goals require effort, but can be easily pursued in tandem with other goals. When discussing the concept of research goals with employees, the practitioner must not get co-opted into letting the employees think that the work will be done for them. Research goals are individual projects. The practitioner may assist and offer guidance, but the work must be done by the person concerned.

The practitioner could assist employees in establishing research goals by developing interview and report-back forms that contain standard questions pertaining to the department(s) being explored. The forms could include questions about the purpose of the functional area as a whole, the function of any subunit being explored and the nature of specific jobs at the employee's own level. Questions about behavioral job demands, skill requirements, working conditions, and the like should also be included. Entries made by employees could note the different people interviewed, the method used to contact them, their level in the organization, and the insights they shared with the employee. An employee could arrange to follow up by reporting back (to a supervisor, counselor, workshop teammate, or other person(s) at a specified time after having conducted the research. Exhibit 4-3 provides a sample exploratory worksheet.

Position/Unit being researched _____

General area of activity _____

1. Who can tell me about the position? _____

2. What other information sources about the position are available? _____

3. What are the duties and responsibilities involved in this position? _____
   _____

4. What appeals to me about the position? _____

5. What might I dislike about the position? _____

6. Will the position develop me for future advancement? _____

7. What kind of ability, experience, and training is necessary in order to obtain this
   position? _____

Exhibit 4-3 Exploratory Research Worksheet

The practitioner could facilitate the exploration process by identifying key contact people in various functional areas who would be willing to act as information resources for employees conducting research, and who could set aside time to be interviewed. Formal presentation by representatives of various units to describe their unit's functional responsibilities can also be arranged. Or supervisors or career counselors can be trained to field questions about other functional areas. Special interest articles concerning work in various units can be published in the company paper or newsletter.

Another important but complementary task is encouraging employees to contact peer level people in other parts of the organization for informal discussions over coffee or lunch. Even an existing job posting system, an existing transfer system, descriptions of job responsibilities in recruitment publications can serve as the foundation for developing informational brochures about work within various organizational components.

These are just a few of the potential sources of information that might be provided. It is likely that the organization already has such systems but is simply not using them in this manner. The more support the practitioner can offer in terms of information resources, the more employees will be helped to see that the organization is in itself a labor market with multiple opportunities for career growth and development.

GOAL SPECIFICATION—THE ROAD TO RESULTS

When first stated most career goals lack the clarity and specificity necessary to inspire action. While individuals may have been urged to set goals for themselves, it is unlikely that they have been instructed in the nuances of setting action-oriented goals or in the wisdom of committing goals to paper and sharing them with others. Typically the resulting goal statements demonstrate only vague desires, such as, "To advance to an administrative position," or "To gain more independence in my work."

In order to assist employees in specifying goals, the practitioner must be both instructor and motivator, instructing employees in how to write clear goals that lead to action plans and results, and motivating them to make a commitment to those goals by putting them in writing and discussing them with others.

Specifying goals requires a step-by-step process of writing, testing, and revising goal statements. And it requires that goals be tangible and action-oriented. Employees will need encouragement and assistance in articulating goals that meet those criteria.

The practitioner can use any one of several delivery mechanisms, or a combination of them, to assist employees with this process. Workshops for setting goals are particularly valuable at this stage, as they can generate an immediate exchange of ideas and can support the testing, and revision of goals. In these settings employees can be instructed in preparing goal statements and can test their statements on others. The peer interaction that takes place invokes commitment to follow through toward attaining goals.

If the organization's career development effort relies largely on self-instruction workbooks, the material should include directions urging employees to test their goal statements with supervisors, co-workers, family members, and friends. If one-on-one counseling is used, counselors must be prepared to instruct employees in effective goal techniques for achieving action-oriented goal statements.

Furthermore, the practitioner must ensure that adequate organizational support systems are in place to supply individuals with the necessary information to specify realistic goals. Structural supports such as job posting and information about career paths provide data for stimulating goal ideas and testing goal relevance.

The Goal Statement

Goal statements move individuals from the intangible to the tangible. To lead to concrete action, they must be

- Specific
- Time-framed
- Relevant
- Attainable
- Measurable
- Visible

The practitioner is now charged with guiding employees to understand the preceding characteristics and to assess their goals in light of them.[7] Each of those characteristic is essential in moving from goal formulation to goal achievement and is half the battle of achievement. Goal Matrix in Exhibit 4-4 can be used by employees to check whether their goals include all categories of movement and have all necessary characteristics.

"Can't You Be More Specific?"   Career goals should be expressed in specific terms that hold the same meaning for the employee, the supervisor, and others who review or hear of them. Formulating specific goal statements means explicitly stating as many details as possible of the position being aimed at. Specificity can be achieved by identifying aspects such as job title, job category, grade level, functions and tasks involved, and location or division.

When designing exploratory career goals, the employee should include the specific departments or divisions to be explored, job categories of interest, and specific questions to which the employee is seeking answers. Job enrichment goals should specify the job enrichment project being considered, the portion of the job to be affected by the job enrichment intervention, new or changed activities, and expected outcomes.

The biggest problem that may be encountered at this point results from employees' lack of familiarity with their organization. It is difficult for them to be as specific as necessary if they do not have enough information about the organization to intelligently identify and define job titles, job categories, grade levels, and functions. Practitioners will often find it necessary to provide assistance in obtaining this information.

GOAL MATRIX	Specific	Time framed	Revelant	Attainable	Measureable	Visible
Vertical						
Lateral						
Realignment						
Relocation						
Enrichment						
Research						

Exhibit 4-4   Goal Matrix

One possible approach is to create a marketing survey form that will allow employees to research their organization as if it were a market in which they wished to introduce a new product—themselves. This survey form could fit the format of Exhibit 4-5, or it could be developed by the practitioner and employees in a workshop session.

Any number of approaches may be useful in helping employees to learn more about the organization. Group projects, tours, guest speakers, and orientation sessions might provide the needed information.

Practitioners may find that they and their staff can compile specific information available into a book. Organizations that have computerized personnel accounting systems may be able to provide a readout of jobs, titles, levels, and codes. All means should be investigated.

Once specific goals have been set, practitioners could ask employees, whether their goal statement specifically agrees with the skills, values, and contexts identified during the profiling stage. The more the goal builds upon identified strengths, the better. Questions the practitioner might ask include

- Is the goal statement readily understandable and identifiable to a supervisor? to colleagues? to employees of another organization?
- Is there any way to clarify this statement further?
- Are the title, function, and division correct?
- Are the specific kinds of projects for exploratory or enrichment goals clear?

Primary Skills to be Marketed: _____

Consumers

Consumer Number One: _____
(Department, Division)

Specific User of Skill: _____
(Specific group, office, and location)

Name of Position: _____
(Job title, category, level)

Skill, Functions, Tasks Required: _____
_____

Consumer Number Two: _____
(Department, Division)

Specific User of Skill: _____
(Specific group, office, and location)

Name of Position: _____
(Job title, category, level)

Skills, Functions, Tasks Required: _____
_____

Exhibit 4-5   Marketing Survey Form

An example of a goal statement that meets the specificity requirement is, "I plan to move from store manager, East City (grade 15), to assistant regional operations manager for the Eastern Region (grade 15) within the next six months." A *specific* enrichment goal would be, "I plan to design a new bonus system for the department and take over responsibilities for initial drafting of the annual budget."

Well-Timed Goals. Time frames for career goals can be set to establish the number of weeks, months, or years within which the goal will be actualized. Exploratory goals should specify research completion dates (for example, "to complete my exploration of the job prospects in the accounting department by March 31"); whereas vertical, lateral, and realignment goals may be more appropriately framed within a given number of weeks, months, or years (for example, "to become corporate controller within eighteen months"). Job enrichment goals should have time parameters in order to encourage immediate implementation upon return to the job. They may consist of incremental job enrichment steps, each of which may have its own time parameter. The nature of relocation goals, on the other hand, may make them more long term.

Target dates strengthen the goal statement by providing milestones against which to measure progress. It is helpful to keep career goals within a three-year range, whenever possible. Setting long-term future goals does not place the same important pressures on the individual as shorter-term goals do. Most effective short-term career planning goals will focus on a six- to eighteen-month period. The strength of establishing a time frame lies in forcing the individual to consider contingency plans if the goal is not achieved within the specified time frame. Checkpoints along the way also provide the individual with ways of measuring progress. Practitioners should recognize that time frames must sometimes be extended, since it is not always possible to complete a goal within the initially defined time period. The employee should also be wary of setting unrealistic time frames. A time frame that is too long will remove any sense of urgency about the goal. A time frame that is too short will make the goal unattainable and may be simply an excuse for failure.

It is almost mandatory that practitioners become an expert at setting realistic and workable time frames. Not only do they have to know how to establish schedules that are challenging but not overly demanding; they must also have a general working knowledge of organizational time constraints that might affect employees' goals. A number of excellent sources on the market can help establish general expertise in time framing. However, only the organization can provide the information needed to aid specific goal statements.

Following are some questions that practitioners may find useful in establishing the validity of employees' time frames:

- Is the time limit reasonable, given the typical rate of movement in the organization?
- Is it reasonable, given current skills development and frequency with which openings occur?
- Is the time limit reasonable, given the length of time on the present job?
- Is it reasonable, given the employee's normal rate of progression from job to job?
- Is the position likely to be needed by the organization by the time one moves into it?

The following realignment goal meets the requirement for timeframing: "I plan to realign (downward) from supervisor to senior key punch operator by June 15, or as soon as a replacement supervisor can be trained, in order to be able to go back on the day shift." (The employee should also identify a reasonable time period to wait beyond June 15, if no suitable replacement could be found by that time, and the option to be followed should that time frame not be met.)

Reasonable Relevance. Career goals must be relevant to current and future employee and organizational needs if they are to amount to more than fantasies. Emphasis on their comparison to profiling information will help employees determine if they have or can readily obtain the skills, traits, and experience necessary to reach the goal. The goal should be congruent with the employees' preferences for work environments, values, and job behavioral demands.

To meet the relevance requirement, individuals must know that the organization has or will have a need for the functions and positions to which they aspire. Goals should not conflict with current policies or projections of future trends. Organizational and individual goals should be viewed as interrelated components for achieving company purpose. Without compatible individual goals the organization will suffer from lack of full human resource effectiveness; without compatible organizational goals, the individual will lack opportunity and sense of accomplishment.

While employees have few problems seeing the importance of their own goals and career plans, they often have a limited concept of the organization's needs and plans. As a result they often feel cheated when they find that their goals are in conflict with organizational priorities. It is incumbent upon the practitioner to provide the organizational information necessary to help employees analyze the relevance of their goals. To do this will require that they be made privy to such information as organizational long-range strategic and short-range plans, future marketing schemes, product or organizational changes being contemplated, and shifts in direction.

Publications such as annual reports, internal newsletters, trade magazines, manpower projection documents, and industry trend reports can provide valuable indications of future directions if other company documents are considered too confidential to distribute. By instructing employees to consider every document or conversation as a potential source of information for career development, practitioners can assist them in concretely assessing the relevance of their goals.

At Security Pacific National Bank, workshop participants are encouraged to test the relevancy of their career development goals by generating lists of changes that are likely to affect the bank over the next ten years. Workshop participants then prioritize ten trends that will affect banking and consider how they will affect jobs and goals. Examples of these trends named include:

- Legislation to impose more government control
- National and international branching
- Banks becoming agents of social change
- Simplified forms; reduced legal jargon
- Automated bill payment
- Electronic funds transfer
- Internal automation

Lists such as this can then be discussed by practitioners to help participants see how changes will impact on individual careers.

Questions the practitioner should be asking about relevance include

- Is the goal in sync with present position, skills and abilities?
- Does the goal match future expectations?
- Is the goal a step in the right direction?
- Is the goal congruent with the organization's present position?
- Is the goal congruent with the organization's future needs and policies?

For example, a relocation goal might say, "I plan to relocate to XYZ Computer Software Company, where I will be able to move out of systems programming and into software sales." If the employee could show that the sales opportunity is closed within the present organization; that XYZ Company could provide that opportunity; that the goal meets with the employee's current abilities; and that it is compatible with future plans of the employee and of the industry, the relevance requirement would be met.

Aiming for Attainability.   Attainability suggests that the goal be within the employee's present competence, or that it represents a reasonable learning and development experience. It should provide strong motivation to stretch beyond current levels or functions, but it should not be an impossible dream.

Like relevance attainability should be questioned from the viewpoint of an individual's skills and abilities and from that of the organization's structure and constraints. If the reality-testing component of profiling has been effectively accomplished, employees should be able to accurately calculate the attainability of their goals within the organizational framework. They should consider how reasonable their actions are in light of their present positions, normal organizational rates of movement, prerequisites for jobs, training opportunities, and availability of information about various segments of the organization.

The practitioner's input may include career path progression charts, information about thresholds between job categories, job groupings by salary grade, and other data about current and future opportunities. One organization found it useful to prepare a graphic representation showing the number of staff at each salary grade level. Employees could then estimate the number of other people at similar grade levels who were competing for higher grade level jobs. The same graph provided them with an estimate of how many such jobs existed within the organization. Such information demonstrates that the number of positions in each higher grade level declines quickly after a certain point, and it helps employees understand the structure of the organization and of the competition they face.

Questions the practitioner might raise at this stage include

- Is this a logical next step from the present position and salary grade?
- Will this move require crossing a job category threshold, and is that significant?
- Is this a typical job progression step that others have taken?
- Is the salary too high or too low to make this move?
- Is there likely to be an opening in that position?
- What is the competition likely to look like? (qualifications and numbers)
- Are the qualifications for the job presently possessed? Can qualifications be attained within the time frame specified?
- How will the employee's qualifications compare with those of the competition?

If these questions can be answered satisfactorily, the following vertical goal statement will meet the attainability requirement: "I plan to move from junior buyer to senior buyer within twelve months."

While it is difficult to precisely measure goal attainment, it is possible to measure desired outcomes in steps along the way to goal attainment. These steps consist of specific verifiable activities or events which, when completed, should logically lead to accomplishing the career goal.

Measuring Milestones. Measurement involves assessing progress at a series of checkpoints along the way. These checkpoints help measure the relative success or failure experienced by the individual while in pursuit of the goal. Checkpoints should be inserted at intervals that permit corrections in defining the target. This allows individuals to test the accuracy of their self-assessments, the accuracy of their original assumptions about time parameters and attainability, and the accuracy of their perceptions about the evolving environment, throughout the career development process. Specifying desired outcomes for comparison with actual outcomes at designated points introduces an ongoing reality-testing mechanism.

Questions the practitioner could ask at this stage of the process include

- How will you know whether or not you are on the right track?
- Can the goal be broken down into a series of subgoals that can be monitored to assure that you are moving in the desired direction?
- What are the signs to look for that would signal adjustments in the goal?
- What contingency plans can be made to adjust the goal?

The following exploratory goal meets the requirements for measurability: "I plan to explore job opportunities within the personnel department by

Studying the department's organization chart	—June 1
Reading a book on organizing the personnel function	—June 15
Reading the last two issues of *Personnel Report*	—June 5
Interviewing Bob Jones, Management Recruiter	—June 8
Interviewing Mary Wilkins, Personnel Specialist	—June 10
Interviewing Sarah Smith, Department Head	—June 18
Attending a Personnel Association meeting	—June 9

Focusing for Clear Visibility. Goals are more likely to be acted upon if they are shared with those who can provide encouragement and with those who can open doors that may eventually lead to their attainment. Practitioners should encourage employees to view peers, supervisors, family, and friends as personal resources who can assist in a variety of tangible and intangible ways.

Employees should share their goal statements with as many members of the organization as possible—supervisors, coworkers, personnel staff, recruiters, and others. The more individuals in an organization who are aware of an employee's specific goals, the more assistance is available. If individuals feel reluctant to share goals with organization members, it is all the more important that the practitioner encourage them to convey their goals to family, friends, and peers from other organizations. Support and occasional nudges are important to keep the employees on track.

In some companies visibility is promoted through using developmental reviews that ask employees to state career goals and to define abilities they wish to develop over the coming year. And in some, career goals are part of performance reviews.

Questions the practitioner could ask to check on the visibility notion include

- How can a goal be made visible within the organization?
- What vehicles currently exist that can help to gain visibility?
- To whom should a goal be visible?
- What kind of assistance would be helpful from these people?

The following job enrichment goal meets the requirement for visibility: "I plan to write a proposal for expanding and modifying my current job accounting abilities, so that I can handle the entire tuition reimbursement auditing process. The proposal and cover memo will be sent to my supervisor, with a copy going to her boss and to the department head."

Getting It Down

Once employees understand the required characteristics of effective goals, the practitioner can offer assistance in actually drafting goal statements. A workshop setting can encourage employees to develop initial drafts individually, to share them with others, and to receive advice from peers and workshop staff concerning any necessary changes. Counseling sessions are another alternative, but they should be supplemented by employees exchanging their goal statements with others outside the individual sessions. No matter which vehicle is selected, the practitioner will need to support employees in four distinct activities:

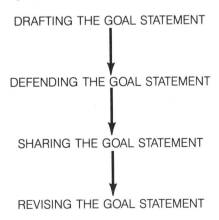

DRAFTING THE GOAL STATEMENT

DEFENDING THE GOAL STATEMENT

SHARING THE GOAL STATEMENT

REVISING THE GOAL STATEMENT

Drafting.   For most employees the most difficult part of setting goals is facing a blank sheet of paper. Practitioners can help by defining and clarifying the six career option categories and by strongly suggesting that goals in each category be established. Such an exercise can provide realistic suggestions to help employees work through mental blocks. Providing employees with a form such as the Goal Matrix (described earlier) can provide a framework for generating ideas.

Employees should be urged to review their personal profiling information as well as data gained about the organization as they set about drafting goals. And they should ask themselves if their statements meet all characteristics of action-oriented goals discussed in this chapter. Goal statements should be continually challenged with questions such as, "Is this goal *specific* enough, in terms of the job title, salary/grade, and duties to which I aspire?" and "Is this goal *relevant* to the skills I now have or could easily develop?"

Goal statements should reflect a match between the realities of the organization and the individual's skills and aspirations. Conflicts, if any, should receive close attention and may warrant rewriting the goal statement.

Defending.   During the defense of goal statements, employees explain why this goal is appropriate for them at this time. They should be able to write or verbalize a defense statement that considers

- How does this goal incorporate my profiling information?
- Is the goal as *specific* as I can make it?
   —Am I able to specify a job title?
   —Am I able to name departments or divisions?
   —Am I able to define concrete actions indicated by the goal?
- Is the goal *attainable?*
   —Does such a job exist?
   —Is it a reasonable move for me?
   —Do I compare favorably with the competition?
   —Can I obtain additional skills I will need?
- Is the goal *time-bound* and relatively short term (six to eighteen months)?
- Is the goal *relevant?*
   —Does the goal match the future I want and expect?
   —Is the goal in tune with information I have about the organization?
- Can I make this goal *visible* to those who can help?

The defense step can be carried out with a counselor, a supervisor, or peers. It may be executed one-on-one, in small groups, or in a workshop setting. In a workshop setting groups of two or three can take turns interviewing one another, using the foregoing questions.

Sharing.   While goal statements have already been shared with other individuals during the defense step, employees should be encouraged to think of additional persons with whom they might discuss career goals. For reinforcement practitioners might find it helpful to have employees design subgoal statements reflecting their plan to share their goal statement. A simple format can be useful in helping to generate ideas, such as Exhibit 4-6.

Revising. As new information is obtained, or as assumptions prove to be in error, the goal statement should be modified. In some cases the new information may be significant enough to require that the individual return to the first step and draft a new goal statement. In others only minor adjustments may be needed.

The practitioner should remind employees that not all assumptions must be or can be tested immediately. Few career decisions are made with all the information at hand. The important point is to make the goal statement as precise and appropriate as possible with whatever information is at hand, to begin actively working toward goals, and to resist the rationalization that "I can't really go after that goal because I'm not sure I'd achieve it anyway."

By the end of the Targeting Stage employees should have developed realistic career-planning goals that have high probability for success. Practitioners can help employees to evaluate their goals' probability for success by using several thought-provoking questions that cause participants to go back through the process step-by-step.

Examples of such questions are

- Do you have adequate information about the organization's current activities and future plans to select personal career goals?
- How can you get the additional information you need?
- Have you considered all categories of career paths in selecting your goal options?
- Do the options you have generated adequately cover a variety of circumstances that may occur in the organization and in specific job areas?
- Should you select more goal options than you now have?
- Do your goals realistically reflect profiling information?

GOAL: _____

Persons to share with:	Occasion/time:	Purpose of sharing:
Husband	After dinner tonight	Moral support
Peer in another organization	Lunch—next Monday	Reality-testing
My secretary	Private meeting	To inform; to solicit understanding of my future actions

Exhibit 4-6 Goal Sharing Format

- Are your goals compatible with organizational goals and plans?
- Are your goal statements oriented toward a specific action?
- Are your goals stated in such a way that their progress can easily be checked along the way?

Structural Supports for Targeting

Thus far practitioners have been invited to design career workshops and counseling sessions necessary to assist employees in exploring and specifying career goals. They have been advised to use vital organizational information to aid employees in making their goal statements more realistic and in sync with the organization's overall goals. The organization has a variety of processes that are part of its structure and that can greatly assist in the targeting process. It is the practitioner's job to learn and understand these processes and to translate them for use at the Targeting Stage. The organizational policy and practice areas described in the following section can serve as a guide, but practitioners must consider their own organization and how its policies might be further tied to the career development process at the Targeting Stage.

Organizational Planning.   Most organizations, regardless of size, have several different types of planning processes. These might be broken down into two general types: the longer-term strategic plans, and the shorter-term operational or tactical plans.

Strategic plans are those long-term schemes that deal with projected changes in direction, growth efforts and velocities, and environmental adaptations. They normally involve major commitments of resources and affect how an organization will proceed with its business in the long run and how fundamental questions of policy and organizational mission will be addressed.

Operational or tactical plans are those that deal with the step-by-step objectives along the route toward strategic goals. These plans may be looked upon as the milestones for measuring progress along the strategic path.

Suppose that an employee, as a result of a career development plan, establishes a goal of becoming a marketing manager in a particular product area. Unbeknown to either the employee or the practitioner, however, the organization's strategic plans call for the termination of that product line in three years. Operational plans are the only ones available to the employee during the Targeting Stage, and these indicate that the product line will continue to exist and even grow during the coming two years. The employee develops the goal and the practitioner, just as ignorant of the long-term plans as the employee, endorses that goal. Three-quarters of the way through the plan to reach the career goal, however, the employee suddenly finds that the career path is a dead-end, that acquired skills are inapplicable, and that a return to the start position is the only logical choice. Who is going to feel cheated? Who is going to find that credibility has been undermined? Who is going to be hurt?

The answers are, of course, everyone concerned. Employees may feel that they have been led astray and that valuable time and effort has been wasted. Practitioners may find their role in the organization diminished, find themselves less trusted by other employees, and find that the whole career development effort has suffered tremendously. The organization may feel that dollars have been wasted on career development, may see a lack of trust in the organization by employees, and may lose an employee who could have been valuable in another area.

To avoid this type of LOSE/LOSE/LOSE situation it is imperative that practitioners have access to organizational planning information and develop the skills necessary to translate and disseminate it. Toward this end the practitioner will have to convince those in authority of the vital importance of sharing with employees as much of this information as possible. Existing documents such as annual reports, company newspapers, industrial trend reports, and current media reports about environmental, cultural, political, and legal changes can be used effectively at the Targeting Stage. In other instances it may be necessary to actually gather raw data that pertains to upcoming corporate changes in technology, product, and market strategy and prepare it for employee consumption. The practitioner can develop files of such information or assign employee task forces to gather it for their departments and present it at group meetings or workshops.

> Security Pacific National Bank has its own in-house futurist who publishes a monthly newsletter called Future Scan that projects changes that will affect the banking industry. Individuals may subscribe to the newsletter and remain up to date on the current trends in banking and in affiliated industries. For many who attend the career seminars, this valuable informative item is first introduced to them when the targeting stage is presented, and becomes a valuable asset for their continuing career futures.

Charts and Titles. Much of the information that can provide a base for targeting is assumed to be common knowledge in most organizations, though in fact it is not widely disseminated throughout the organization. Organizational charts and lists of titles and grades are often considered to be of value only to personnel department staff. Some organizations keep these charts confidential. However, these charts can assist all employees in setting more specific goals for movement within the organization, and practitioners should not fail to consider them.

When specific job titles, grades, or qualifications are not readily available to employees, practitioners might consider preparing special career information reports that contain as much of this data as can be gathered and easily understood. Job titles and classification listings can be categorizing into job families and task groups for easy identification of functions and skills. Career path examples can demonstrate grade level clusters and major thresholds between categories, such as nonexempt and exempt, exempt and managerial, and managerial and executive levels.

At California Institute of Tehcnology, employees who can attend career development workshops are provided with lists of current job title series in various functional areas, such as administration, accounting, payroll, and secretarial. The lists indicate exempt and non-exempt status, as well as grade levels. For example:

Exempt

Division Administrator (A7)
Senior Administrative Assistant (A4)
Administrative Assistant or Assistant to (A2)
Administrative Aide or Assistant to (A1)

Non-exempt

Senior Administrative Aide (O7)
Executive Secretary or Administrative Aide (O6)
Senior Administrative Secretary (O5)
Administrative Secretary (O4)
Secretary (O3)

While the information may seem simple and easily attainable, employee reaction is usually one of insight and appreciation for clarity of grades, steps and job titles which were heretofore vague.

Organizational charts can assist employees in understanding reporting relationships between individuals and between divisions and units. These charts presents visually a great deal of information that may not be as easily understood if presented verbally. This information will be of particular benefit to those who have research goals but who do not realize the expanse of the various organizational units (for example, that personnel includes placement, training and development, employee relations, compensation, job analysis, employment, benefits, and research.)

A great many organizations are now putting together organizational charts that display pictures of key personnel. These can be valuable to employees in identifying those within the organization who may be contacted to gather more information about the viability of a particular goal. Practitioners in organizations that do not have pictures displayed on charts may want to make available to employees photographs of key personnel. Familiarity, even through a photograph, can ease the research process for those employees who need to learn more about a position before selecting their target.

Company Goals and Trends. To ensure the integration of company and personal goals, individuals must understand overall business objectives before formulating their personal plans. Since the success of the organization requires that each of its employees be working toward achieving company objectives, employees must be aware of overall organizational goals and must understand them, in order to be committed to the role that they are expected to play in achieving those goals.

A great many organizations have facilitated this process through Management by Objectives (MBO) programs, which not only clarify organizational goals, but also provide a mechanism through which individual goals can be coordinated with organizational goals. Ideally MBO programs provide for the formulation and promulgation of clear, concisely stated objectives from which action plans are developed. These action plans can be monitored and their progress measured because they are quantitatively stated and give a time frame. MBO plans also provide for taking corrective actions to keep efforts on track.

Ideally an MBO program provides for a series of objectives that relate to goals down through the organization, so that individual employees, regardless of level, can determine exactly what must be accomplished and by when.

Organizational objectives define certain desired results in each major area of the organizational hierarchy. Each division addresses those objectives through a series of statements about specific actions. Each department takes those objectives that relate to it and determines what actions will be necessary to accomplish those objectives along with any others that its management may desire to pursue. The process continues to filter down through groups and subdepartments and, finally, to individuals who determine what part of their group's objectives they can accomplish.

There is a recurring fear that MBO imposes objectives and schedules, rather than letting the organization's individual units and employees determine what they wish to accomplish. This is somewhat true, but MBO does provide a means by which organization-wide objectives can be stated and coordinated. Some organizations have experimented, with varying degrees of success, with bottom up MBO, wherein objectives begin at the individual employee level and work their way up to the organizational level.

Practitioners who work in either top down or bottom up MBO organizations will find that coordinating personal career development goals with organizational objectives is easy. Information is easier to come by than in most other organizations, and employees have a better understanding of organizational directions and trends.

Job Posting. In addition to their use in internal job placement, bulletins announcing job openings can give employees a sense of the types of employment available and of the changes taking place. Employees who keep informed about potential jobs—even those for which they do not intend to apply—will begin to see company trends in employment and trends in growth or decline of certain functional areas. For example, they may get their first clue about expansion of a branch office by noting the number of jobs posted for that site. Or they may note that while many jobs are opening in the Marketing Division, they tend to be clustered at the lower levels with little turnover at the top. Simply seeing the variety of jobs that become available can generate ideas for goal options that employees may not have previously considered.

To be effective a job posting system must include all openings and must be part of an honest effort to objectively select from among applicants. In many cases, however, job posting is simply a routine that is followed because of regulations, when in fact a candidate has already been selected. Since this practice is not likely to change dramatically, the practitioner may need to candidly caution employees to be realistic in their expectations. Some organizations make it a policy to at least have a face-to-face discussion with applicants from within—explaining selection procedures and reasons— rather than simply sending them the same form letter that others may receive.

Job announcements should be posted where all employees will see them (for best effect, in a number of locations) and should display as much information as possible about the job. This includes title, salary, experience and education requirements, and major duties. Also useful is an enumeration of how many persons have held the position over the past five to ten years and a description of the potential career ladder(s) that could result from the job.

The practitioner can supplement this information by compiling statistics on who has moved where over the past several years. A simple list can be disseminated with items as

- Personnel Analyst III (1975-77) Personnel Supervisor (1977-79) Assistant for Labor Management Relations (1980)
- Secretary, Marketing (II) (1974-76) Office Manager (1976-79) Assistant Account Supervisor (1980)
- Supply Clerk, Public Rel. (1975-77) Asst. Office Manager (1977-80)

This kind of information offered in a workshop setting can help employees to be more realistic in their attempts to set goals.

Succession Planning. Generally used to plan and clarify progression in managerial ranks, succession planning assists the organization in training backup personnel who are likely to fill certain positions.

Often these succession plans are made behind closed doors—individuals are not cognizant of the specific targets being developed for them. As a result individuals often end up determining several specific targets, while the organization has designed a radically different game plan. One result of this approach can be that the heir apparent, not knowing of the secret selection, begins looking elsewhere for opportunity. The first that the employee knows of management's plans and the first that management knows of the employee's disgruntlement is when the employee tenders a resignation, citing a lack of opportunity. By then it can be too late to rectify the situation. The organization's intent is usually to keep all options open, but the new opportunities finally offered to the employee are often turned down or met with mixed emotions.

One method of succession planning involves the incumbents naming and training their successors. This gives the successor direct contact with and instruction from the predecessor as well as visibility among others in the unit. However, this practice can result in questionable selection criteria if incumbents are allowed to be the sole judge in replacing themselves.

A more formal method of succession planning is a team selection approach, whereby a team of managers evaluate potential candidates, generally nominated by their own supervisors or identified through a testing procedure, for higher positions. Those who prove to be superior performers are then placed in a fast track development program, designed to give them extensive experience and training in preparation for advancement. They continue to be evaluated in order to determine their specific placement in the organization. This system relies heavily on training or job rotation to develop multifunctional employees who have potential for management.

If practitioners could make succession plans available to individuals during this stage, individuals would have enough time to contemplate their option and consider whether or not the organization's plan meets with their own career goals. The more thought that individuals have given to their skills and desires during the Profiling Stage, the better they will be prepared to actively pursue the next step of their career development needs. Clearly the practitioner and the organization need to give serious thought to the succession planning issue and to sharing that information with employees at the Targeting Stage.

Shared Responsibilities

It is apparent that the Targeting Stage requires a partnership of individual employees, practitioners, and the organization as a whole.

At Union Oil Company of California, recruitment forecasting and succession planning provide both the company and employees with a valuable data base for decision making and planning. The programs are backed by information from the company's extensive skills inventory (with cross-referenced information on employee education, experience, skills, and interests) and its organizational change model (a mathematical simulation which tracks demographic distribution, functions, employee ages, departures, status and new recruits).

The organizational change model supplies estimated attrition rates which, along with the company's human resource needs, forecasting, and other data, provide the basis for development of a company-wide recruiting forecast. This forecast, in turn, becomes valuable input for the succession planning process.

A key element of succession planning at Union Oil is a managerial needs forecast, covering about 500 positions and supplied annually—by unit—to each unit head. The document received in the units predicts numbers of openings over the next five years and provides a list of unit members that notes those who will reach average retirement age within the forecast period.

The managerial needs forecast is used by succession planning groups in each unit who apply personal knowledge and skills inventory information to determine potential candidates for key managerial positions that will come open. The candidates' preparation is linked to an individual development plan, designed to help them ready themselves for advancement. Responsibility for seeing that the plan is carried out—including deadlines for specific developmental activities—rests with each candidate's manager.[8]

Individuals can set goals for themselves, but they cannot do so in a vacuum. The organization must be prepared to share information that is necessary in generating goals, and the practitioner must develop ways to translate that information into usable, meaningful terms.

During the Targeting Stage, managers and supervisors must be prepared to help employees push toward their goals. Managers and supervisors can set targets for subordinates and challenge them to meet those targets. They must give honest performance evaluation to their subordinates and help them to increase their skills. And finally, they must be sensitive to their subordinates, to the work environment, and to how individual goals mesh with those of the organization. Practitioners must be prepared to help managers and supervisors fulfill these responsibilities.

The practitioner, thus, is an intermediary who may need to prod top management to provide information and may need to encourage and instruct employees to use it in setting goals. Where necessary the practitioner may need to guide employees to sources of information about career opportunities outside the organization. The practitioner may also become involved in designing programs to assist employees in setting goals.

Once career plans have been identified and tested against the realities of organizational life, employees will be ready to begin designing the action plans that will enable them to pursue their goals in an organized manner. During the Strategizing Stage employees work to make their goals operational. The practitioner continues to play the vital role of information supplier and facilitator.

MAPPING MOVEMENT
the strategizing stage

" . . . goals are only half the problem; it's planning the way to reach them that requires real ingenuity . . . "

Once goals have been established, the next stage in the career development cycle is formulating a comprehensive strategy to accomplish them. All too often the career development process moves along to the point of individual goals being set, and the practitioner assumes that employees will be able from that point to function on their own.

Goals do not stimulate action. Action results from a carefully thought out and meticulously structured plan that describes how a goal is to be accomplished. The practitioner's job is to help employees develop those plans, to aid them in discovering potential problems, and to give them means of overcoming the problems en route to accomplishing their goals.

In the opening scene of Meredith Wilson's musical comedy, *The Music Man,* a group of traveling salesmen are discussing the infamous con man, Professor Harold Hill. Professor Hill's goal is clear to all of the salesmen: he goes about the country bilking the locals out of their money under the guise of selling uniforms and musical instruments for boys' bands. Hill's plan for doing this is carefully planned. The salesmen go to great lengths in describing Professor Hill's ability to sweet-talk, con, and spellbind his potential customers. One salesman, however, keeps saying that Professor Hill will never succeed because, "He doesn't know the territory!"

As anyone who has seen *The Music Man* knows, Professor Hill proves that he not only knows the territory, but that he has also planned in his strategy for reaching his goal, planned for nearly every contingency.

Despite all efforts to upset him, he makes his sales, and River City, Iowa, gets its boys' band.

Practitioners of career development can learn a great deal from Professor Harold Hill. Although they are certainly not involved in a con, their job *is* to help others attain their goals, and to do this they must be prepared to help their participants to

1. Know the territory, by thoroughly understanding their organizations; and
2. Develop workable plans to achieve their goals, by effectively synthesizing that information into an achievable course of action.

The practitioner must, therefore, be able to plan interventions that promote *understanding* of the organization and facilitate the *synthesizing* of information. This two-part process takes planning out of a vacuum and makes the goal statements and the process of achievement come alive.

This is the Strategizing Stage: expanding the planning process to take into account opportunities and obstacles that might otherwise be overlooked; and investigating the formal and informal organizational factors that can aid or impede accomplishment of goals.

Surmountable Obstacles

The strategizing process is not easy. The first obstacle is resistance to change. Strategizing confronts individuals and pushes them to name specific actions and events that they may encounter immediately. This new concern often brings with it a sudden realization that lives could really change. Practitioners who have an understanding of the whole change process will find it particularly useful at this stage.

Change is particularly difficult for people who aren't sure where they are going. Whatever aspect of a person's life causes the need to reassess, forays into the unknown are often followed by hasty retreats to a more stable condition. Sometimes a work situation must become physically unbearable before a person is willing to risk even minor movement. The practitioner's efforts at the Strategizing Stage can help counter fears of change by providing individuals with an opportunity to learn how to plan for change. The whole purpose of strategizing is to gain control over the changes in one's career. A large part of the practitioner's job during strategizing is to help participants develop skills in analyzing organizational realities, in assessing alternative paths toward achieving goals, and in developing a realistic plan for what to do and how to do it.

It is easy for career development practitioners, as well as others in the organization, to simply ignore the importance of strategizing. The goal-setting process results in such a tidy end product that it is difficult to recognize it as only the beginning. People need to realize that nothing can happen without continued work and commitment. Goals that have been established require follow-up to bring them to fruition.

UNDERSTANDING THE SYSTEM

Organizations are comprised of more than just structures, rules, procedures, and policies. Organizations are made up of people. Not only is there the formal, established, traditional organization; in addition, a host of informal norms appear in response to the social and personal needs of the people involved. In order for effective action planning to take place, it is necessary for the practitioner to understand both the formal and the informal organization. An employee who attempts to achieve a career development goal based upon a plan that considers only the formal organization will encounter difficulties as that plan moves into areas influenced by the informal system.

Formality and Informality

Interest in informal organizations began during the 1930s, as a result of studies conducted by Elton Mayo and Fritz Roethlisberger in the Western Electric Company plant at Hawthorne, IL. These studies showed that the differences shown in Exhibit 5-1 exist between formal and informal organizations.

The structure of the formal organization is based upon the jobs to be performed by the organization as a whole as well as by its individual component parts. Although there may be some overlap of functions within an organization, each department, group, or division has its own hierarchy of managers, supervisors, and executives. The informal organization is

Factor	Formal	Informal
Structure	Hierarchical and Functional	Social and Based on Personal Preferences
Establishment	Authority and Organizational Requirements	Spontaneous and Meeting Personal Needs
Maintenance	Through Organizational Rules and Regulations	Through Mutual Meeting of Needs
Permanence	High Depending upon Life of Organization and Environmental Factors	Low to High Depending upon needs satisfied and personal factors

Exhibit 5-1   Formal and Informal Structures

usually social and based upon individuals' preferences for persons and personalities with whom to associate.

The formal organization is established by rules and regulations designed to facilitate the fulfillment of organizational requirements. Informal organizations, on the other hand, spring up without planning or overt intention and are aimed at meeting the personal needs of individual members.

The formal organization is maintained by a system designed to promote order and focus efforts toward organizational goals. Informal organizations tend to exist only so long as personal needs are being met by and for their memberships. When members have new changed needs that the informal organization cannot satisfy, they will move on to another group more capable of meeting them.

Formal organizations tend to have a great deal of permanence. They are established for accomplishing specific purposes, and as long as those purposes are being accomplished the organizations will continue to exist. Informal organizations may be temporary, lasting for only a few days, or permanent, lasting the entire lifetimes of their members. The deciding factor in determining the length of an informal organization's life span is based on the strengths of the associations formed and the needs being fulfilled.

Later research has shown that for every function or system that operates within a formal organization, parallel or shadow functions of systems operate within the related informal organizations. It is imperative, therefore, that the practitioner understand these functions and systems in order to assist career development program participants in understanding them.

To aid the practitioner with the process of organizational analysis, eight separate functions or systems will be identified and described. Most organizations will have these functions or systems operating within them. However, some may be more explicit than others. Practitioners may find it necessary to study their organizations to discover the systems in operation and how they may be different from or similar to the ones analyzed here.

Understanding the system means knowing about

- Relationships
- Power
- Politics
- Support: Mentors, Networks, and Task Groups
- Information and Communications
- Culture
- Values
- Technology

Meaningful Relationships. In most informal organizations, relationships are work oriented, system imposed, and hierarchical. An employee has a function that has been established as necessary in order to accomplish certain organizational goals and objectives. The employee is situated in the work place around other employees who have specific functions and jobs. All employees within a common work place have a supervisor, appointed by the organization. That supervisor works for another supervisor, who, in turn, works for another supervisor, and so on up the chain of command.

In the informal organization, on the other hand, relationships are socially oriented, are established by the group and its individual members, and are sociometrically based. Regardless of their functions within the organization, members make individual decisions about their associations. Though members of the informal group may be friendly with all others in the organization, certain close ties will be formed with certain individuals more than with others. These relationships all affect the action plans developed by individuals as they pursue career goals.

Suppose, for example, that a machinist set a lateral career goal of moving into quality assurance. The practitioner in this case might want to help the machinist understand not only the formal organizational relationships of the quality assurance group, but the system of informal relationships existing there as well. Machinists would in this case have to examine their own needs for special relationships and determine if those needs would be fulfilled in and by the new group. Current friendships could certainly be affected. Barriers could also be encountered in such a change of relationships—some internal to the individual making the move, and some within the group to be joined. The practitioner would perhaps need to assist the machinist in considering how those barriers might be overcome or effectively neutralized.

While practitioners are not expected to be thoroughly conversant with the actual informal system of relationships in order to facilitate organizational changes, it is helpful for them to understand the impact of these informal relationships on potential career moves. As usual the process is the concern of the practitioner while the content is the concern of the employee.

Power and Influence.   Practitioners who understand the use of power and influence in the organization will be able to funnel that information to employees for assistance during the Strategizing Stage. Learning to effectively utilize power and influence is often integral to achieving certain goals set by employees at the Targeting Stage, and although practitioners are not expected to point out the precise paths to such power, they can educate program participants in the subject or perhaps offer training programs that build these vital skills.

Sometimes such education lies in explaining the primary sources of formal and informal power so that program participants understand these sources. One view suggests that there are eight sources of power, which vary according to their acceptance by others in the system and according to the permanence of their effect on others. These include:

- *Positional Power:* The authority granted by virtue of one's position in the organization or relationship. Positional Power is usually well defined and limited by the association's structure and agreements.
- *Expertise Power:* The ability to influence outcomes or create control, based upon one's background, education, experience, and acquired knowledge. Expertise Power is limited by the area(s) in which one's knowledge actually applies.
- *Charismatic Power:* The ability to guide the actions and decisions of others through the strength of one's own personality, style, and charm. Charismatic Power is measured by how much others desire to be associated with persons, or are willing to do for them, without thought of reward or fear of punishment.
- *Influential Power:* The power derived from one's associations and mutual support networks, or control over the rewards, services, or resources desired or needed by others. Influential Power is generated and, in turn, limited by one's willingness to form associations with and perform services for others, who then obligate their power to the initiator.
- *Implied Coercive Power:* The power derived from the ability to withhold rewards, services, or resources from another, even though the threat to do so may never be openly communicated. Implied Coercive Power is based in both one's Influential Power and one's Actual Coercive Power.
- *Actual Coercive Power:* The ability to influence another by actually withholding rewards, services, resources, or favors, until the desired action is accomplished or the desired behavior is demonstrated. Actual Coercive Power is established when the holder actually uses it. Until it is used, this power is Implied.
- *The Power of Applied Pressure:* The power derived from one's ability and willingness to apply sanctions, cut off resources, or deny services to others, in order to accomplish an objective.
- *The Power of Raw Force:* The ability to remove, shunt aside, overrun, or eliminate an obstacle presented by another person or conflicting group. Raw Force is limited by one's ability to maintain it long enough to effectively and permanently neutralize the opposition.[1]

Practitioners might use this information in designing strategizing modules devoted to understanding these power sources. This assists employees

---

The Circles of Power model was used in a series of workshops conducted for the Inland Air Conditioning and Refrigeration Contractors' Association, Inc. Supervisors and managers from a number of member companies were shown how power sources can influence the basic organizational structure and resulting relationships. Though Positional Power may be largely centered in one particular person, or group of people, participants were shown that recognition of their own Circles of Expertise, Charismatic, and Influential Power may be used to accomplish long-term objectives and goals. In addition, they developed techniques by which the negative uses of all sources of power, especially Implied and Actual Coercion, Applied Pressure, and Raw Force, could be avoided. Through simulation, the constructive uses of all eight circles was demonstrated. Participants came to recognize that though they may have previously felt "power-LESS" they could be "power-FULL" and more effectively understand the system and their relationship to it. (For further information contact Hugh R. Taylor, 6661 Bobbyboyar Ave., Canoga Park, CA 91307).

in evaluating their own strengths and in projecting the difficulty or ease of entering another part of the organization, where the environment and type of power used is different from where the participant is currently located.

One of the most renowned current organizational theorists, Rosabeth Kanter, defines power as the capacity to mobilize resources to get the job done. She suggests that power can be accumulated through activities and alliances. Activities must be extraordinary (innovative), visible (noticed by others), and relevant (of importance to the organization) if they are to add to an individual's power. Alliances may be used to accumulate power; alliances with peers (who can offer an exchange of favors), mentors (who can open doors or cut red tape), and powerful subordinates (who can bring notice and enhanced reputation to their bosses) are vital to the individual.[2]

Goodmeasure of Cambridge, Massachusetts has developed an inventory which analyzes the power dimensions of jobs by using Rosabeth Kanter's theoretical model. Their questionnaire is designed to help individuals analyze the current aspects of their jobs that contribute to effectiveness (the way things are done now) and asks individuals to think of future actions that can develop specific parts of the job that would contribute to their organizational power. Questions concern *visibility*, the extent to which an individual's work is known in the organization, *autonomy*, the amount of discretion in the job; *relevance*, the value of the job to pressing organizational issues and relationships, and the supports and alliances on the job. (For further information contact Goodmeasure, 330 Broadway, Cambridge, MA 02138).

Practitioners can use questionnaires such as this to assist individuals in understanding their own position in the power system, and in determining steps to detail a plan during the Strategizing Stage for acquiring the power needed to move in a particular direction.

Practitioners may be able to assist participants in operationalizing Kanter's suggestions by educating employees about these ideas and by perhaps helping them take advantage of opportunities to form such alliances or helping them seek involvement in activities with the characteristics mentioned.

Other approaches help employees to understand power by encouraging them to identify their own personal influence style and to practice using a range of styles through simulated situations. With sufficient training, employees can, in fact, increase their effectiveness in this area.

Another approach to this subject would be for practitioners to educate program participants in the subject of personal influence by direcing them to closely observe managers who have power. Questions the practitioner might use to help individuals understand the use of power in the organization could include

Situation Management Systems (SMS) of Boston has developed a training package called *Positive Power and Influence.* The program uses a questionnaire which assesses the influence styles an individual uses most and least frequently and also provides questionnaires to others who can judge the person on the same dimensions to provide a reality-testing component. During the five-day training program, employees are provided with additional assessment opportunities as well as self-directed time to practice utilizing and fine-tuning particular styles. Before concluding, employees complete an application plan which applies learnings in the workshop to a real influence problem at work. Intensive coaching is provided by skilled facilitators throughout so that participants can be assured of expanding their repertoire of influence styles. (For further information contact SMS, Box 476, Center Station, Plymouth, MA 02361)

- Who in this organization (department or unit) has power? (Who has been consistently promoted? Who chairs important committees and meetings? Who confers with those at the top? Who seems to have the inside information?)
- What is the source of this power? (position/title, relations to peers, sponsorship by others)
- How did they acquire this power? (visible accomplishments, personal trappings, response in crisis)
- How do they use this power?
- How might they help you? (provide role models, give advice, intercede on your behalf)
- Is it necessary for you to acquire more power in order to reach your career goals?
- If so, what are some things you can start doing immediately to make this happen?

These questions can be raised in small one-to-one encounters or in group settings during workshops. The subject of organizational power is important, and information about it is plentiful. The practitioner's job is to have enough knowledge to inform participants or to guide them to appropriate sources of information.

Politics Out of the Closet.   Another area with which the practitioner must be familiar is that of organizational politics. While books such as Dubrin's *Winning at Office Politics,* Jenning's *Routes to the Executive Suite,* and Harrigan's *Games Mother Never Taught You* flood the marketplace, individuals are still at a loss to understand the meaning of politics, and many still see it as a dirty word. While employees know that something besides long-term goals and hierarchical structure influences what happens within an organization, they are often reluctant to admit that their organization, like every other, is rife with political influence. This myopic view can hinder the progress of those who are strategizing to achieve career goals. Only by recognizing, studying, and understanding the internal political system can they fully structure their plans to deal with the barriers it presents and take advantage of the opportunities it affords.

Organizational politics do not have to be seen in as negative. The practitioner who agrees that organizational politics should be discussed will probably have to point out that politics has a very positive side:

> If we define politics as an astute awareness of the human dimensions; as reality orientation and sensitivity to the frequently unspoken needs and feelings of others; as noticing and respecting others ethical but differing values, anxieties, and interpersonal styles; as concern for the best possible solutions incorporating the best of everyone's ideas (as opposed to a defensive not-invented-here syndrome); and as a carefully, consciously developed set of interpersonal competencies for taking all of the above into account when we want to accomplish change or improvement—politics can be very positive.[3]

It may take a great deal of effort by the practitioner and the participants to get organizational politics out of the closet. Even though most people in formal organizations pride themselves on their discretionary use of power, they find it difficult to admit that this use of power is the basis for well-planned and executed political maneuvers. While it is considered an organizational tabu to play office politics, everyone admires the skilled artist who is able to obtain the impossible, soothe ruffled feathers, and get ahead in the competition for scarce resources. Practicing organizational politics means skillfully balancing power, saving the work group's face in bad situations, bartering and horse trading where necessary, working out compromises and keeping intergroup relationships harmonious, being able to think on one's feet in tough situations, and exercising tact and diplomacy.

John F. Kennedy once said that every mother wants her son to grow up to be President—but she does not want him to become a politician. Most employees want to become successful and influential managers and supervisors, but they do not want to play office politics in order to get there.

The career development practitioner must realize that politics are an important part of the formal organization and must be able to help employees develop skills in reading political climates and structures. Practitioners must be prepared to help participants develop the skills necessary to survive the political structure and to become adept in working within it.

Politics have become an accepted part of informal organizations. As politics become more overt, great skill is required to practice it. Informal group politics are almost an art form. Politically it would be the kiss of death to ignore another member of the group. The glue that holds together most informal groups is the mutual satisfaction of needs. Common sense tells the members of the informal group that to admit that one does not wish to satisfy another member's needs would be destructive to the

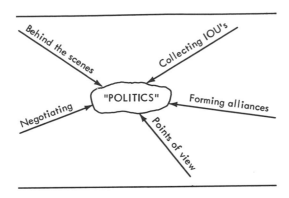

Exhibit 5-2   Organizational Politics

group, so group members engage in compromise, tact, diplomacy, and power balancing. Politics become the life blood of the informal group.

One group exercise that practitioners can use to help individuals revise their notions about politics might invite individuals to

1. put the word "politics" in the center of a flip chart with arrows pointing to it.
2. brainstorm the meaning (associated words) of "politics."
3. write statements on arrows as they are called out.
4. when ideas have been exhausted, individuals can divide the information into three lists: positive, negative, and neutral. (A thought: If all ideas generated are negative, how great is the possibility that individuals in the group are not using politics to their advantage?)
5. generate group discussion, emphasizing the fact that politics can be positive or neutral as well as negative.

Practitioners may be able to help individuals recognize that the system of organizational politics (formal and informal) is largely a matter of relationships between people and the influence of those relationships on how decisions are made. It is a subtle set of activities information, for sharing, building reputations, and gathering influence that usually happens outside formal channels. Politics often shape organizational decisions by answering questions such as, "Who will win or lose if we do this?" and "Whose opinion really counts the most?" Appointments of committee chairpersons may be based as much on their ability to get the attention of top management as on their expertise in the subject matter at hand. A decision to reorganize part of a company may be influenced by the opportunity to give more control to likeable rather than knowledgeable people. Those who excel at playing office politics put themselves in a position to gather inside information and to get the attention of those with organizational influence.

Practitioners can usually suggest a variety of clear approaches to thinking politically. Such thinking may involve

- *Visibility*—making sure that accomplishments become well known, by sending memos, circulating reports, and making presentations at meetings.
- *Attention*—getting the ear of people who are in positions of influence and power.
- *Association*—forming friendships and networks with valuable contact people at lunches, coffee breaks, and conferences.
- *Information*—gathering inside information from such diverse sources as secretaries, mail clerks, auditors, and managers.
- *Aspirations*—making career advancement ambitions known to those who can assist.
- *Demonstration*—finding opportunities to demonstrate abilities by volunteering for committee assignments, special projects, and oral presentations.

Though it can be difficult for the practitioner to openly encourage the study of the politics permeating the organization, and though to clearly delineate such a study might be seen as threatening by some within the organization, employees can surely benefit from such study during their strategizing efforts. Practitioners might find they simply need to instruct employees to closely observe (1) internal periodicals of the organization: What individuals and departments consistently get most play? What types of programs and activities seem to get most mention? (2) memos and reports: Who sends documents to whom? Who is on the internal routing list and in what order? How does the follow-up on reports occur? (3) information flow: Who seems to know everything that goes on? Where is information exchanged (formal meetings, coffee breaks, lunches)? Why is some information shared and other information withheld? (4) power success: Who has the best offices and furnishings? Who spends time with the top brass? Whose subordinates get promoted? Who were the big winners in the last reorganization? Who is responsible for major personnel changes?

Once participants thoroughly understand the relationships, power, and political systems, they will already begin to have some knowledge about how people within the organization assist each other and provide support to one another.

Systems that Support.   When informal groups and organizations were initially recognized as operating within formal organizations, many managers and organizational leaders saw them as potentially dangerous and counterproductive to the goals of the formal organization. In some cases that assumption was valid, but for the most part, informal groups and organizations are valuable support adjuncts to the formal organization. For this reason employees strategizing to accomplish career development goals should understand the informal groups within the organization and the other support systems operating there.

All organizations, formal and informal, have three main systems that provide support for their members.

- *Networks*
- *Mentors*
- *Task Support Groups*

In addition, of course, formal groups often receive a great deal of support from the informal organizations and groups within them, even though this favor is not always returned with any great enthusiasm.

Networking is a relatively new term for a very old practice. Only recently, however, has the practice received recognition and official sanction as a means of providing support for those at the lower levels of formal organizations.

A formal organizational network might work to solve specific organizational problems in a way similar to one currently operating in Los Angeles.

It became abundantly clear that a large aerospace organization's technical library could not keep up with the phenomenal rate of technological change being experienced. Material could not be written, printed, and distributed fast enough to make certain of its availability to those who might need it. It was known, however, that within the organization there were a great many people working on projects, or having recent experience in certain areas, which were among those which progressing with the greatest rapidity. A far-seeing director of technology carefully researched and indexed every field and subject in which his division of the company was working. He then requested that every person within the company who had worked on these areas, or projects related to them, make themselves known to the technical librarians and, through the librarians, available to others who might be seeking help in a job related to that particular expertise. The network worked beautifully. In effect, he established a walking, breathing library of human books and created a technical expertise network. Now, when a particular question comes up, in any field, two lists are checked at the technical library: the printed books available and the walking books in the network. Research delays have been cut significantly.

Similar networks exist, formally and informally, in many companies and organizations. Practitioners can provide invaluable aid to those seeking to accomplish their career development goals by helping program participants join those networks or initiate them with some specific goal in mind. Informal support networks within an organization can be especially valuable to women, minority group members, the physically handicapped, and those contemplating a major job area shift. Those who have blazed the trails are often willing to help others avoid the pitfalls they have encountered.

Many networks are now being established outside organizations. Practitioners might investigate these and make information about them available to participants for use during the Strategizing Stage.

There was a time when every entrant into a career field received the help of a patron, sponsor, or **mentor.** This type of support system was the mainstay of the early guild and craft union apprentice programs. The industrial revolution more or less ended the concept of mentors for those in the so-called labor force, though it has continued, mostly informally, at the managerial and junior executive level.

Fortunately for the career development practitioner, the mentor concept is being formally and informally reestablished in many organizations at all levels.

There is no substitute for personal advice, assistance, and support from somebody who knows the ropes and is in a position to help others up the ladder. One-on-one mentor-protege relationships are a major component of the informal system for individuals aspiring to achieve career goals. The design of effective strategizing activities should include helping employees to initiate one or more mentor relationships and to plan how to best use those relationships to reach goals. Mentors are important throughout the career development model described in this book, however, they carry slightly different responsibilities at each stage. Exhibit 5-3 describes those differences.

After strategizing, the career development participant will need somewhat different resources from a mentor, who may or may not be the same individual sought for strategizing assistance. The mentor should be someone who can provide not only support and guidance, but also active

Career Development Activity	Mentor Contributions
Profiling (Skill definition and self-awareness)	• Feedback about reality of profile • Added information for profile • Guidance in analysis of profile
Targeting (Goal Setting)	• Feedback about reality of goals • Advice on fit between goals and profile • Guidance on alternatives
Strategizing (Planning)	• Added information for developmental plan • Review and guidance regarding obstacles • Role model
Execution (Taking action)	• Intervention on behalf of employee—remove obstacles to acceptance into training programs • Support to generate continued enthusiasm for skill acquisition • Introductions to other key persons/programs • Guidance • Sponsorship for OJT or job rotation • Role model

Exhibit 5-3   Mentor Roles

assistance in removing obstacles to executing the plan. This may be an individual who can nominate an employee for tuition reimbursement programs or provide the employees with a rotational assignment in the employee's own or another unit.

For help during strategizing, practitioners might advise the employee to look for mentors who have done substantial overt career planning of their own and have experienced obstacles and successes in moving toward career goals. Such an individual can help test the validity of the action plan developed by the employee, suggest alternative actions, and present ideas for working around obstacles. Additionally he or she can teach from experience the workings of the informal system, share information generated from the informal system, and advise on ways to best use it.

Clearly mentors are important liaisons throughout the process but particularly during the Strategizing Stage. A number of studies of successful executives have verified that those "who have had mentors, do, in fact, earn more money at a younger age, are better educated, are more likely to follow a carefully delineated career plan, and also mentor others."[4] The practitioner may wish to arrange a formal or informal system that establishes these relationships, knowing that the payoff is considerable.

A mentor can be anybody inside or outside the organization who can be drawn upon for career assistance. It is generally useful for career development program participants to seek out several different mentors who can provide different types of assistance. One may be a role model whose successful career strategy can be emulated by the protege. Another may be a direct superior who can suggest or sponsor choice assignments or developmental activities. Still another may be a particularly skillful counselor who can listen to personal information and give pertinent career guidance. Four specific ways a mentor can provide assistance at the Strategizing Stage are to

1. Actively prepare the individual for new responsibilities and higher positions (suggesting opportunities for relevant experience and training).
2. Coach the individual in using the informal system (including appropriate associations, behavior, and dress.)
3. Provide specific advice on career plans.
4. Protect the individual's interests in the organization (suggest specific ways to become visible, to be considered for good assignments, and to obtain developmental opportunities).

One way that practitioners might gain participation from prospective mentors is to point out that the mentor-protege relationship is not a one-way street—mentors also stand to gain much from it. Some people become mentors simply out of good will, often seeing themselves in the younger or junior person they are helping. Others recognize that they, too, have much to gain from the relationship. Fast track junior employees on the way up, for example, can lend credibility to mentors or assist them by preparing special reports, undertaking new projects, and sharing valuable information that may not be accessible to the mentors.

The practitioner has several alternatives for increasing the possibility that mentor relationships will form during the Strategizing Stage. These include soliciting interest in mentoring from mature, experienced employees (a good job enrichment idea too!) and directing them to specific individuals whom they might take under their tutelage. The alternatives can also involve designing activities that simply make these potential mentors more visible to individuals who are actively participating in the career development effort. This might involve sponsoring one or more discussion groups where specific topics can be addressed and where potential linking can occur on a less formal basis.

For the practitioner conducting career development workshops it might be useful to give an assignment to participants.

- Whom have I identified since the last session who might be able to act as a mentor to me?
- What can I hope to get from this person? (advice, information, role modeling)
- What can I give in return?
- How can I initiate a mentor-protégé relationship?

Mentors are not the cure-all for career development programs, but they provide a strong conduit for the teachings of the informal system. A strong mentoring effort can make the practitioner's job considerably easier and can provide a wealth of information for the participant.

Another means of support that exists in many organizations and that combines the best features of networking and mentorship is *task support groups.* These are groups of people with wide and varied experience in certain fields who make themselves available to help other individuals or groups work on problems related to their jobs. The medical profession pioneered this type of support through the establishment of special consultation groups, which are available to doctors in a particular area or hospital. The idea soon spread to other industries, and today special troubleshooting groups are available in nearly every organization. Many of these groups operate as part of the formal structure, while others are informal and have only quasiofficial status.

The career development program participant who desires to move up or horizontally into a new area of expertise can learn a great deal from these groups. Practitioners can help by locating task support groups and preparing participants to learn from them. Questions such as the following would aid participants in investigating new or unfamiliar areas:

- What are some of the major problems encountered by people in this area?
- What is the general atmosphere for newcomers into this area?

- What areas of expertise should be developed by a person *before* moving into this area?
- How is help requested and provided in this area?

It may take effort on the part of practitioners and participants to locate task support groups operating within the informal organization. These are usually ad hoc groups that spontaneously spring into existence when a problem is encountered and just as quickly disappear once the problem is solved. Rather than becoming a written record of the problems encountered, processes employed, or solutions generated, the aid offered by these groups becomes part of the informal group's oral history. The preceding questions will serve to generate some data, but it may be necessary to penetrate the informal organization before the information can be obtained. Practitioners may find that their greatest value to participants is in designing informal group penetration strategies. These strategies will necessarily include investigating the relationships, power, and political systems of the target organization.

Organizational support systems, networks, mentors, and task support groups can be the career development program participant's greatest source of information at the Strategizing Stage. Practitioners should begin their efforts to help these systems surface early in the cycle if they are to be called on during this stage.

Channels to Information and Communication. Many organizations and the people within them still operate on the premise that knowledge is power. When this is the case, the information flow and communication networks are closed and closely guarded. Information is made available only to those with a demonstrated need to know, and communications are highly structured and closely screened to make certain that never is too much information is released. Practitioners and participants operating in such organizations will find gathering data, analyzing it, understanding the system, and building successful action plans difficult.

Closed formal organizations usually result in relatively closed informal organizations operating within them. The intragroup information flow may be fairly open, but intergroup communications or those with outsiders may be quite closed.

However, even the fact that information is difficult to obtain can be of value to participants building plans. Those who are operating in or come into contact with closed organizations will need much more detailed action plans and more time for accomplishing their plans than those who are dealing with open systems.

To help determine the nature of the formal or informal organization, practitioners can suggest that participants investigate

- The general attitude toward sharing, holding, and withholding information:
  —Is there a free flow of information?
  —If not, is information held until a need to know is established? or
  —Is information withheld as a means of establishing power and control?
- The general nature of communications:
  —Is information spread verbally in order to avoid putting things in writing, or just because this has been established as an effective informal means of passing data?
  —Are memoranda carefully drafted so that only necessary information is circulated? or
  —Are memoranda casual, containing full details of projects, problems, and plans?
  —Who can sign memos?
- The flow of information:
  —Is information passed vertically or vertically *and* horizontally?
  —Is there a two-way flow of information, or are orders and questions passed downward and answers upward?

Two of the preceding questions ("Who can sign memos?" and "Is information passed vertically or vertically *and* horizontally?") can give participants and practitioners a great deal of insight into the nature of the political and cultural systems of the organization.

A sure sign of a closed organization in which politics is a major factor is one in which only managers and supervisors are allowed to sign communications going out of the work group. This might be done for two reasons:

1. Managers and supervisors must approve any and all information going into or out of the organization or work group to give assurance that data is controlled.
2. Those in nonsupervisory positions are kept in relative obscurity with low levels of visibility.

Conversely, of course, open organizations will allow subordinates to sign memos going out of their work groups. It will be much easier to investigate, develop plans for, and make decisions about the desirability of these organizations.

Similar indications can be gleaned from the flow of information and communications in an organization. If all information must go upward to the supervisor or manager before going to other working levels within the organization, the group is probably fairly closed. On the other hand, those organizations in which communications are freely passed between horizontal levels are more likely to be open and will be ones in which gathering data is easier.

As was stated earlier, informal organizations will often follow the model of the formal one of which they are a part. A closed formal organization in which only approved information is passed will very often have cliquish informal groups operating within it that which do not share information with others. Open organizations normally give birth to a system of informal groups that exchange information with ease.

There are times, of course, when informal groups operating within the environment of a closed formal organization will react in a totally opposite manner. Sometimes when this occurs an "us against them" attitude develops, and there is an open and free exchange of information horizontally while everything possible is kept from the boss(es).

Practitioners who are aware of these patterns can be of great service to participants who are trying to learn more about the environment. They may find that participants have questions about moving into these environments. Employees can experience culture shock if they have been working in an open organization and suddenly find that the assumed Utopia of their career development goal is closed or greatly different than they had imagined.

The communication networks, politics, power distribution, relationships, and support systems of formal and informal organizations, are factors that help determine culture of groups within the organization. For this reason the issue of organizational cultures must be examined carefully.

A Not-So-Foreign Culture. The culture of an organization has its roots in formal and informal systems, written and unwritten rules, and spoken and unspoken approval or disapproval of individual behavior. The culture is influenced by the organization's origins and history, by the type of work in which the organization is engaged, by the kinds of employees the organization attracts, and by the organization's physical surroundings and geographical location. All this distinguishes each organization as a unique entity. And within each organization there are subcultures among departments and divisions, which have unique identities of their own.

A questionnaire developed by Roger Harrison identifies four very specific ideological orientations that can describe the character of an organization. These four organization ideologies include (1) a power orientation—an organization that is power oriented tends to dominate its environment and vanquish all opposition; (2) a role orientation—organizations aspire to be as rational and orderly as possible; (3) a task orientation—achievement of a superordinate goal is the highest of value, and (4) a person orientation which exists primarily to serve the needs of its members. Harrison argues that the failure to understand these ideological differences causes conflict between organizations as well as within them. Harrison's questionnaire characterizes an organization's orientation and may be helpful for the practitioner to introduce to employees during the strategizing stage. (Available from University Associates, 8517 Production Avenue, San Diego, CA 92126, 1975 Annual Handbook for Group Facilitators).

Career development practitioners will need to give some thought to their own organizational culture and to consider ways to transmit their understanding to employees.

Like human cultures, any given organization operates with a set of assumptions that signal acceptable conduct and activities within its culture. It is essential that practitioners assist employees to clarify these assumptions for themselves as part of the Strategizing Stage, in order to ensure that their plans fit with the realities of existing norms. For example, if administrative leave to attend a year of special study is totally counter to organizational tradition, the employee will want to consider the repercussions of planning such a leave. If it is an acceptable organizational norm to substitute experience for a college degree in order to obtain a certain position in the organization, then employees can examine how this has been done in the past so that they can determine proper strategies.

Practitioners might encourage employees to build a normative profile of the organization and of their departments and divisions. Employees could review this profile with their own managers or with a member of the career development staff in order to determine the fit between their plans and current organizational norms. A number of exercises can be built around such a profile, which ask for input in several categories.

Performance

Is there a standard of excellence, or is mediocrity acceptable?
How is exceptional performance encouraged and rewarded?
Is quality or quantity more important to decision makers and policy makers?

Teamwork

Are cooperation and communication highly valued?
Do people get ahead by being team leaders and members or by being individual entrepreneurs?

Leadership

Are supervisors rewarded for skills in working with subordinates or for controlling subordinates?
Are supervisors concerned more with production or with people or with both?
How important is it for supervisors to ensure that subordinates adhere to written rules and regulations at all times?

Creativity

Are new ideas encouraged and rewarded?
Do people feel it is risky to do things differently than they have been done in the past?
Are people promoted and hired because they fit a traditional mold or because they contribute something new and different?

Employee Development

Are adequate resources committed to training and development?
Are individuals personally encouraged to seek developmental opportunities?
Are jobs and tasks structured to provide opportunities for learning and new experience?

Open Communication

Are people afraid to share opinions with one another?
Is negative feedback about operations discouraged?
Does anyone listen?

Cost Effectiveness

Are employees encouraged to find means of increasing productivity?
Does management consider cost effectiveness in decision making?
Is cost effectiveness considered in reviewing the performance of various units?

An exercise useful in building such a profile might consist of the following steps:

1. A group in a workshop setting answers the previously listed questions pertaining to organization-wide norms.
2. Subgroups (by units within the organization) answer the same questions about their units.
3. Each individual reviews the lists of answers and asks which norms could create problems for reaching my career goals and why.
4. Small groups (three or four persons) exchange individual information and assist one another in identifying ways to alleviate the problems they have identified or select new routes to career goals.
5. Small groups report highlights of their discussions and what they have learned.
6. Groups discuss the general influence of norms on strategizing efforts.

Exploring norms at this point in the career development effort develops an important awareness. While employees work within the culture every day they rarely take time to consider how it affects their mobility. If they don't take time for such exploration, they may find out too late that cultural realities present insurmountable obstacles to attaining their career goals. If this becomes apparent early, they may be able to adjust their goals, select alternative methods for pursuing their goals, or look for other departments or organizations with cultures more amenable to their aspirations.

Employees can use their knowledge of organizational norms to their advantage in working toward goals. They may determine that adhering to certain norms of conduct and appearance can help them. Or if they discover that certain personal associations and professional memberships are within the norm of the job they want, they may find it beneficial to initiate and maintain those relationships. Understanding the organization as a culture gives employees another informational tool for successful career planning.

The Value of Values.   Just as conflicts between cultures can cause shock and disturb employees' goals, differences between organizational values and the personal values of employees can represent a primary cause of employee dissatisfaction and low productivity. Practitioners who encourage employees to move into areas where values differ greatly from the employees' own do their program participants no favors. However, those practitioners who help participants who understand and weigh this factor make significant contributions to overall organizational and individual effectiveness.

The value systems of formal organizations develop from a number of sources. They may originate with organizational founders and may be tempered by a succession of inputs from organizational leaders, boards of directors, stockholders, major customers, and environmental factors. An organization, for instance that was founded by a person who was creative, innovative, and adventurous, might have retained those characteristics through the years. However, a succession of organizational leaders who placed high value on sound business judgment, judicious expansion, and fiscal restraints might cause the company to shift emphasis from innovative exploration and research to research designed to meet established, low-risk customer needs. If the organization served customers who placed high value on product reliability and economy, the organizational values could again be altered so that producing high quality goods at the lowest possible price could become the priority.

Informal organizations are often an amalgam of their individual members. People with similar values will generally group themselves together. Minor differences in values will be resolved through compromise or through ignoring those differences. People with major differences in values seldom form close groupings. The good time crew hardly ever hangs around with the workaholics, and the three-martini lunch bunch contains few members of the health food crowd.

Practitioners can aid participants during the Strategizing Stage in identifying the basic values of an organization or group they might consider joining, by having them investigate and report on items such as

- The questions asked in organizational interviewers during the hiring process.
- The espoused, if not innate, values systems of those who have experienced rapid promotion within the organization.
- Statements of work group policy and procedures.
- Values systems of major customers and suppliers.

- Values of the organizational leadership, those who have made it within the system.
- Reasons for recent discharges and separations.

How can values cause conflicts?

Suppose that a secretary has set a goal of entering project administration in another department of the organization. In the secretary's current job, the major operational values are task accomplishment, interpersonal harmony, and effectiveness, as opposed to efficiency. The department that has been targeted, however, places emphasis on promptness—arriving at and leaving from work on time regardless of task status, competition, or neatness, and even at the expense of accuracy.

The practitioner in this case must help the secretary understand, evaluate, and plan for a change in values systems if the secretary is going to make that plan work. The practitioner might be guided in providing assistance by considering

1. What are the secretary's innate values?
2. Has the secretary accepted and espoused the values of the organization where the secretary currently works?
3. What personal values must the secretary change in order to accept and adapt to the target organization?
4. How will those changes affect the secretary's personal life style and ability to effectively function in the new job?

The secretary will also have to examine the values systems of the informal groups within the target organization. If everyone in the new group enjoys jogging, physical fitness, and health foods while the secretary prefers gourmet cooking, minimal physical activity, and sedentary leisure activities, there are going to be some conflicts. How will the informal organization accept a person with different interests? Can such persons with different interests adjust their current values? If not, how will they bridge the gap?

Practitioners may find that certain employees can adjust their values with little or no trouble. Some may be able to understand and cope with the relationships; the networks of power, politics, communications; and the cultural systems within their target groups without difficulty. However the last system to be analyzed and understood, the technological system, may pose a gap that cannot be bridged.

Terminal Technology. A short true case study helps to explain the problems often encountered when investigating the technological system:

Bob H. was a brilliant young business administration major who, after receiving his bachelor's degree, took a job in the shipping department of a large manufacturing firm. His goal was clear. Bob intended to use the shipping department position as an entree into the company. As soon as an opening occurred in the organization's accounting department, he intended to make his move into his chosen field.

Bob did *most* of his strategizing well. He studied the formal and informal organizations of the accounting department thoroughly. He understood the relationships, power structures, political atmosphere, support systems, and the flow of information and communications. He found that the culture and values systems of the accounting department were in complete agreement with his own. He felt that he was ready to make the move as a position opened.

Shortly after completing his research Bob learned of an opening in the accounting department, and he immediately applied. He was interviewed by several supervisors and managers within the accounting department and felt that everything went well. He settled back to await his transfer.

When the job was filled, however, it went to someone from outside the organization. It was not until then that Bob realized that he had failed to consider an important aspect of his targeted job. The computer system used in the accounting department was totally different from those with which Bob was familiar. Even though Bob seemed perfect in every other respect, the accounting department management had decided that they could not afford the time necessary to train him in their system. It was easier, they reasoned, to train an outsider who was already familiar with the computers about company policy than vice versa.

How could such an error occur? Easily. Very often assumptions about technology are made that make both the employee and the boss believe that there is a natural fit. In this case everyone was lucky. What would have happened if Bob had been hired and then the technology problem had been discovered? He might have been out of a job altogether, and the accounting department would have had to begin the whole job search again.

Had Bob considered all aspects of the strategy necessary to move toward that particular career goal, he might have detected the difference between the technological system and his expertise, and this would have helped him develop a plan to bridge that gap.

It may sound elementary, but organizations are littered with Bob H.'s, people who lacked the technical skill to move up but did not realize it until too late.

Practitioners must be alert to employees' technological deficiencies and not only help them to overcome their shortcomings, but very often develop programs aimed at correcting the deficiencies. Effective career development plans must provide for technical skill evaluations that look at

- Requirements
- Personal Skills Available
- Skills to be Developed
- Methods for Attaining those Skills

Informal groups often form around technical skill areas. Research and development people, for instance, will form social groups based on their common technical interests. The same is true of doctors, lawyers, short metal workers, lathe operators, and steam plant engineers. Members of these technical groups may belong to other informal groups that focus on athletic preferences, literary interests, or political persuasions, but at least a part of their social lives usually centers around technical expertise. A newcomer to a work group who demonstrates a lack of technical expertise will be excluded from the informal structure and will continue to be an outsider. Practitioners should recognize this and help prepare participants so that they can overcome those shortcomings.

Getting to know the territory includes a great many subsystems and functions that must be considered and investigated during the Strategizing Stage. The eight discussed herein are not meant to be all-inclusive or the only ones that will be encountered. The practitioner's job is not to provide all the answers for every participant, but to become as familiar as possible with the organizational system in order to help the employee to see the forest as well as the trees.

One way to undertake a more systematic analyses at this stage might be to develop a matrix, such as Exhibit 5-4, that addresses specifics of the various systems just discussed. This tool can be helpful to employees who are just beginning the strategizing process.

Knowing the territory does not in itself enable the program participant to start marching down the streets of River City, followed by seventy-six trombones and one hundred and ten cornets. The participant must now determine if there is a demand for a band in River City.

"To Market To Market"

One final aid, therefore, through which practitioners may might help employees to further understand the system is to present the organization as a marketplace for individual development and career advancement. In this setting the employee becomes a professional marketer who is concerned with product research and development, packaging, salesmanship, competition, economy, and all other marketplace features. This concept can help employees understand the reality of the environment in which their products (skills and experiences) must be marketed if their career goals are to be achieved.

SYSTEM	FORMAL ORGANIZATION	INFORMAL ORGANIZATION
Relationships	Work oriented Imposed by organizational structure Hierarchical	Specially oriented Voluntarily established May be hierarchical, but often tend toward sociometric alliances
Power	Structurally imposed, with emphasis on position, expertise, implied influence, actual coercive influence, applied pressure, and raw force	Tacitly established, with emphasis on charisma, implied influence, actual coercive influence, and applied pressure
Politics	Covert—based on power structures and on games within the organization; tied to the flow of information	Overt—based on charisma and power structures of influence; determines the flow of information
Support	Based on expertise 1. mentor 2. work group	Based on charisma and influence 1. mentor 2. networking
Information	Vertical flow Work related	Vertical and horizontal flow Social and work related
Orientation	May be that of task, role, power, or person, in either the people area or organizational area	Probably has people area orientation only—but may be that of task, role, power, or person
Communication	Formal written or verbal	Grapevine approach—verbal or written.
Culture	Organizationally imposed, resulting from history and traditions	Usually composite of the culture of its members
Values	Established by organization, reflect organizational leadership and traditions	Established by membership as a result of needs, cultures, and goals

Exhibit 5-4   Strategizing Matrix

To adequately study the market the employee needs to examine three major areas: the product, the market, and the competition. Questions the career development practitioner can help the employee address are

The Product

- What are key tasks you have successfully performed in past positions?
- What skills do you offer?

- What reputation do you have among others in the marketplace?
- What are the limits to what you'll be able to produce?
- Will others provide the support necessary for you to fully utilize your strengths?
- Will personal values and needs limit your ability to fully utilize your strengths?
- How is the product packaged? How do you present yourself and your skills to others?
- What can you do to improve the products you have to offer?

The Market

- Is there a market for your skills?
- Is the demand for your skills great or limited within that market?
- Is there a way to strengthen or expand the market?
- Are your strengths transferable to a variety of situations within the market?
- Who are the most likely customers for your product?
- How effective are you at selling your product to potential customers?
- How can you improve your marketing position?

The Competition

- Who is your competition?
- What does the competition offer?
- How are your skills and experiences distinct from those of the competition?
- What marketing strategies are the competition using?
- What advantages do you have? Does the competition have?

Part of employees' strategy should be to improve their market position, which may mean enhancing one's product or competitive position. The preceding questions can be used in a workshop setting, in a counseling situation, or in a workbook so that employees can ponder their meaning whenever they have the opportunity.[6]

The practitioner's job in this first phase of strategizing is to assist employees in understanding the system in which they operate. Unless they understand the system, with all its subtleties, employees will be hard pressed to come up with an effective plan to use that knowledge toward reaching a career goal. Since this is one of the least formalized phases of the entire effort, the practitioner will want to thoughtfully design approaches for thinking about the system in new and creative ways.

SYNTHESIZING INFORMATION

With a greater understanding of the system in which strategizing takes place the employee is now ready to synthesize ideas and information and to frame a coherent plan of action. This phase includes considering opportunities and obstacles and drafting a developmental plan for pursuing each of the career goals determined during the Targeting Stage.

The career development practitioner can assist employees during the synthesizing phase in two major ways: 1) by introducing them to tools and techniques that can help them analyze what they know and structure it into a planning format; and 2) by making available to them any organizational information that might help them generate realistic analyses and plans. This helps employees to acquire the skill and the information necessary to complete the planning process.

Synthesizing Information

- Determining Forces
- Understanding Obstacles
- Decoding Messages
- Assessing Knowledge Areas

Analysis without Paralysis

Analyzing all the data that employees have acquired about themselves and their organizations is the step that facilitates establishing relationships between the diverse pieces of information gathered. During this step practitioners will need to help employees think back to past experiences and think forward to potential obstacles and opportunities.

A variety of techniques can be used to organize and coordinate this effort, many of which are probably already familiar to practitioners. They are all aimed at helping employees to structure their thinking and to arrive at concrete results. Most of these techniques could be solo activities, with employees sitting down with pen and paper to generate ideas. However, sharing the strategizing process with others is likely to enhance it. Workshops can be designed in which employees use the various techniques on their own and then share the results in small groups whose members exchange ideas and help one another test their viability. The same techniques can be further used by practitioners

- As counseling tools for individuals who have made career decisions, but are unable to move toward them.
- As training tools for supervisors/managers who might use the exercises as part of their career counseling activities.
- As diagnostic tools for the organization, to assess its effectiveness in providing career opportunities.

Determining Forces.   For every goal that employees set during targeting, there are circumstances, personal beliefs, and other factors that push them toward or away from that goal. Sometimes these factors are obvious, such as lack of training needed to perform a sought-after job. At other times the forces holding individuals back or propelling them forward are more subtle, such as lack of faith in personal ability, or strong personal ambition for greater challenges.

The contributing and restraining forces combine to hold a situation in a state of equilibrium, where it will remain until those forces somehow change. It is important that program participants have a thorough understanding of what they have working for them and what is going against them.

An excellent tool for helping participants to recognize their strengths, weaknesses, aids, and obstacles is a simple variation on the open system map or relational planning model, which follows:

This model may be used in either individual counseling or group workshops. The practitioner shows the model and asks each participant to draw in and label as many factors as possible that might affect accomplishing the goal. If participants have conducted an organizational analysis similar to the one outlined in the first part of this chapter, a great many resources and obstacles will already have been identified.

In any case some examples of obstacles are

Personal:
"I'm overweight."
"I can't speak well in public."
Environmental:
"I had to take a job because I didn't have money for college."
"I lost my last good job when the company went bankrupt."

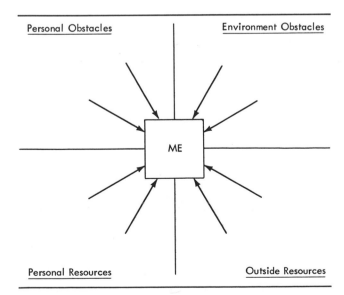

Exhibit 5-5   Planning Map

Some examples of resources are

Personal:
"I am good at listening to others' problems."
"I write well."
Outside:
"My spouse encourages me in my career."
"My subordinates really try to make me look good."

Once the personal and environmental resources and obstacles have been identified, their actual effect on the career development goal(s) should be determined. Kurt Lewin's Force Field Analysis model is an excellent tool for aiding participants in this process.

Personal and environmental resources, those factors which participants see as aiding them in accomplishing their goals, become driving forces in the Force Field. The obstacles, of course, are the restraining forces, those factors that are hindering achievement of goals.

The practitioner can help by suggesting that participants write out their goal statements and begin to consider the driving and restraining forces in a format such as Exhibit 5-6.

The statements from the open system map are written on as many arrows as necessary to show the driving and restraining forces.

Examples of restraining forces are,

"I don't have the required three years of experience."
"My spouse wouldn't like the long hours it requires."
"I'm not really confident I could succeed."

Examples of contributing forces are,

"My boss has encouraged me to apply for the position."
"I need the additional money I would make in the new job."
"I feel the challenge would be stimulating to me."

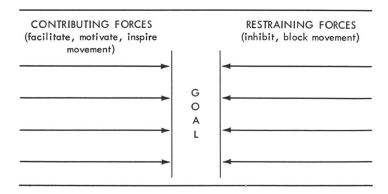

Exhibit 5-6   Force Field Analysis

After individuals have listed as many forces as possible, they can begin to synthesize the information. One method of analysis is to determine the degree of impact that each force has on reaching the goal, by assigning a weight—on a scale of one (least impact) to five (most impact)—to each force. This helps clarify which forces need to be strengthened or weakened in order to pursue the goal.

It is also useful to code forces as to whether they are 1) environmentally imposed, 2) organizationally imposed, or 3) self-imposed. Practitioners should be aware that individuals often find it hardest to work on the self-imposed forces, since individuals are often resistant to such change. Forces stemming from the organization or environment are easy to blame as restrainers, although they may also require extra time and resourcefulness to work through.

There are several ways of working on a Force Field once the forces have been defined and analyzed. One is to look at the tension between the forces to determine if one kind of force seems to override another. If forces are equal, no movement will occur, and participants should strive to have the contributing forces outweigh the restraining forces. Options are

- Add to the list of contributing forces
- Increase the magnitude of existing contributing forces
- Remove restraining forces
- Decrease the magnitude of existing restraining forces
- Move restraining forces to the contributing side of the field

It is also important that employees examine their assumptions about the forces. The feelings of others or barriers created by the organization may be only *assumed* rather than real restraining forces.

Understanding Obstacles. The next step is to consider the obstacles to achieving goals and to determine whether or not these obstacles are real. Employees often make obstacles seem larger than they are or fail to recognize how obstacles can be related to resources and even neutralized by them.

To effectively deal with obstacles or restraining forces it is necessary to determine their sources. When initially listed the obstacles were shown as originating from the individual or the environment. These sources may be more specifically identified by listing them as being

Self-Imposed
System Imposed
Boss Imposed
"Other" Imposed

Now participants can make a similar determination about resources. Tie-ins will immediately emerge, and participants will get ideas for generating additional resources to remove obstacles. For each of their restraining forces, participants can be encouraged to ask such questions as

- Is this obstacle something that others would see, or is it simply my own invention?
- Am I using this resource to my greatest benefit?

Decoding Messages.   The practitioner should at this stage encourage participants to recognize the messages they receive from others that can strongly influence the outcome of a particular goal. Every personal contact of the employees (spouse, friends, superiors) has attitudes that are verbally and nonverbally sent to the employees about their aspirations.

As employees receive these messages, they tend to adjust their strategies and goals accordingly—often without analyzing the contents of or sources of the messages. The employee may even misconstrue the meaning of the message. When someone says, "Wow, that's an ambitious undertaking," it is easily translated as, "I'm not capable of achieving that goal." Or if someone says little or nothing about another's goal, the interpretation of that message may be, "They think it's ridiculous."

If the practitioner can assist employees in specifying the messages received, or those likely to be received, and considering strategies for accepting them, rejecting them, or negotiating changes in them, employees will develop more effective strategies. This could be done by introducing a written format such as Exhibit 5-7.

Using this format, practitioners and participants can effectively analyze messages and their underlying meanings. Strategies for responding can be discovered with relative ease.

SENDER	MESSAGE	UNDERLYING MESSAGE	STRATEGY FOR RESPONSE

Exhibit 5-7   Message Decoding Form

While such an exercise may seem unduly laborious, it is a valuable tool for realistically clarifying messages. Practitioners may find that this cannot be done unless the employee discusses the messages to be analyzed with at least one other individual.

Assessing Knowledge Areas. A good check-back procedure before employees develop a plan of action is for them to ask themselves, "Do I really know all I need to know in order to strategize effectively?" In this way they can take one final look at the factors affecting career plans and ascertain whether or not they have acquired the essential information related to each. Managers who are involved in the process will want to test the employees' readiness to begin executing their career plans.

Areas that the employee should consider checking could relate to the job, the family, peers, subordinates, supervisors, or even the organizational structure. Individuals might test their knowledge in each of these areas by using a series of questions and rating their answers on a scale of one (I don't know anything of what I need to know) to five (I know all I need to know).

Examples of questions that might be used follow.

Job-related issues:
- What is the relationship of this target job to other jobs in the organization?
- What technical and administrative skills are required?

Organization-related issues:
- What specific organizational politics affect this job?
- What are this division's long-term goals?

Supervisor-related issues:
- What are the actual span and the limits of my boss's job?
- How much concern does my boss really have for my development as an employee?

Employees undertaking this exercise should be encouraged to develop as many check-back issues as possible.

Framing the Plan

When all available information about self and system—including developmental needs, organizational resources, and possible barriers—has been generated, employees are ready to frame a developmental plan for pursuing career goals. The developmental plan (1) defines the specific actions that will be taken, (2) relates them to needs and to specific skills and experiences, (3) pinpoints the necessary resources, and (4) sets time frames for completion actions.

The value of the developmental plan is that it sets forth a detailed strategy that can easily be monitored at each step for progress.

The Management Readiness Program (MRP) at Merrill Lynch is experimenting with a development plan for all program participants. The plan directs employees to state a development goal (discovered during the workshop portion of the program) and to identify the (1) skills the employee wants to develop, (2) activities that will help develop those skills, and (3) sources of assistance in improving those skills. Suggestions are made as to how employees can track their own progress and measure their success in skill mastery. Mentors and managers comment on the choice of development ideas and show their concurrence by signing off on their employees' development plans.

Needs and Desires. Determining needs and desires is directly linked to skill, knowledge, resource deficiencies, work values, and context preferences that the employee identified at prior stages of the career development effort. With the practitioner's help the employee should now be able to state these needs on a detailed developmental plan that makes each more specific.

The listing should include not only skills and knowledge to be acquired, but also certain experiences and relationships with others, not necessarily directly related to work, that can facilitate movement toward career goals.

Examples of statements about knowledge or skill areas are

- to feel more at ease and present a positive image when addressing large groups,
- to have experience in or exposure to at least two organization-wide task forces,
- to understand how to effectively communicate through management reports to higher levels and how to verbally obtain information from all levels,
- to become conversant with the goals of the sales management group so that I can effectively explain them to other groups within the organization,
- to be confident about proposing and evaluating budgetary requirements in my own division, and
- to increase my skills in and knowledge of computer functions, policies, procedures, scheduling, and workload.

The more detailed the description of need, the easier it will be to determine specific actions and resources to meet that need.

Actions. Actions that are specified in the plan are the tasks to be undertaken in pursuit of career goals, and they assist the employee in answering the question, "What can I do to get where I want to go?"

It is important to emphasize two key elements that often cause problems in stating actions. First, action statements must often be divided into specific steps rather than one general task. For example, the action that is stated, "Complete the remaining requirements for my advanced university degree," may be better set forth as, "Apply for tuition reimbursement; apply for admission to courses X,Y, and Z; and complete my thesis."

Secondly, actions should be stated with a great deal of specificity, so that there is no doubt as to whether and when they have been completed. The action, "Form mentor relationships with persons who have experience in the same career progression," can be more specifically stated as, "Invite John Doakes to lunch to discuss his similar experience, and initiate an ongoing mentor relationship with him."

At TRW Management Systems, a "Career Counseling Record" is provided to aid employees' career planning. The use of the format is optional, and it is designed to encourage employees to define and complete actions with the support of their supervisors.

The record begins with a two-page format to be completed by employees, who fill in the following categories:

1. Summary of work experience to date
2. Summary of education and training
3. Special skills, capabilities, or experience
4. Long-range career objectives
5. "Reasonable next assignment," or "change in current assignment" directed toward achieving long-range career objectives.
6. Voids in experience, knowledge, or skills that need to be satisfied if progression toward career objectives is to be realized.
7. Actual/proposed action plan—including list of actions and time frames.

The second part of the record is a one-page "Supervisor's Appraisal" which asks the supervisor to comment on the employee's self-evaluation and action plan, and to specify a date for an action plan progress review.

The third part of the record is a one-page progress review format to be completed and signed by the supervisor and the employee. It asks that they state the status of the plan, further required actions, and any additional remarks.

This recording process is an excellent method for making career planning a truly joint venture between employee and supervisor and for providing a formal method for developing a plan and periodically checking on its progress.

There are a number of opportunities for employees' goals to be discussed with managers. The regular performance appraisal session provides a perfect vehicle.

Action plans can also be discussed in specially designated support groups, which meet to help group members brainstorm about actions they might take to reach specific goals. They can be shared in workshops through exercises carefully designed to help employees help themselves. Some personalized coaching on the part of the career development practitioner is needed. The practitioner should recommend actions that can be carried out, to which the organization can readily respond, and that seem to have the greatest return on investment for both the individual and the organization.

Resources.   Each plan should include a definition of resources that are needed to make the actions a reality. Major resources available include people, money, and time. When considering resources, employees should ask, "Are there others who can help?" "What financial assistance is available?" and "What time can be committed?"

Practitioners can stimulate thinking about resources by pointing out the myriad of resources available. Personal resources include the employee's family, friends, colleagues, boss, peers, professional associations, and community networks. Monetary resources can be found in the organization's tuition reimbursement program, the organization's bonus plan for special development, or the employee's own savings account! The precious resource of time might be discovered in an employee's accrued leave (to attend a training session) or in simply asking for and receiving four extra hours a week to take on a special project. Resources come from the individual as well as from the organization.

Resources provided by others often need special attention because many individuals are reluctant to call upon other people for assistance. However, giving such assistance is rarely considered a burden, and may require only that someone make a phone call, give occasional encouragement, or offer advice. Using outside resources can give employees a sense of support: "Others are pulling for me; I don't want to disappoint them." Practitioners who develop resource listings of people in specific departments who are willing to help will find that this planning puts employees ahead of the game.

Deadlines.   Finally, a complete plan includes specified times for completing each step. While deadlines must be realistic, they must also be demanding enough to stimulate continual movement toward goals. Deadlines may be set by working backward from a final deadline for goal attainment or by setting incremental time frames forward from the earliest step to be completed. Although it is likely that deadlines may need to be revised as various actions are taken, this practice should be discouraged except when it absolutely cannot be avoided.

Often employees do not know enough about their own limits and organizational red tape to be able to plan effectively at this point. Practitioners can play an important role by offering sound time management advice and helping the participants establish realistic deadlines. These practitioners who are uncertain about how to help the participants establish deadlines would be well advised to seek help from others within the organization who are experienced in this area. Nothing will destroy a plan or discourage a participant faster than unrealistic deadlines. It is imperative that time schedules be workable and well thought out and, at the same time, involve effort and challenge for employees.

An abbreviated example of a well-developed workable action plan appears in Exhibit 5-8.

Structural Supports from Within

Two ongoing human resource development activities that are particularly valuable in the Strategizing Stage are establishing career paths and specialized counseling. These provide the employee with guidance and assist the organization in planning for the future and using employees efficiently.

Needs/Desires	Actions	Resources	Deadlines
Increased writing skills	1a. Apply for tuition reimbursement for college course.	1a. Tuition reimbursement program.	1a. Dec. 15, '80
	1b. Take "Written Communication 103" at Norton Community College.	1b. Time: two nights a week, ten weeks.	1b. Mar. 30, '80
	1c. Volunteer to draft Division submission to organization's annual report.	1c. Boss.	1c. Feb. 28, '81
	1d. Complete draft submission and discussion with supervisor.	1d. Boss and peers.	1d. Apr. 5, '81
Greater visibility	2a. Discuss with boss my profiling, goal, and plan information.	2a. Boss 2a. Two to three hours time	2a. Jan. 5, '81
	2b. Discuss with at least two managers in Division X my goal of movement to that division.	2b. My counterpart in Division X can introduce me to managers. 2b. Three to four hours time.	2b. Feb. 5, '81

Exhibit 5-8   Action Plan

Employees should not strategize in a vacuum. Without organizational support mechanisms their plans become pipe dreams that are unrelated to what the organization is able or willing to do. Employees need to know the organization's plans and objectives concerning the development of its work forces. They also need material support and encouragement from the organization for their strategizing efforts.

Career Paths.   Information about career paths and progression lines within the organization is essential for realistic action planning by an employee. A career path is a written projection of a logical job progression sequence that may realistically occur for an employee. The progression includes alternatives related to the experience being acquired in the job and may include lateral or downward movement or movement to jobs outside the current department or unit. It may state the specific skills and knowledge to be developed as a requirement for each job.

Career paths must reflect the employee's personal skills and experiences that can be acquired through a series of job moves, and the organization's intentions with regard to recruitment, placement, and manpower utilization. Career paths should

- "represent real progression possibilities, whether lateral or upward, without implied 'normal' rates of progress or forced technical specialization
- be tentative and responsive to changes in job content, work priorities, organization patterns, and management needs
- be flexible, to take into consideration the compensating qualities of a particular individual
- specify acquirable skills, knowledge, and other specific attributes required to perform the work on each position along the paths, and not merely educational credentials, age, or work experience which may preclude some capable performers from career opportunities."[7]

To initiate a career pathing program, the practitioner will need to first analyze positions to determine the various tasks performed and the time and importance given to them. Jobs with related activities can then be clustered into groups of jobs that require similar skills and knowledge and among which skills can be transferable. It is then possible to determine alternatives for progression among related job areas, producing a network of career path possibilities.

A handy tool for analyzing the skill areas needed for designing career paths is the matrix described in Chapter 3, which specifies the skills needed in the technical, human, and conceptual areas at each level in the organization.

Program participants who are planning a horizontal move from one nonsupervisory position to another can then get an accurate picture of requirements for moving into the new position at the initial level and for moving upward after the change has been made.

Practitioners may need to show how not only the nature of the required skills changes as a person moves up within an organization, but the relative emphasis on different skill areas also shifts.

At the lower levels emphasis lies on the technical skills with secondary importance being given to human relations skills and very little attention being given to the conceptual area. As a person moves upward or enters at higher levels, the emphasis on different skill areas shifts, and the technical aspects become less important as the conceptual areas receive more attention. The emphasis on human relations skills should remain constant, even though the scope of the requirements for human relations skills expands from interpersonal to intragroup to intergroup to intraorganizational to the organization as it relates to other organizations and the environment, when one reaches the executive level.

Employees who are aware of the career paths open to them by starting with the jobs they now hold or desire to hold can use this information to develop more realistic action plans. They may see new alternative routes to future jobs that they had not heretofore imagined. Or they may recognize that the route they had planned to take does not provide the appropriate experience or training to attain a job that they seek. Often, too, the paths to a certain job may include elements that employees have little desire to pursue, in which case they may decide that an entirely different line of work would be a more appropriate goal.

Visualizing career paths charted by the organization also gives employees a broader view of requirements for a wide variety of task areas. For example, a common response is, "I hadn't realized that supervisory jobs in Department X require experiences so similar to those in my own department." Employees can also see how lateral moves and even downward moves can ultimately lead to career progression into new areas.

> One of the principles which is at the foundation of the Sears Roebuck and Company approach suggests that the identification of a rational sequence of job assignments for a person reduces the time required to develop the necessary skills for a chosen target job. If a particular job results in skill development then a series of specific job assignments could very well produce even more development over the course of a person's career. In the Sears program, the use of a well planned sequence of job assignments is specifically designed to maximize career growth. This use of career pathing actually encourages the learning of new skills. Putting together rational career paths on the basis of the skills that the paths will impart is a way of moving from folklore to fact about what jobs will best aid career growth.[8]

The practitioner is encouraged to do everything possible to make career path information accessible for all interested employees. In fact, when a job opening occurs, the career path into which it fits should be made available to potential applicants so that they can consider how it fits with their past experience and possible future progression. Managers are also encouraged to review career paths within the organization that are relevant to their subordinates as an aid in identifying training needs, planning for future needs, and counseling employees on career development.

Practitioners may have to design and offer special training sessions or handbooks for managers in order to acquaint them with ways of reading and using this information.

Because of its size and diversity, Aetna Life and Casualty recognizes that its employees could often work in isolation—unaware of the many other job possibilities which exist—possibilities which might better tap their own interest and skills. To improve the matching of people's talents to the jobs available, Aetna provides a Career Path Handbook as a beginning step toward providing vital information. The Career Path Handbook is given to supervisors as a tool for assisting their employees to choose individual development and training activities which will guide them along the road to further self development.

The Handbook is divided into fourteen sections which describe the principal job clusters or fields within Aetna. The fields are not all inclusive but were chosen because they are areas in which a natural career progression exists for a large number of employees. The Career Path Handbook is designed to help employees gain a sense of where they want to go through an understanding of what major directions are open to them. With the supervisor's help, a clear developmental plan for activities for the coming year can be stated.[9]

Career paths enable employees to see the skills needed for certain jobs and the steps that are possible within those jobs. Career paths allow employees to compare their own plans with the organization's maps for employee progression. This can result in developmental efforts that are a mutually beneficial joint endeavor.

Establishing a career path system can require a substantial commitment to analyzing jobs, categorizing them into related job families, and determining logical progression alternatives. But, the potential rewards for establishing are great.

Practitioners may themselves want to directly impart information about career paths, at meetings or in one-to-one discussions. Some practitioners feel that it is not good to put career path information in writing because it formalizes the system in a way that gives the practitioners and individual managers less flexibility.

Many organizations, however, have followed the example of Aetna and have produced handbooks that actually describe the skills needed for jobs and the steps possible within those jobs. Handbooks are useful in that the employees might turn to them on their own to see what kinds of jobs might be a better fit for them, and they might then be able to seek out experience and education toward their goal. Handbooks also help facilitate the dialogue between employer and employee about career opportunities, and they are especially useful in forming the developmental plan. Still another way to share career path information is to deliver it within a workshop itself. Career path information can be disseminated, for example, by delivering a short lecture on the numbers of people at nonexempt, exempt, and first line management levels in the organization and by providing statistics about the numbers of people who move from one level to another.

> At the California Institute of Technology, a simple pyramid was drawn for participants during the course of a workshop. The pyramid had lines which showed the major dividers that corresponded to different levels in the organization and current employment statistics showing how many people were at what level, what their salary grade was, and what the potential movement was from level to level. This gave workshop participants an idea of what could and could not be done within their own positions and still did not push the organization to formally publish career pathing information.

Practitioners must make the point that career paths are flexible and do change. Career paths should be seen as another tool to be used in the Strategizing Stage.

Counseling for Career Change. In an effective career development program counseling is available at each stage to help employees understand their own strengths and weaknesses, assess organizational opportunities, set realistic goals, and develop plans for career progress. This individual counseling, offered by human resource practitioners themselves or provided through supervisors, recognizes the unique situations and needs of each employee and complements individual planning activities and group workshops. Counseling may range from straightforward advice to supportive pep talks to provide motivation.

One particular type of counseling that becomes relevant at the Strategizing Stage is outplacement counseling. This service, which is experiencing increased use in organizations throughout the country, is generally aimed at individually assisting those who are being involuntarily separated from the organization. In some organizations it is also offered to those who voluntarily resign. Since strategizing about career options can sometimes lead to a decision on both sides that moving out of the organization is the most logical move, outplacement counseling can be a valuable support program, and practitioners may wish to develop the capacity to offer this service within the organization.

Typical objectives of outplacement counseling include

- To reduce negative psychological impact on terminated employees
- To provide guidance in identifying new job opportunities
- To improve the employee's skills in job search and application
- To help employees place themselves elsewhere as quickly as possible
- To ultimately bring the best match between people and available jobs

Outplacement counseling may be provided by the career development practitioner, by designated members of the HRD staff, or by skilled outside consultants. While the practitioner's own staff are often better able to assess an individual's strengths and weaknesses, outside consultants add a greater sense of anonymity and objectivity. Outside consultants may also be necessary if internal expertise is not available.

Most comprehensive outplacement services include

- Information about organization policies (such as compensation and accrued leave)
- Job search strategy training
- Employment interview training
- Resume preparation assistance
- Office support service (for typing resumes and taking phone calls)
- Information about job leads
- Personal counseling
- Attitude awareness training
- Resource appraisal
- Salary negotiation practice

Organizations benefit in a number of ways from viewing outplacement as a responsibility and an ongoing HRD activity. One obvious payoff is public relations a company might receive from becoming known as forward thinking and sensitive to employee needs. In this way an organization may be seen as an attractive potential employer. And heightened sensitivity affects not only the morale of terminated employees but also the attitudes of current employees toward their place of work.

Often, as a result of some initial thinking during the Targeting Stage and some additional planning at the Strategizing Stage, employees may recognize their own need to leave the organization and seek a job elsewhere; but they are reluctant to take such a step into the unknown until their current situation becomes unbearable. A good outplacement counseling program can encourage these employees to take action to find another job that better fits their career needs, before their own work and personal life suffer as a result.

Cleveland Trust has developed an Outplacement Service as part of its comprehensive Career Development Program. An employee in the program is assisted in a wide array of self-assessment, goal setting, and planning activities. These are accomplished through individual counseling, workshops, and workbook preparation. If it becomes apparent that the bank does not provide the appropriate or desired career future, the Outplacement Service can assist the employee in pursuing careers elsewhere.

The Outplacement Service provides: counseling (by personnel department counselor), employment interview practice, office and phone answering facilities, typing and printing, and resume writing assistance.

The service is offered both to voluntarily and involuntarily terminated employees. Additional personal counseling is provided for those who are involuntarily terminated to assist them to realistically identify performance problems and to alleviate negative psychological effects.

Such a service encourages the idea that termination and job change need not be considered bleak and traumatic if adequate support is available from within the organization.[10]

Active Support—Practitioner and Manager

During the Strategizing Stage the practitioner must be prepared to act as a designer/facilitator by guiding employees in conceptualizing ideas, and as a generator of organizational interest by seeking continued support for career development programs. As designer/facilitator, the practitioner seeks to supply ideas and techniques that enable employees to assess their own situations, to size up the organizational environment, to identify potential obstacles, to determine appropriate alternatives, and to set forth a realistic developmental plan. This role includes responsibility for providing informational materials and perhaps organizing group workshops and counseling. While practitioners may not be directly involved in all of the design or conduct of such activities, they have primary responsibility for stimulating staff members to pay attention to the Strategizing Stage and to support its actualization.

In addition the practitioner must develop a deliberate strategy for informing managers and motivating them to actively support the strategizing process. Managers can play an active role in providing the encouragement, information, and organizational support mechanisms that facilitate strategizing. They can help employees understand organizational expectations, opportunities, and limitations. If they are willing to spend extra time with individual employees, they can provide reality-testing assistance by reviewing plans with subordinates and suggesting alternatives or changes. They can also develop opportunities for on-the-job experiences that facilitate acquiring the experience and knowledge called for in specific developmental plans.

There is substantial payoff at the Strategizing Stage as employees continue to dynamically use their organizing and synthesizing skills. These skills can be drawn upon to assess situations in which individuals operate and to help them continually plan and replan in light of a changing environment. By internalizing the strategizing processes, individuals acquire the flexibility to maximize their efforts and successes under conditions of organizational or environmental change.

Strategizing can provide the organization with valuable information about its employees and their developmental needs. The more actively the organization supports this process, the more it enhances its utilization of existing work force capabilities and its ability to plan future work force needs.

Strategizing clearly lays out a detailed plan of what individuals must do in order to move toward the next step of their career goals or to enrich their present position in the organization. A careful monitoring and documentation system structured by the practitioner at this stage can provide the early warning signals needed by the practitioner to begin making sure that the Execution Stage can assist individuals in operationalizing their goals. At the Execution Stage, individuals follow their developmental plan to acquire the tools, skills, and knowledge that in the Strategizing Stage, they discovered were necessary.

The career development practitioner and the program participant are not quite ready to lead the band down the street to the blare of trumpets and the oompah of the bass drums. It has been established at this point that the participant knows the territory and has a plan; the uniforms and instruments—certain training and the skills—must still be acquired. And that is the next stage: carrying out those plans to accomplish goals.

PURSUING PLANS
the execution stage

"If only there were a way to make training activities more cost effective."

EXECUTION!

The call to action! Skills have been identified, goals have been set, and a plan has been developed. The career development program participants are now about to move toward their career goals. They know what they want, and they have developed strategies for achieving their goals. They can now begin acquiring the skills, training, experience, and personal support systems necessary for moving ahead.

What is the practitioner's next step? What will the organization be called upon to provide? Who else must be involved at this stage if the program is to succeed?

Shared Responsibilities

During this stage each player is asked to participate in a specific way. Organizational involvement is essential and complex. Shared responsibility is the watchword.

The employees participate in activities aimed at acquiring new skills; brushing up on old skills; acquiring new contacts for personal support, information, or instruction; and supplementing professional/technical skills with growing capacities for leadership, communication, or group interaction.

The organization is at the same time concerned with providing financial support for off-site education and training, developing in-house training and development opportunities, structuring on-the-job experiences (OJT) to promote learning and development, structuring and encouraging informal learning and support among employees at various levels of the organization, and providing access to information about available resources.

Individual managers will find that they must act as channels through which program information is passed to employees, encourage and support employees in accomplishing their plans, provide the time needed by employees to pursue their plans and acquire training and development, establish means by which the new skills being developed by employees can be practiced, and provide means of recognizing employees for their motivation and effort.

Practitioners become the middle people during this process. In addition to facilitating the fulfillment of organizational responsibilities, practitioners make certain that the functions and programs developed are cost effective, are based upon actual needs, and are focused on the goals to be accomplished. They work with participants to ensure that they do not lose sight of their career goals. They work with managers to make certain that they thoroughly understand the skills that participants will now need to acquire and that they provide the support and environment necessary for program success. When displayed as a coordinated effort, these responsibilities and functions create the picture shown in Exhibit 6-1.

The Execution Stage culminates in specific present and future benefits for the organization and the individual. These benefits include

- Personal understanding and growth
- Skill development in the present job
- Increase in challenge and job interest
- Better understanding of the organization, other employees, and the informal structures within the system.

These results are achieved through completing the two phases of execution: (1) acquiring the resources necessary to attain a goal, and (2) demonstrating the new skills within the organization.

A Cost-Effective Approach

There is often concern within organizations that the efforts to help employees acquire skills at this stage are aimed toward moving people out of the organization altogether, toward transferring people from jobs where their talents are being used to more glamorous jobs within the same organization, or toward encouraging upward mobility in cases where it might not be justified. These fears can spring from the fact that too many

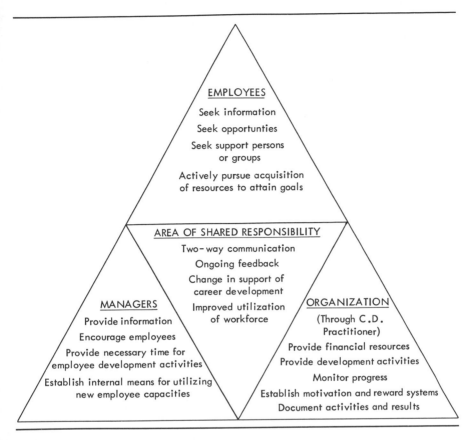

EMPLOYEES
Seek information
Seek opportunties
Seek support persons
or groups
Actively pursue acquisition
of resources to attain goals

AREA OF SHARED RESPONSIBILITY
Two-way communication
Ongoing feedback
Change in support of
career development
Improved utilization
of workforce

MANAGERS
Provide information
Encourage employees
Provide necessary time for
employee development activities
Establish internal means for utilizing
new employee capacities

ORGANIZATION
(Through C.D.
Practitioner)
Provide financial resources
Provide development activities
Monitor progress
Establish motivation and reward systems
Document activities and results

Exhibit 6-1   Shared Responsibilities at the Execution Stage

development programs are established without adequate people-planning and are aimed at a multitude of needs that have never been clearly identified. Programs that are planned this way are indeed costly.

The Smorgasbord.   Many organizations approach training and development by offering employees too many choices and by filling the schedules of the participants with many programs while leaving the participants' needs unfulfilled. This kind of career development effort is easy to establish and looks wonderful to the casual or nonprofessional observer. It can provide off the shelf programs that are easily acquired from internal and external sources, and it may generate a great deal of interest from those who pursue training and development without clear objectives. Smorgasbords are usually quite economical in the short run, but in the long run they can be very expensive. By failing to fulfill specific needs, by diffusing career development efforts, and by failing to support career development goals, smorgasbords can confuse participants.

Often in a misguided effort to make a smorgasbord program cost effective, or to show that the organization supports career development efforts 100 percent, management will allot quotas for minimum program participation. In some cases top management will, based on their own intuition, direct what courses will be made available and then direct that certain employees or percentages of employees participate in them. Such policies may make the program look good and may accomplish some training purposes, but do they achieve the desired career development goals?

"Let's try this" is a phrase that often determines what will be included in a training program. A training director hears about a course and says, "Let's try this." An administrator reads a brochure and says, "Let's try this." A potential instructor reads two or three books and says, "Let's try this." Before long a smorgasbord has been set up, and all are busy filling their "plates" without considering the consequences. An alternative to this approach follows.

The Diet.   A professional athletic team gathering at the beginning of training camp has a goal: to develop the skills, strategies, physical assets, and teamwork necessary to have a successful season. The coaching staff knows that the members of the team will work hard and will have huge appetites, but they also know that fat detracts from physical dexterity and causes muscular and mental fatigue. The dietitian who plans nourishing meals that designed to help the team meet its goals plays an important role.

The alternative to the smorgasbord approach to career development is a carefully prepared diet plan that avoids fat and excess but meets the needs of participants, the needs of the organization, and the needs of management. Practitioners can look upon their role as being similar to that of a skilled dietician.

By the time the career development effort reaches the Execution Stage, a solid foundation for training and development programs has been established. One of the great advantages of the career development process outlined in this book is that each stage has contributed toward knowing what training opportunities are needed and how these needs should be addressed.

During the *Preparation Stage,* for example, the process of gathering information about employee and organizational training needs was begun. Existing training programs and systems were investigated, and this information can now be used to determine future directions for the Execution Stage.

By the conclusion of the *Profiling Stage* practitioners had learned a great deal about the strengths and weaknesses of program participants. Specific knowledge about the need for individual skill development was acquired.

At the *Targeting Stage* employees set specific goals which, when weighed against their individual profiles, gave another forecast of what would be needed to meet those goals.

By the end of the *Strategizing Stage* participants had developed comprehensive action plans that identified the specific training and development efforts which would be required.

All this information should go a long way toward helping the practitioner decide what specific training and development will be needed so that these needs can be appropriately met at the Execution Stage. Exhibit 6-2 demonstrates the contribution of the first four career development stages to the Execution Stage.

With this information practitioners can build effective programs that provide maximum benefit. The main concern now becomes locating internal and external resources to meet those needs.

This brings the career development program to the first of the two phases of the Execution Stage, the acquisition of specific resources.

RESOURCE ACQUISITION

The first thing that comes to mind when the practitioner plans programs to assist employees in reaching their career development goals is planning the most effective training and development programs for them. Although formal programs are attractive, the practitioner will probably recognize quickly that they are not all that is needed. Employees build skills and capacities through informal processes as well as formal ones. The practitioner needs to be well informed about three categories of resources:

- *Training and Education:* Those programs conducted on-site or off-site, by internal or external training and development people that addresses technical skills, personal growth and development, and management training.

From Preparation	What skills do our preliminary needs assessments suggest will need development?
From Profiling	What skills do employees already possess? (What training is not needed?)
	What skills are weak or absent? (What training will we need?)
From Targeting	What skills will be needed to assist employees in reaching stated goals?
From Strategizing	What areas are suggested in action plans that demand the acquisition of specific skills?

Exhibit 6-2 Information that Contributes to Planning of Training Programs

- *Experience-Based Training:* Those experiences and efforts aimed at expanding skills through on-the-job training (OJT), new job experiences, and job rotation or project assignments in a variety of areas.
- *Support-Guided Development:* Those efforts that call upon the skills of others to provide growth and development and include such resources as mentor arrangements, professional organizations and instructional groups and teams, and informal support groups and networks.

Program participants will be acquiring skills in each area while the organization is providing the necessary resources and individual managers are encouraging and helping their employees. The practitioner not only oversees the establishment of the programs but makes certain that all who are involved understand their roles and the range of options available to them.

Training and Education

It is particularly important that practitioners help the others involved understand the differences between training and development. Training is the process through which skills are acquired, improved, or expanded. Most of the work done in the technical area is training; however, certain activities in some nontechnical areas also aim at building skills and are by definition training. For example, a program aimed at certain management or leadership skills, though nontechnical in nature, might be classified as training. On the other hand, development efforts in the leadership area focus on behavioral and attitudinal change and problem solving. Programs that seek to expand or enhance interpersonal and organizational capacities are development activities. They are usually longer term, broader in scope, and aim at a wider range of on-and off-job situations.

There are four general areas in which training and development efforts can be focused:

- Technical Training: Technical skills to be acquired, improved, or expanded may range from operating new or different equipment to using new methods of data processing or accounting to acquiring specialized knowledge through a university degree in the given area. The focus lies on technical proficiency through which one's current job or any future jobs may be performed more effectively.
- Leadership/Management Training and Development: The skills, behavior, and attitudes that enhance individual capabilities in goal setting, problem solving, time management, employee motivation, report writing, and work flow analysis all fall into this category. These programs may be aimed at presupervisory level personnel, supervisors, managers, or executives, though program content will vary at each level.
- Interpersonal Development: Programs in this area are designed to enhance and expand individual capabilities in the area of interpersonal relations, including communications, group leadership, teamwork, conflict manage-

ment, and interpersonal problem solving. Development in this category may be necessary at all levels of the organization, with focus and design varying at each level.

- Organizational Behavior Development: Skills in understanding the norms, values, and politics of the organization are generally acquired informally through others who can help provide awareness of the environment and knowledge of organizational power and influence. Programs often contribute to the employee's knowledge of the organization, the industry, and the basic procedures pertinent to the job.

Practitioners must make participants aware of each of the four categories and of the differences between them. It will be necessary to help the employees see that opportunities are available beyond the traditionally perceived areas of training and development and that some opportunities will be available only outside of the organization while others are best provided from within it.

The Inside Story. If the information acquired through the earlier career development stages is accurate and complete, it will have provided an excellent data base for examining in-house training currently offered by the organization. If, for example, financial management training has aleays been offered but reviewing the career development plans set by employees during the Targeting Stage indicates that it is not needed, then this may be the time to question the efficacy of such a program. On the other hand, if many employees felt they needed to acquire systems planning skills, the organization may be able during the Execution Stage to develop in-house training in this area.

The organization may also want to consider revising some of its in-house programs. Employee career development goals, for example, may indicate that behavioral science teachings should be added to an existing basic supervisory program that emphasizes management science concepts. The key here is that the organization can use the information it has already acquired as a rich resource for guiding in-house training decisions before the organization seeks off-site programs to fill the gaps.

In-house training in business and industry ranges from executive development programs in which participants spend several weeks or months studying all aspects of the organization to lunchtime sessions that for an hour or two a day provide updated skills information. They may be classroom sessions or off-site weekend retreats, programs for people who work together or workshops for employees from different units.

In seeking resource persons for in-house training, the organization has the option of using its own training staff—employees who have special expertise in instructing others (which can be ideal job enrichment for those employees)—or of hiring individuals from outside who can develop and conduct on-site training aimed at specific organizational needs.

The Nuclear Energy Business Group at General Electric offers many in-plant courses after hours which improve employee skills. These are open enrollment courses for all employees. These courses are not all offered each semester. Employees are requested to check the Employee Course Bulletin each semester for classes available. Employees register through self-nomination with immediate manager approval and are accepted on a first-come, first-served basis. Employees are encouraged to select courses applicable to their developmental needs; they are also warned to not misconstrue these courses as a replacement for on-the-job training.[1]

The advantage of in-house training is that it can be specifically tailored to the organization concerned. During training sessions examples and experiences can be used that have immediate relevance to organizational tasks and structure. This often replaces theoretical material being covered with material that fits the context of the organization. For example: The case study method has long been a favorite means of training and development. In workshops and seminars that draw from a wide range of organizations the cases often wind up being stereotyped and often concern problems and situations foreign to many of the participants. An internal program, however, might be able to draw cases from the participating group that illustrate the same principles. These cases, then, become meaningful for participants. Additionally employees pursue their learning with others whom they are likely to work with or meet in the future. This provides an internal support system that can enhance their instructional experience and that may continue once the instruction ends.

Increased knowledge about team management and group dynamics are examples of development objectives that can be most effectively achieved through in-house training. They can be practiced with actual working groups, and problem solving and long-range planning can be related to existing issues. Participants who are also coworkers can begin to practice their newly acquired knowledge immediately, and they can provide each other with support for continuing to use it over time. Interpersonal skills such as open communication, candid feedback, and participatory problem solving often seem risky in practice and are more likely to be applied when several colleagues have been trained and have experienced them together.

In addition, in-house training can include the development and monitoring of follow-up activities to encourage transferring newly acquired knowledge to the job setting. Follow-up activities may range from evaluating the changes in the units staffed by employees who have completed training programs to implementing the application projects developed during the training.

The View from Outside.   It is impossible to expect that any organization has enough resources to provide training and development programs

A five-day training program for middle- and upper-middle managers at Inland Steel has included topics such as team building, communications, leadership, interpersonal effectiveness, and job enrichment. To help insure follow-up, participants develop, share, and critique action plans for on-the-job application. Later, members of the company's personnel staff act as consultants to assist participants in implementing action plans.

sufficient to meet all of its employees' needs. Very often practitioners will, in a frantic attempt to keep the program internally based, with good intentions establish a smorgasbord. On the other hand, all that is good does not come from the outside. Just because a local college or university, professional organization, or consulting firm offers a particular program does not mean that the same program of equal caliber could not be offered at a lower cost by internal personnel or professionals.

The opposite holds just as true. Each day training and development professionals and career development practitioners receive a vast amount of mail, brochures, announcements, and catalogues extolling the virtues of a host of programs and plans. It is essential that practitioners exercise discretion in incorporating these offerings into the training and education package. (Because of this it is also essential that communication between the career development practitioner and training and development professionals continues on a frequent basis).

Once again information gathered from the earlier stages of this model can provide guidelines for determining what resources should be obtained from the outside. Practitioners should, therefore, review the data gathered during earlier stages to determine

- Needs to be addressed.
- Resources that are available internally.
- Organizational capacity for career development programs.
- Employee levels within the organization.
- Budget that is available.

If this information makes apparent that the best resources in a particular area lie outside the organization, then that is where the practitioner should look. Exhibit 6-3 describes the types of companies that use internal and external resources.

Practitioners should be aware that often the training and development conducted for top management is off-site in luxury hotels or major universities, with all expenses paid and recreational facilities available. Middle management receives their training and development in full-day sessions off-site and in conditions only slightly less plush than top management. By the time the training and development program gets down to the

	Organization Size		
Program Level	Medium to Large, Less Than 2,000 Managers	Very Large, 2,000-8,000 Managers	Giant, Over 8,000 Managers
Executive	Programs largely individualized. Primarily out-company, some internal on contract, some completely ad-hoc. Oriented toward conceptual skills and strategy.	Programs divided between in-house and out-company. Oriented toward conceptual skills, strategy, and environmental understanding.	Programs largely in-house and centralized, supplemental lectures, some out-company exposure. Oriented toward interface of internal and external environment.
Middle	Programs mixed between in-house (supplemented by lecturers) and out-company. Oriented toward human and conceptual skills and analytical abilities.	Programs largely in-house, with little out-company. conducted on centralized corporate basis. Oriented toward human and decision-making skills, geared to company policy.	Programs predominantly in-house, either corporate or division centralized. Orientation is toward human, decision-making, and conceptual skills.
Supervisory	Programs on-site in division. Orientation is on basic technical and human skills, geared to company procedures	Program on-site in division. Orientation is on basic technical and human skill, including company procedures.	Programs on-site in division. Orientation is toward basic technical and human skills, including company procedures and policy. Program instructors are centrally trained.

Exhibit 6-3   Program Type and Level Versus Organization Size[2]

supervisory or general employee level, much of it is after hours on personal time in makeshift classrooms located at the work site. A demotivating second-or third-class citizenship feeling develops, which can torpedo a development program before it has a chance to get started.

The caveat, therefore, is this: Practitioners should carefully determine needs in conjunction with the impact that the site will have on a group before deciding whether to conduct a program internally or schedule it in a location outside the company. Arbitrary decisions destroy the most carefully designed programs.

Outside off-site programs may fill a need for the organization by allowing its employees to select from a broader range of education and training options. However, transferring learning from the training sessions back to the job may be difficult when the employee has received education as a solo activity with little opportunity for support or sharing among

General Electric sponsors a series of professional development courses put together by the California State University and College system in cooperation with the American Management Association's Extension Institute. The courses may be taken singularly or as part of a program to earn a Certificate in Business Management. The courses are designed to give information to three groups of people: those who would like to seek promotions to become managers; those who are newly appointed managers; and those who would like to brush up on management techniques. A variety of seminars, conferences and workshops are also available through the extension programs of San Jose State, UC Berkeley, and Santa Cruz. Information about course offerings can be obtained by contacting Training and Education.[3]

colleagues. Practitioners and managers must be alert to this phenomenon and be prepared to lend support.

Whether training and education is off-site or in-house, it is essential that the organization consider ways to encourage, recognize, and reward its use. One way to do this is through providing rewards to managers who take an active interest in career development and begin to allow employees to undertake new projects that will apply their learning. A more formal approach to this problem is to include in official performance appraisals factors relating to the learning acquired, giving employees an opportunity to report on their recent training and development and how it is being applied to their jobs.

Financial Assistance for Education. Early in the twentieth century the American ideal was the Horatio Alger hero who, in ragged but always clean clothes, after working long hours in a factory, attended night school to become a doctor, lawyer and tycoon. The Alger model lives on today, but numerous organizations have made the task easier by instituting financial aid programs which encourage personal and professional education and development.

The methods and structures for administering these programs vary greatly in terms of who receives the assistance, who decides to whom it will be given, and how much assistance is made available. Any number of options are available in setting up a tuition or financial aid program. The major considerations are

- Who will receive the aid
- The amount to be paid
- Deciding who will get how much
- Deciding which institutions will deliver the education programs
- What the restrictions are
- How budgets will be established and administered

PROGRAM DECISIONS	OPTIONAL METHODS
RECIPIENTS OF AID	All employees eligible
	Limited to certain levels of employees
	Limited to employees in certain job categories
	Cut-off number, with first come, first served
	No set limits
AMOUNT OF AID	Ceiling on individual amounts—same for each employee
	Ceiling on individual amounts—adjusted for length of service and salary
DECISION ABOUT WHO AND HOW MUCH	Central unit (personnel office) decides
	Department heads decide
	Immediate supervisors nominate or decide
PROGRAM DELIVERY MECHANISMS	All off-site learning programs eligible
	Only accredited educational institutions eligible
	Central unit develops roster of approved delivery institutions
RESTRICTIONS	Must complete courses satisfactorily for reimbursement
	Must show job relatedness
	Must show career relatedness
	Must commit future amount of time for working for organization
	No restrictions
BUDGET STRUCTURE	Central (personnel office) budget for financial aid
	Decentralized—from budget of each department
	Each employee given personal annual budget for education and training

Exhibit 6-4 Financial Aid Decision Guide

Exhibit 6-4 shows ways in which these considerations have been handled by some organizations. Practitioners may find that their organizations prefer one of the methods shown or a combination of options or that they desire something totally different. Methodologies should fit the character and traditions of the organization so that employees see the financial aid program as an opportunity and not as a change that must be approached with caution.

Particular care must be taken to ensure that decisions made about educational assistance are fair to all employees. Decisions should be made in the open, with employees clearly understanding what is available and how they may take advantage of it. If organizations decide what financial aid is available on a case-by-case basis, with total amounts buried in a variety of budget items, employees do not have equal access to the system. And if departments or divisions are left to pull educational assistance resources from tight budgets, without having budgeted specifically for that purpose, it is likely that some will allow for no employee development while others allow for a great deal.

The Educational Opportunities Plan at Kimberly-Clark Corp. allows each employee an annual self-development allotment in a personal "bank account." The size of the allotment is tied to a formula based on the employee's performance rating, salary, self-development plan, and the company's earnings. It is scheduled such that lower income employees are likely to receive higher allotments. Courses taken need not be directly job-related and can also include pursuing cultural interests; however, the vast majority of those selected by employees have been related to the immediate job or company business.

The program also includes a family education savings plan in which the employee and the company contribute to savings for educational expenses of the employee or immediate family members.

Practitioners may find the following questions helpful in establishing the training and education programs that are necessary to support their career development efforts:

1. What training programs have employees identified as needed?
2. Are these programs currently available within the organization?
3. If the answer to #2 is no: Is there sufficient need within the organization to merit the establishment of an internal program?
4. If the answer to #3 is no: Are the programs available from external sources?
5. Are training and education facilities within the organization sufficient to allow additional programs?
6. Is the training and development budget sufficient to allow needed program expansion?
7. How can additional resources be made available?
8. How is our outside program financial aid being administered? Are changes necessary? How can these changes be affected?
9. Am I operating a diet plan for a professional training table or a smorgasbord?

Experience-Based Training

There are other ways to develop the necessary technical personal and management skills besides taking courses. One of the best alternatives is sometimes referred to as learning by doing, or experience-based learning, which provides employees the opportunity to observe and practice new techniques and skills on the job. This approach enables individuals to realistically determine how the new work they are performing fits their needs and abilities.

The work place has often been called the ultimate classroom. It is likely that employees will discover a range of self-development opportunities while learning on the job. In addition to increasing their technical skills, they may enhance their leadership and interpersonal abilities and their capacities for understanding organizational behavior.

Experience-based learning may derive from formal on-the-job training or from job rotation programs or from less formal activities through which current job roles and assignments are refined to provide new experiences.

Practitioners should examine the advantages and possible problems associated with each of these learning approaches so that they can be used where applicable at the Execution Stage. Keeping in mind the "diet plan," however, practitioners should use approaches that will benefit employees and the organization.

Training while Doing. Probably the most extensive training device used by organizations to develop their people is on-the-job training (OJT). Commonly used as a method for breaking in new workers, OJT introduces employees to new tasks under the guidance of an individual who can instruct and coach. This provides employees with a chance to "learn the ropes" and gives supervisors an opportunity to observe and correct the methods of new employees.

OJT also has broad applications for the more experienced worker who suddenly finds it necessary to learn new skills related to changes in equipment, procedures, or work routines. It can be used as a means of cross-training to provide back-up support and to ensure that important functions will be covered in the event of temporary absences, illnesses, or vacations.

Two primary questions about OJT must be answered to ensure its effective utilization: 1) Who is the most appropriate person to act as instructor? and 2) How will the training period be structured to provide the necessary steps toward full learning? If employees are to profit fully from on-the-job training experiences, the assistance they gain should come from those who have acquired greated wisdom and experience. The learners in this situation are provided the opportunity to observe the teachers, to see what they themselves have been doing wrong, and to correct their own mistakes. One of the most obvious candidates for the instructor role is the immediate supervisor. The coaching that takes place during on-the-job training is more informal and continuous than that which occurs during the performance appraisal process, which also attempts to place the supervisor in a coaching role.

The coaching role in OJT involves observing employees in order to analyze their performance and assist them in improving it. Assistance is provided in the form of instructions, comments, criticisms, questions, and suggestions offered to motivate employees to develop themselves further. On-the-job training that focuses on work achievements is much more effective than that which concentrates on individual inadequacies. OJT coaching can contribute to a better relationship between supervisor and subordinate since the supervisor no longer has to constantly look over the subordinate's shoulder.

Good OJT coaching requires that supervisors provide good examples for subordinates by establishing high standards of performance for themselves and for their subordinates to observe. Supervisors must demonstrate confidence in their subordinates, which in turn requires that they have adequate confidence in themselves.

Although immediate supervisors may have sufficient knowledge of the tasks to be performed, they may not have enough time or interest in guiding subordinates as closely as necessary. Often, employees perform OJT functions for their peers. When an employee who is already performing the job acts as instructor, OJT becomes an apprenticeship experience for the learner and a job enrichment experience for the teacher. The employee has an opportunity to observe all tasks related to the job and to practice them under the tutelage of someone who knows them intimately. The learner may feel more comfortable asking questions and risking occasional floundering with a peer than with a supervisor. The teachers in this case may be experiencing their first responsibility in that role and may find it challenging and meaningful.

> The Naval Air Arm of the U.S. Navy has long been a major proponent of OJT. Personnel assigned to aircraft squadrons have usually attended a formal school on the general systems associated with their ratings and have received training on the specific aircraft upon which they will be working. However, no one is allowed to perform any but the most routine maintenance functions on his/her own until completing a rigorous OJT program and check out. Only after satisfying command requirements is the individual considered qualified to work on the complexities of the system. OJT is a way of life in naval aviation that all aircraft maintenance work periods are designated as OJT sessions.[4]

To ensure that OJT will include the elements necessary for effective learning, the practitioner should understand the steps involved in effective OJT. These steps include

1. Develop (or update) a description of the job, identifying tasks to perform, special techniques to apply, and indicators of effective accomplishment.
2. Determine what the trainee already knows and what new learning will be necessary.
3. Determine a time frame for the training period.
4. Select individual(s) who will act as instructor(s).
5. Provide instructor training in educational and interpersonal skill building.
6. Conduct general orientation to familiarize trainee with all aspects of the job.
7. Demonstrate and instruct trainee in specific tasks, phasing them in according to difficulty and trainee ability.

8. Encourage employee to practice and ask questions.
9. Observe, suggest changes, and note favorable progress.
10. Phase out instruction, giving trainee more individual responsibility and conducting periodic follow-up checks (including opportunities for the trainee to solicit information about the job).

Why do some OJT programs fail while others succeed? Practitioners should consider a number of possible reasons before establishing a program. The supervisors selected to conduct OJT must not only be highly motivated but also effective as instructors. Teachers who do not have patience, empathy, and the ability to communicate thoughts and processes will destroy the employees' desire to learn.

Participants in OJT programs must be just as carefully selected. Those who do not have the motivation to learn, the capacity to learn, or interest in the given area of training can slow the process and stall the effort.

All employees in the program must be dedicated to the programs success. Lukewarm or surface allegiance to OJT will cause it to create more problems than it solves. The time frames established for the OJT effort must be realistic. Time frames that are too long may result in frustration and burn-out. Making them too short may lead to inadequate training and corners being cut.

Other employees who work alongside OJT participants must be cooperative and supportive of the effort. They can help the OJT participants to see the importance of their efforts and should be willing to provide help. Derision and the use of terms such as "new kids" or "rookies" degrade the OJT participants and may cause them to withdraw or drop out.

The organization should see OJT as a legitimate training function and fund it properly. OJT activities ought to be provided with adequate space and suitable tools and training aids. Even the best instructors cannot accomplish their goals without having adequate materials available to them. Practitioners may have difficulty finding resources, or facilities that can provide equipment mock-ups or simulated work environments, but they will find that their efforts pay dividends in the long run.

One advantage of OJT for the organization is that OJT can be arranged fairly informally within departments and divisions and requires little formal, organization-wide structure or policy making. However, the organization should encourage and recognize those units that are using OJT as a method for developing employees and learning about valuable skills they may have.

A Moving Experience. Job rotation, the movement of employees to different tasks at specified intervals, enables them to develop and practice new skills and to determine areas in which they can best use their talents. Additionally this practice allows the organization to add depth to its personnel by developing people who are prepared to function in a variety of capacities and by discovering where individual talents fit best in the organization. Job rotation provides a greater variety of work experiences that can broaden the knowledge and understanding that employees require to develop further in their career.

The length of a rotational assignment may range from weeks to months. It may be a single event to give an employee a closer understanding of a different function, or it may be a "revolving door," meaning the employee continues to rotate back and forth between two or more jobs. Some common types of job rotation and their objectives are depicted in Exhibit 6-5.

Depending on its objectives, job rotation may take place within a department or division or between different departments and divisions. The goals that employees identified at an earlier stage of the career development process can help guide the organization in determining how the system should be structured and in identifying which jobs are likely candidates for rotation. While rotation must be structured and planned as a comprehensive system, it can provide flexibility for different types of programs in different units. Some may only occasionally rotate employees who volunteer for a temporary "swap" in duties, while others may exchange all employees with certain duties at set intervals on a continuing basis.

TYPE OF ROTATION	OBJECTIVES
New Employee Exposing new employees to a number of jobs before placing them in a permanent position	• Provide understanding of operations in different areas • Test skills • Determine appropriate placement
Personal Growth Moving employees temporarily to jobs they have not undertaken in the past	• Learn variety of skills • Learn new skills • Opportunity for advancement • Opportunity for lateral moves
Executive Development Moving managers or managerial candidates to various units of the organization	• Assess managerial potential • Understand total organization • Determine next move
Revolving Door Shifting employees back and forth between jobs at predetermined intervals	• Reward for level attained • Broaden skill base • Alleviate boredom of doing same job
Continuing Reassignment Reassigning employees to different units or geographic locations at set intervals	• Provide depth of talent through cross training • Geographic relocation • Facilitate new ideas through diversity • Prevent employees from getting stale in one place • Use employee talents in diverse settings

---

Exhibit 6-5 Job Rotation Alternatives

Colt Industries in New York rotates recent college graduates through three and sometimes four challenging assignments during their first three years of employment. Participants selected for the program are chosen on the basis of early identification of management talent. Each new manager spends approximately one year in each of three jobs with the first job selected in areas that match their indicated strengths and the second job chosen to indicate the true limitation of any weaknesses revealed by their initial assignment. All spend time in staff function, such as industrial engineering, and all of them work in a job in the area of finance and budgeting.

Colt Industries feels that by the end of their three year rotation they will have had the chance to demonstrate possession of most of the skills necessary to be a general manager in a highly divisionized corporation that operates in several segments of heavy industry. An indication of the success of this job rotation program is that the number of managers chosen for the program's fourth year was double the size of the original group.[5]

In planning for rotation, the practitioner might consider the following questions:

- What are the objectives of rotation?
- What types of rotation will be used?
- How should eligibility be determined?
- Which jobs can and cannot be included?
- Will specialized training be necessary for participants?
- Will there be limits on the number of persons rotating at any one time?
- What will be the time frames for rotational assignments?
- How will performance appraisal of rotated individuals be determined?
- How will the results of the system be measured?

Since it is usually not feasible to train individuals who have higher level managerial responsibilities by rotating them, their skill, knowledge, and experience can be broadened by making lateral promotions for them through different departments in the organization.

Positions, for example, in industrial engineering or personnel can provide excellent experience for managers who need to learn more about these areas. Working in these departments brings candidates into contact with nearly every other department in the organization and, as a result, increases their knowledge of the overall organizational structure. Lateral promotions, like rotational assignments, provide an opportunity for individuals to receive guidance from a variety of other managers and to observe many management methods and techniques in action. If these sorts of developmental activities are suggested during the Strategizing Stage, a job rotation program might fill the bill.

Training for Cross Purposes. Common to both job rotation and OJT is the concept of cross-training—increasing skills so that individuals are able to perform a variety of duties. This gives the organization a broader base of talent and increased options for placing personnel where and when they are needed most.

Cross-training represents a hybrid approach to skill development that combines some of the features of OJT with some of those of job rotation. The object of cross-training may not be to permanently change an employee's job, but to provide in advance for organizational needs during peak times or vacation periods. For example, one division or department in an organization may have a high seasonal need for additional employees. Through cross-training the valley and peaks of seasonal demand can be leveled out by having employees in these divisions and departments with low seasonal load provide back-up assistance for those divisions of departments with high demand. During the season in which the demand is reversed the flow of assistance is also reversed.

Cross-training as a seasonal aid has several advantages:

- Organizational needs are met with permanent personnel rather than through hiring temporary help.
- Employees are exposed to different skills and functions that can help them to make career decisions.
- A team spirit is developed within the work force that enhances morale and feelings of mutual support.
- Monotony and routine can be broken up.

Not all cross-training efforts are seasonal. Cross-training can also serve as a basis for increasing job enrichment efforts, expanding the awareness of organizational objectives, developing improved relationships between functions or departments, and exploring career alternatives. Most cross-training efforts involve shorter periods of time than OJT or job rotation.

An essential component of the word processing system at Eastern Airlines, Inc, is the rotation of secretaries between administrative and correspondence units. Cross-trained to handle all functions within each unit, secretaries move among various work stations (such as check preparation, mail handling, or phone handling), as well as between units, on a planned rotational schedule. Depending on the secretarial tasks and the needs of the department supported by secretarial services, individuals may rotate every six weeks or may remain in a job for six months to a year. A coordinator for each unit plans rotational assignments.

The system provides for learning and challenge, and prevents secretaries from becoming "stuck" repeating any single task. It enables the company to shift secretarial personnel to areas where the need is greatest at a given time, to balance workloads, to back up for absences, and to capitalize on individual talents.

Practical Projects.   Another method of experience-based training is to assign temporary projects that can result in learning and practical experience. These projects may be undertaken individually, such as research assignments; in teams, such as problem solving and planning assignments; or on committees where employees have an opportunity to gain more responsibility and diversified experience.

These endeavors are often undertaken on a less systematic basis than OJT or job rotation, with employee and supervisor or career development practitioner simply recognizing a skill that should be acquired and matching it with a special project that can give the employee a chance to practice that skill. Action plans developed by employees during strategizing can guide the selection of projects. For example, individuals who want to move into financial management may be able to research alternative inventory accounting systems for their division. A secretary desiring to advance to administrative assistant may be placed on a project team that reviews the departmental communications and paper flow system. Projects such as these enable employees to learn and practice specific skills and simultaneously provide the organization with valuable information.

A more comprehensive formal system for providing project assignments is provided by a relatively new organizational structure known as matrix management.[6] This department-wide or organization-wide arrangement superimposes the management of individual projects onto the traditional functional system, drawing employees from various areas to tackle problems that cross functional lines. Project teams are created to address distinct problems and programs—often to research a special issue, to develop a new product, or to initiate a new system. Numerous projects, under different project managers, may exist at varying stages of progress at any given time, and team members may return to their functional specialties or new project teams when the project is completed. The system can introduce employees to a variety of issues and expose them to as many as three or four bosses—one functional and two to three project managers.

As with an innovative management approach the matrix system has certain advantages and disadvantages.

Employees engaged on a project have two people to whom they are responsible, the functional boss and the project boss, and very often they develop divided loyalties. When not engaged on a project, employees sometimes feel their talents are underutilized and become frustrated especially during periods when business is slow.

Both functional and project managers are very often placed in competition for limited human resources. Functional managers, especially, often feel pressed between the demands of competing project managers and the desires and needs of employees. Project managers may feel that they spend more time competing for the limited skills available than in conducting their project.

At Mattel, Inc., executive secretaries participated in a career development effort that utilized the project concept as a way of enriching jobs and preparing participants for possible future career moves.

After participants had worked through a long process of profiling and had met individually with a consultant and a member of IR staff to select career goals (job enrichment in this case being the most important), the development of the project concept process began. Participants were asked a "riddle":

> What is it that this company needs that
> it presently does not have that it would
> challenge you to do—i.e., you would practice
> new skills, utilize old ones and grow as a result of it?

Participants answered the riddle by suggesting a range of projects that they thought might benefit both the organization and themselves.

Each project had to meet a series of criteria before it was sanctioned. Criteria combined job enrichment principles developed by Richard Hackman (described in the Targeting chapter) and characteristics of power defined by Rosabeth Kanter. (Is your project extraordinary? Relevant? Visible? Does it provide an opportunity to make new alliances with peers? Subordinates? Mentors?) Participants assisted one another in the selection of projects and in discussions regarding the return-on-investment for them and the organization. The organization was apprised of the projects so that commitment could be assessed before commencement.

Projects selected by the group were team developed and provided each woman with a chance to practice or learn specific new skills. Projects ideas included: (1) the design and dissemination of an information handbook that described specific non-job related skills that Mattel employees possessed (e.g. speaks Spanish, is a Notary, does calligraphy). It was felt the project widened the "alliances" of each member of the project team and provided opportunities to use design, art, and creative writing skills. (2) The development of a temporary task assignment system for all nonexempt employees. This provided access to alliances outside the organization (participants interviewed other organizations who had similar programs) and an opportunity to practice proposal writing. (3) Redesign of a course for executive secretaries—this project gave its team members the chance to design and develop a survey, interview dropouts of the original course, decide on selection procedures, and actually teach the new course.

During slow business periods, organizations find that they have a great many people, some of them highly paid and possessing premium skills, who are doing little or nothing productive. The organization cannot afford to turn these people loose, however, because a sudden project acquisition can cause them to be needed immediately.

Practitioners find that people employed on a project are seldom available for training and development. However, when not engaged on a project these people are often available and eager for career development activities.

Despite all this the matrix organization can provide a great many opportunities for practitioners to use imagination and creativity in meeting particular skill development needs. Familiarity with its structure and operation can help smooth out the problems before they emerge.

Employees in the internal audit division of a large wholesale bank were given wide exposure to a variety of supervisors as they worked on audit assignments in various units of the Bank. One outcome of these multiple bosses was that subordinates experienced greater demands on their abilities because of differences in supervisor expectations. No longer could they anticipate and predict what would be expected of them. Frequent contact with higher level supervisors also caused subordinates to feel closer to the source of power, increasing their opportunity to contribute to the organization.

Another stimulus to career development was the frequency and openness with which managers in the internal audit division talked about task-related issues. The sharing of task-related problems contributed directly to employee growth by: (1) broadening employees reference group to include people higher up in the hierarchy; (2) helping employees internalize organizational goals; and (3) making supervisors look more human, therefore, helping employees to identify with them.[7]

Support-Guided Development

A great many development opportunities during the Execution Stage come simply from getting employees together with others who can provide instruction, guidance, and support. This may take place within groups of individuals who share some common need or goals or between two individuals who are helping each other. Support groups within organizations can generally be categorized by 1) profession (such as engineers, accountants, or personnel managers from various units within the organization); 2) level or rank (middle managers, administrative aides, or department heads); 3) special interests (women, minorities, or young managers). These groups may be formally sanctioned by top management, or they may be formed informally by a few interested individuals. Many organizations formalize support groups and mentor relationships by initiating a structure for their development and arranging times and places for meetings.

Informal support groups can also effectively promote professional development, with individuals meeting over lunch or after work to discuss a variety of issues of common interest. In addition employees may join support groups outside the organization in order to exchange ideas and promote learning along with others who are in the same profession or have like interests.

Following a 3-day development program at Merrill Lynch, participants were assigned to "development quartets"—support groups organized to meet on a continued basis during the six month period following the workshop. The groups were provided with a variety of activities that could be discussed at meetings and were assigned mentors who met individually and with the entire group to discuss career goals and development plans. The "development quartets" were organized to represent a cross-section of two major departments within the organization as well as male/female and ethnic diversity.

Typical activities of these internal groups include

- Sharing information about operations in various units.
- Helping individuals learn and grow.
- Identifying issues that need to be brought to the attention of top management.
- Conducting special projects concerning issues of interest to group members.
- Encouraging favorable treatment of members by the organization.
- Providing a sense of togetherness and comradeship that is supportive of group members' career mobility.

Occasional meetings that cross departmental lines can provide learning opportunities as well as support. Most organizations have regular meetings of department heads and division heads, and some have periodic meetings of budget analysts, personnel specialists, and others. The practitioner may want to institute special days during which individuals from various departments meet to discuss and demonstrate the operations of their groups. This can be set up as a display hall environment, with booths and tables where departmental operations are discussed and literature is made available. Employees can be invited to circulate through the area and meet people from different departments and functions in order to learn more about the organization and the opportunities it offers.

Mentor as Teacher.   One of the most effective supports for growth and development is the mentor/protégé relationship. An individual who finds another person (generally with longer tenure in the organization) who can teach, coach, and advise gains access to information and assistance that can contribute to acquiring the skills necessary to reach a particular goal. Three major roles of the mentor during the Execution Stage are

- Grooming an individual for new responsibilities or advancement.
- Coaching and counseling an individual in behavior and skills that can facilitate career progress.
- Sharing information and expertise that have been specially acquired.

The environment created by this relationship is unique in the way it fosters learning and enthusiasm in the employee-protégé. Mentors must be willing, however, to let the protégés learn on their own, which includes permitting the protégés the freedom to make mistakes. Protégés are allowed leeway to question their mentors' opinions so that they can learn and understand. The protégés must be able to accept criticism without becoming defensive, while also asserting individual feelings and views. The structure of the mentor relationship makes this possible. Since mentors are not forced to protect their jobs and the protégés are not evaluated as protégés, the environment is conducive to learning. The mentors must be willing to devote time to aiding, supporting, and instructing a protégé. The protégés must also be willing to devote time, often outside of work hours, to the relationship.

Typically the mentor arrangement is an informal one, adopted by two individuals who simply feel comfortable with each other. However, many organizations have formalized the system, generally by asking for volunteers to form a pool of mentors and matching them with individuals who are relatively new to the organization. Their informal meetings are supplemented by structured occasions to bring all mentors and protégés together for discussion and learning sessions. Other organizations develop mentor programs for select groups of employees who may be on the organizational fast track.

Support from Afar.   The proliferation of professional groups has resulted in an organization for almost every line of work. These groups and societies provide an excellent opportunity for learning and growth. Many individuals might not be aware that they are eligible for the specialized services of a number of associations. For example, an accountant in a government agency may find opportunities available from an organization of professional accountants or from an organization of government employees. If the accountant is female, she may also discover opportunities in a group representing professional women. Through their meetings and training programs these groups can provide a good source of personal contacts and professional learning. Since these organizations contribute substantially to the development of their members, many employers pay for membership dues and conference travel expenses and grant time off for attending meetings.

Other groups outside the organization address special interests and development needs. Public speaking groups, for example, are an excellent vehicle for skill development. They have had particular success in helping members learn and practice the delivery of speeches and presentations. Similar groups range from those that help members develop writing skills to those that assist members in starting their own small businesses.

Clearly the acquisition of skills does not have to be restricted to the confines of the organization. Ambitious employees will use all the sources

Security Pacific National Bank developed a special program mentor role for participants in its Advanced Opportunities Program (AOP). The purpose of the Advanced Opportunities Program is to prepare a group of individuals to assume certain targeted senior management positions and to aid the Bank in meeting its affirmative action goals. The Bank carefully selected program participants from throughout the system and assigned a technical mentor to each one. The mentors included individuals who were

1. Senior members of management.
2. Interested in and capable of developing others.
3. Willing and able to commit the time required to act as a mentor.
4. Knowledgeable about the necessary technical skills and the developmental requirements for the targeted area.
5. Able to convey that knowledge of the technical area to others in a coaching situation.
6. Willing and able to provide coaching and to share insights about the political fitness and organizational norms appropriate to the targeted area.

In addition to the above characteristics, the role of the program mentor includes the following responsibilities:

Developmental Guidance. It is the mentor's responsibility to provide information and make suggestions to his or her protégé concerning the skills, knowledge, experience, training, and other developmental requirements an individual would need in order to qualify for the senior management level. Whenever possible, the mentor would be expected to suggest sources for acquiring this expertise.

Technical Expertise—The mentor is expected to be an ongoing source of high-level technical expertise for the protégés as they develop their skills in these areas.

Program Feedback—Mentors' comments and assessments of participants' progress are solicited and considered by the program designers throughout the life of the AOP program.

The program mentors play a vital role in meeting the AOP program objectives by sharing their time, knowledge, and experience with the protégés to which they were assigned.

available to them both outside and inside the organization to execute career goals. The practitioner's job is to help employees discover these opportunities and become involved in them.

As organizations find themselves operating in more severely restricted environments with definite limitations on expansion, they will need to seek a variety of ways to provide the necessary training for their employees. Even though expansion may be somewhat restricted, organizations expect their employees to be increasingly better educated, up to date, and career oriented. It is important for practitioners to recognize that skills can be learned in a variety of contexts. Skills can be acquired through any of these activities:

- In-house training and development classes
- Outside training and development classes
- On-the-job training
- Job rotation
- Special projects
- Mentor relationships
- Professional societies
- Support groups

Where Can Support Be Found?

One of the most time-consuming and complex tasks encountered by practitioners during the Execution Stage is that of helping employees to locate the educational, training, and developmental resources required to reach goals set during the Targeting Stage. To accomplish this practitioners might emphasize not only the importance of employee participation in the search for information about resources, but also the necessity of communicating that information to the practitioner for: 1) entry into a central resource file to help future career development program participants; and 2) the documentation of the Execution Stage.

Employee Responsibilities.   At this point in the cycle the employee-participants become active on their own behalf. This requires a great deal of self-direction, motivation, and tenacity as the employee searches for and pursues resources that will be necessary to implement the career development plan. The primary responsibilities of employees are to 1) identify specific ways in which they can acquire resources to facilitate their development; and 2) use those resources to develop the skills and relationships necessary to move toward career goals.

The first of these roles is largely an information function. Employees need to continually search for information about training and development opportunities, experiences, and support that may assist their progress. They may need to talk to colleagues in other departments, supervisors, and friends to gain evaluative information and advice about what specific training is beneficial. They may need to investigate opportunities offered by local educational institutions or through professional associations. In some cases, they may need to talk with supervisors about special projects or job revisions that could be undertaken to provide developmental work. Employees themselves may also need to initiate ideas for on-the-job training and job rotation. A check list such as Exhibit 6-6 can assist employees in thinking through their choices and gaining appropriate recommendations.

Using those resources is simply a matter of following through by taking courses, attending training, completing special projects, trying new skills

Personal Resource Directory		
Skill Desired	*Potential Outside Resource*	*Recommendation/Evaluation*
Assertiveness	*UCLA Extension*	*Program is excellent, takes only one day. Serves as a good introduction. (Sally O.)*
	Action Seminars	*Longer intensive program. Builds support groups. Expensive (Cathy B.)*
	Book: The Assertive Woman by Phelps and Austin	*Best introduction. Easy to read and digest. The perfect starting place. (Jackie S.)*

Exhibit 6-6   An Individual Personal Source Directory

on the job, and forging new relationships with others. This requires an expenditure of time and sometimes money, as well as a willingness to stick with it when the initial excitement of doing something new wears off. (Practitioners can often tell if an employee is truly committed by the amount of energy invested at this stage.)

At the same time employees should continually appraise their experiences and look for ways to capitalize on them for career growth. They should keep managers and career development practitioners informed about their activities and their future plans. And they should try not to operate in a vacuum but rather to seek support and guidance from others in pursuing career development resources. Anything that the practitioner can do to engender this spirit in employees will contribute substantially to the program's success.

Practitioner Responsibilities. The role of the career development practitioner during this effort is to ensure that the organization is operating in a manner that makes it possible for employees to implement career development plans. The career development practitioner needs to see that the resources employees want to use are made available by the organization and that employees are informed about these resources. To do this the practitioner needs to track and monitor information gained from the other stages of career development. Additionally the practitioner serves as liaison between top management, employees, and the direct managers of career development participants in order to inform each of these groups and guide them in contributing to the program.

One early task of the practitioner is to review existing in-house developmental resources such as training programs, tuition assistance, and job rotation and to ask some of the following questions:

- What additional resources should we consider developing?
- Do all employees have equal access to the organizational resources?

- Are employees at all levels adequately informed about resources that are available?
- Do we have a system for tracking how organizational resources are used?
- Have I done all I can to encourage employees to actively seek resources?

It is at this point that practitioners might consider revising old internal programs, terminating those programs that appear to have outlived their usefulness, and instituting new ones that may be required. It may be, for instance, that people within the organization have been discussing the institution of a job rotation program, a broader application of tuition aid, or an after-hours technical training effort. Practitioners armed with the requirements defined by employee career development goals are in an ideal position to help organizations recognize their needs, to help direct the organizational response, and to serve as a prime element in making changes.

The practitioner must also identify which resources can best be provided outside the organization to meet a variety of training needs. This may include gathering information about these methods as well as keeping up to date on the programs offered by local colleges and universities, training organizations, professional associations, and adult education institutions. The practitioner will need to ensure that time and money are available for employee career development pursuits. The organization's top management should be encouraged to adequately budget for learning needs and to set policies that allow employees time to pursue their developmental plans.

Ensuring that employees are informed about developmental resources available within and outside the organization is another responsibility. This may be done through written communications, face-to-face information sessions, and an open-door policy that invites inquiries about what is available.

One extremely effective device for disseminating information is publishing a manual that outlines sources of training and education, developmental experiences, and personal career development assistance. Such a manual can include the identification of both internal and external development resources, a discussion of company policies relating to employee development, a list of individuals who are charged with responsibility for overseeing career development program activities, and an explanation of the other human resource development activities (discussed earlier) that support career development efforts.

Another method of facilitating information exchange is to conduct sessions to orient employees about available resources. These can include presentations by training personnel, by employees who have used various programs, and by individuals representing outside resource institutions. Such a session can be separated into a series of shorter briefings with themes such as "Tuition Reimbursements: Getting Your Fair Share,"

"Unraveling The Mysteries of Job Rotation," and "The Local Colleges Want You."

Northwest Energy Company publishes an "Employee Development and Organization Catalog" annually to provide a schedule of programs and services available to meet developmental needs. This high-quality, glossy publication includes information concerning development guidelines (policies and management's role); in-house training (schedules and course descriptions arrayed according to relevant employee classifications and divisions); outside training (conferences, seminars, and courses offered by others); and suggested projects and services various units can undertake to help enhance employee development.

During development of the catalogue, personnel from throughout the company contributed to a "needs assessment" to help identify programs that would be most relevant to specific learning needs.

The career development practitioner can expect to be everybody's source of reference for questions, concerns, and comments about activities undertaken during the Execution Stage. Employees will want to be provided with the programs and resources they need to carry out their plans. Supervisors of these employees will need information and assistance that allows them to guide their subordinates. Top management will need recommendations and reports to help make policy decisions.

In working with employees the practitioner's primary role is to establish strong ongoing two-way communication. This means listening to concerns, reviewing goals, answering questions, and facilitating the implementation of plans. The practitioner must be available and visible to employees and must continually analyze their needs to determine what the organization should be doing to lend its support.

One warning to the practitioner—don't do it *all* for the employee. All employees need to take responsibility for their own continuing education. One way to operationalize this might be to develop a form that encourages employees to state why they want a particular training course or job rotation assignment—which career goal is it directed toward? Employees should not be able to execute their career plans without having a clear focus. This is essential for the employees' own goal achievement and also to ensure that "diet" plans are being established instead of smorgasbords. When a course is specifically aimed at a goal or group of goals, it has legitimacy and is not being offered merely to justify a budget or provide a rationale for a professional staff's existence. Explaining to the practitioner their need for a particular skill should cause employees to think before acting. Exhibit 6-7 is a form that could be included in the performance appraisal system or could be an attachment in a training and development catalogue.

I plan to take the following course over the next year: _____

It contributes to my career goal in the following way: _____

I can use the course on my present job to do the following: _____

I can use the course in the future in order to do the following: _____

Exhibit 6-7   Skill Acquisition Plan

Another way of encouraging self-management on the part of employees is to initiate a self-monitoring chit system for spending training and development dollars. Under this system each employee is given a limited number of chits, representing dollars, for time spent in learning experiences. Employees themselves decide how and when to spend these chits on developmental experiences. This system combined with thoughtful career goal setting encourages employees to make responsible decisions about how to spend their development resources. An employee whose career goal is to move into a financial management position, is likely to spend more chits on accounting courses than on assertiveness training.

As practitioners continue to encourage employee self-management, they will need to encourage top management to support any necessary organizational changes. This may mean going to bat for increased funds for the tuition assistance program, recommending a more equitable arrangement for funding membership dues for professional associations, or encouraging a more liberal policy on interdepartmental job rotation. To pave the way for these suggestions practitioners should continually inform top management of program activities and results. This may be accomplished through periodic briefings and memos that report on what is being done and demonstrate the benefits accruing to the organization. (If the planning task force begun at the Preparation Stage is continuing its meetings, they are an excellent forum for this kind of reporting and discussion.)

Managerial Responsibilities.   Throughout this stage of the career development effort practitioners must constantly ask themselves the question, "Is what we are doing actually meeting the needs of the employees?"

This question has a multitude of answers, not all of which will be within the power of practitioners to answer. The best sources of information about the appropriateness of the various programs and efforts will be the managers and supervisors directly involved with the employee-participants. The supervisors and managers must be prepared, therefore, to provide direct one-on-one assistance to participants. Special orientation and training sessions may be conducted to help supervisors develop coaching skills, field questions about courses and seminars, determine ways to develop on-the-job learning experiences, and understand how to best provide an arena for the testing of new employee skills and abilities. Supervisors should be encouraged to use the career development practitioner as a consultant who can help iron out problems, answer questions, and interpret policies. This may range from clarifying who is eligible for tuition reimbursement to suggesting how completed seminars, workshops, and training programs can be included in performance appraisals.

A variety of responsibilities can be undertaken by managers, who directly supervise and appraise the performance of career development program participants. In some companies, managers have primary responsibility for counseling employees and identifying opportunities that will help them learn and grow. In others this is the responsibility of career development practitioner or the personnel staff, with managers simply approving requests for time-off.

The options for managers at the Execution Stage can be visualized on a continuum ranging from least active to most active involvement:

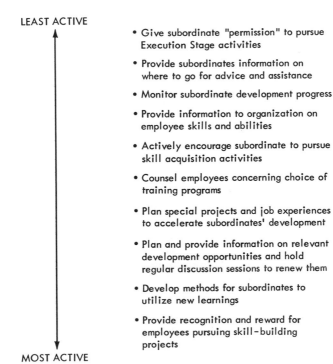

LEAST ACTIVE

- Give subordinate "permission" to pursue Execution Stage activities
- Provide subordinates information on where to go for advice and assistance
- Monitor subordinate development progress
- Provide information to organization on employee skills and abilities
- Actively encourage subordinate to pursue skill acquisition activities
- Counsel employees concerning choice of training programs
- Plan special projects and job experiences to accelerate subordinates' development
- Plan and provide information on relevant development opportunities and hold regular discussion sessions to renew them
- Develop methods for subordinates to utilize new learnings
- Provide recognition and reward for employees pursuing skill-building projects

MOST ACTIVE

Decisions concerning the degree of managerial responsibility largely depend on how the organization views such factors as the time to be spent by managers on career development activities; the availability of other resources, (such as personnel staff); the organization's practices pertaining to involvement of managers in existing human resource development activities; the attitudes of managers concerning employee career development; the existing capabilities of managers in career counseling; and the willingness and ability of managers to structure developmental experiences for subordinates.

An organization can conduct a highly effective career development program regardless of the degree to which it decides to involve managers. There is no single right way. The advantages of less involvement by managers include the following:

- Little additional time is required of managers when the career development program is initiated.
- Special training of managers is not necessary.
- Employees establish closer ties to other resource persons—personnel staff— who are likely to speak with one voice when counseling and coaching and who could become mentors to these employees.
- Employees may assume more personal responsibility for identifying and suggesting learning opportunities on their jobs.

Less involvement of managers will in turn require more involvement of practitioners, who will be required to provide the counseling, guidance, reassurance, and hand holding needed by employees to keep their career development efforts focused on their goals. Managers will require the support that in many cases only practitioners will have the background, knowledge, and information to provide.

Advantages of more managerial involvement include the following:

- Closer ties are established between manager and subordinate.
- Individuals closest to the actual work situation devise ways to increase its learning potential and to give rewards and recognition.
- Employees can turn to the most available resource for advice and information.
- Managers are more likely to fulfill ongoing responsibilities with employee career development in mind.
- Less time is required of personnel staff or other career development practitioner resources.

When managers do take an active part in the Execution Stage, career counseling about developmental opportunities is their primary responsibility. And this is often the function for which they are least prepared unless they are given special orientation and training. Organizations that do decide to have managers act as career counselors are likely to find they need to conduct training for managers in these roles. Managers need to acquire both substantive knowledge that can be passed on to employees and the process skills that will help them conduct counseling sessions.

The areas of substantive knowledge are

- Knowledge of the organization's career development program activities
- Knowledge of basic manpower requirements and plans in the organization
- Understanding of the resources available—internally and externally—that can facilitate employee development
- Familiarity with roles of others in the organization who may be able to provide further information and advice to employees
- Understanding of ways that developmental experiences might be structured in the immediate work setting

Process skills include

- The ability to effectively ask questions about career development goals
- The ability to actively listen
- The ability to give feedback
- The ability to establish an environment of trust and candor
- The ability to advise without putting others on the defensive

Managers who are prepared with appropriate information and skills should be able to conduct discussions which give employees advice and suggestions as well as general support and encouragement to select means of building skills. Discussions at this point may review previous stages of career development or may be limited to Execution Stage activities—enrollment in a course that an employee is contemplating, on-the-job training an employee has completed, or a job rotation assignment that an employee is considering. Managers should review employees' career strategy or action plan and any other pertinent information. The discussion is generally open-ended, using broad questions that allow the employee to discuss a wide range of development concerns.

At Hughes Aircraft, Space and Communications Group, a "communications exchange" is held six months prior to the performance appraisal. During the communications exchange, (Step 1) boss and subordinate each complete a ten question "fill in the blank" inventory that asks specific questions about career goals, plans to achieve those goals, and hoped-for developmental activities that might support the achievement of that goal. Supervisor fills out the form, employee fills out the form, and during the communications exchange, a third generalized form (Step II) is completed by both. Both maintain their own copy (Step I) and uses it only as a discussion tool. The communications exchange allows discussion to be centered around career-related problems and concerns and gives an opportunity for the supervisor to support developmental activities.

Most likely some of this discussion will take place in annual performance appraisals. Semi-annual discussions provide even greater information and support, and the manager should offer an opportunity for employees to initiate counseling whenever they feel a need for it.

The manager who takes an active role in assisting subordinates' at the Execution Stage will also take responsibility for planning ways in which the present job can help subordinates learn. Career discussions should provide a good information base for developing on-the-job experiences that provide such growth.

As a resource planner at the Execution Stage, the manager is called upon to exercise a high degree of creativity and to work closely with subordinates to develop new opportunities that do not conflict with accomplishing the necessary ongoing work.

The manager will need to recognize and reward employees for their activities at the Execution Stage through giving them personal feedback and through visibly calling their activities to the attention of others in the work unit. Completing special projects or assuming new responsibilities that lead to some visible change in operations, some clear benefit to the organization, give employees a sense of accomplishment and worth. This provides one of the most effective rewards for employers.

Two key questions should be continually asked by the manager who acts as resource planner:

- What can I do to help employees learn and grow?
- What can I do to reward their efforts to learn and grow?

Obviously the manager cannot promise that learning will immediately result in new job opportunities, and he must take care not to raise expectations unrealistically. Career discussions at the Execution Stage may include conveying to employees that the skills they gain may not immediately lead to actual job changes. They are, nevertheless, valuable to both the organization and the employee in the short term and, with proper assistance, will brighten the long-term prospects for all concerned.

DEMONSTRATING COMPETENCIES

How Do We Know What They've Learned?

So far in this discussion of the Execution Stage attention has been mostly focused on the role of the practitioner in establishing training programs and that of the manager in providing support and guidance. What sort of a responsibility do the participants in a career development effort have in making certain that the Execution Stage effectively achieves the plans they developed to accomplish their career goals?

The proof of the pudding is said to be in the eating. The proof of developmental efforts is in demonstrating the newly acquired skills, techniques, and behavior gained from the execution of career development plans.

The Four Stages of Learning. Before acquiring a particular skill, employees are at the first stage of the learning process, the level known as Unconscious Incompetence—they don't know (even what it is they need) but they don't know that they don't know. So they continue making errors and *not* demonstrating expertise in the desired area.

As employees begin to learn about themselves and what they want to accomplish, they begin to see new opportunities for growth and development. Slowly they begin to realize how much they do not know in a certain area and, as a result, they are able to name specific areas where they need further skill development. Thus they reach the second level of the learning process, Conscious Incompetence—they don't know, but now *know* that they don't know.

After goals have been established, plans have been developed, and resources for learning have been discovered and pursued, participants can begin to learn specific new skills and to develop new behavior. Step-by-step they achieve the third level of learning, Conscious Competence—they *now know,* but they *know* only well enough to be able to perform with a great deal of concentration and effort. (This may be achieved at the end of the Execution Stage).

This is the most uncomfortable stage of learning. The skill being learned, the behavior being attempted, the technique being practiced can only be done by applying determination and effort. Often the natural inclination at this point is to quit, walk away because doing it is too hard. The urge to go back to the comfort of the Unconscious Incompetence is great. At this stage employees will need all of the support, encouragement, and help that practitioners, managers, supervisors, peers, and the organization can muster. If they receive that support, if their efforts are noted and rewarded, employees will reach the fourth level of learning, Unconscious Competence—where they know, and know so well that the newly acquired skills and behavior become automatic, and they are ready to progress onward with those skills to some new career opportunity.

The purpose of the Execution Stage is to help employees achieve the

IV	Unconscious Competence
III	Conscious Competence
II	Conscious Incompetence
I	Unconscious Incompetence

Exhibit 6-8 The Four Stages of Learning

third level of learning, Conscious Competence, and to know that the fourth level, Unconscious Competence, can also be achieved through continued effort.

Come Blow Your Horn. Most people have a tendency to be modest about their achievements. So employees will, for instance, enroll in an educational or developmental program that could greatly enhance their careers, but through modesty or reluctance to toot their own horns they fail to let managers, practitioners, or anyone else within the organization know about it.

Practitioners must ensure that employees keep the organization informed about what they are doing, how they are doing, and what help they need.

Demonstrating skills gained through career development efforts is more than just letting others see what has been learned. At the level of Conscious Competence, employees will be trying to demonstrate these new skills, but because these skills are not fully internalized (to the point of Unconscious Competence,) mistakes will be made. If these mistakes are noted and the reasons for them are not appreciated, employees are very likely to give up or at least be reluctant to attempt the demonstration of other learning.

Another reason for "horn blowing" is so that the counseling that takes place during performance appraisals will have a basis for evaluation. Progress toward goals must be known so that support and reward can be given.

Practitioners, therefore, have a very special responsibility to: 1) encourage employees to make their efforts known; 2) document those efforts; and 3) keep managers, mentors, and others involved informed as to where participants stand.

The responsibility for the demonstration of competencies is, of course, that of the employee. Only the employees can show what they have learned, and only they can build upon those learnings to advance their career development efforts.

Practitioners and managers have the responsibility to provide support and feedback–support that encourages progress and feedback the participant aware of progress already made.

In addition, practitioners must make every effort to keep a clear, accurate record of employees' progress toward their goals. A great many methods and means exist for this documentation. Sample forms for this documentation are shown in Exhibits 6-9 and 6-10.

From these activity sheets, the practitioner can develop a file, cross-referenced by names of employees and types of activities, that gives easy access to an overview of career development progress. Exhibit 6-9 and Exhibit 6-10 are sample forms.

These reports can help the practitioner monitor individual progress,

Name: (Susan Jones)   Title: (Administrative Aide, Marketing Division)
Activities:
  1. Oct.–Dec., 1979
      On-the-job training—bookkeeping
  2. Jan., 1980
      In-house workshop— "Supervisory Practices"
  3. March, 1980
      Association membership: Women in Business, Inc.
  4. May–Aug., 1980
      Adult education course, Cranston College—Business Finance
Career goals:
Advancement into some phase of financial management—probably starting with
bookkeeping or junior analyst position.

Exhibit 6-9   Execution Activities: by Employee

Course title: _____   Date & Location: _____
Attendees:

_____   _____
_____   _____
_____   _____
_____   _____
_____   _____
_____   _____
_____   _____

Overview of learning reported:
Overview of use of learning reported:

Exhibit 6-10   Execution Activities: by Activity

assess the value of various activities, and report on progress to top
management. The problem with most documents, however, is that once
filed they are often never again seen. Establishing a system to periodically
review files on individuals in the career development program in order to
assess their progress at the Execution Stage would have many benefits.
When the organization is considering offering certain programs, for
example, the practitioner should use the file to check the results of similar
programs offered in the past. In this way the practitioner can keep up the
momentum of the career development effort and assure its fullest benefits
to individuals and the organization.

   The Execution Stage is an important one in which the organization, the
practitioner, and the individual all play strong roles. The results of
successfully completing this stage are worthwhile—employees acquire new

skills and become more proficient in their present jobs while preparing themselves to move on to one or more targeted career goals. The organization gains employees who manage their own growth and development and who are, due to the energizing and quality of this stage, more productive. The next chapter investigates methods of evaluating the entire career development experience in terms of its return on investment for the individual, the organization and the practitioner and methods of rewarding all of them for their efforts.

REAPING REWARDS
the integration stage

*"What will it cost us if we install the program?
What will it cost us if we don't?"*

The Integration Stage is the time to measure the change which has taken place, ascertain the value and effectiveness of the career development effort, and provide rewards for its managers and participants.

Although these functions rightly occur as the last stage of the career development effort, they have been major considerations from the beginning. In fact, unless they were built into the program from its inception, it will not be possible to effectively measure success or provide rewards. The basis for this final stage was considered and planned for when the effort was designed at the Preparation Stage. The major questions to be addressed now include: What have been the changes in the way human resources are to be used? What are the payoffs and benefits for individual employees and the organization in general? What are the effects of the program on individual and organizational productivity? How are individual participants to be rewarded for their perserverence and effort? What can be offered to managers who have encouraged employee growth, movement, and change?

To properly integrate the career development effort into the fabric of the organization so that it becomes a permanent ongoing program rather than a one-shot phenomenon, the practitioner must examine both the evaluation and the reward systems and determine how they can be best applied. However, since each organization is subject to different regulations, different contracts, different environmental factors, different customer-client-supplier relationships, and different policies and procedures, it will be necessary for practitioners to develop integration efforts that are tightly tied to their own particular circumstances.

This chapter provides guidelines based upon successful efforts in other organizations. Practitioners will have to choose those that might apply to their organizations, but they should also search for other means of evaluation and reward when necessary.

EVALUATION EFFORTS

Developing systems that effectively evaluate career development efforts is a headache for the practitioner. Although elaborate methods of human resource accounting are constantly being developed, practitioners still find that evaluation methods are inadequate and that it is difficult to judge the quality of organizational career planning practices. Despite much research in this area, it is difficult to quantify the specific return on investment that organizations receive for their human resource development efforts especially in the area of career development.

A recent survey of 225 organizations that had initiated career development programs showed that while the vast majority (82.9 percent) found them to be "effective" only 3 percent thought that they had been "very effective" and 54 percent rated their efforts as only "partially effective." Just under 75 percent thought that their programs were "very ineffective." The same survey, however, showed that the programs helped to fill management jobs from within organizations, helped to identify training needs, gave needed emphasis to high potential women and minorities who might have otherwise been lost in the corporate shuffle, and aided employees in their efforts to become more effective problem solvers and decision makers. A great many felt that the educational programs established as a part of the career development effort were successful![1]

It is felt that the results of this survey reflect less upon the effectiveness of career development programs than on the difficulties encountered in designing and carrying out effective evaluation mechanisms. The survey shows the need for establishing innovative and creative means of determining the effectiveness and benefits of career development programs.

Interestingly enough, many organizations underestimate the importance of evaluation and are content with a cursory evaluation from participants following the workshop portions of the career development program. Practitioners may be swayed by management to avoid this step (after all, it's costly, time-consuming, and may not provide the desired results) but should argue for its inclusion. Several ideas for evaluation are suggested in the preparation chapter since, ideally, evaluation technologies should be established at the inception of the program and continue throughout all six stages. The evaluation section of this chapter is designed to remind the practitioner of some crucial questions (Who?, What?, When?, and Where?), to elaborate on some simple "how's," and to press for, at minimum, a tracking or documentation of the various program components.

Who? All too quickly practitioners choose the program's participants to be the primary source of evaluation. Often the program audience is *not* the best group with whom to test the waters. Program participants may be overly optimistic because a trainer has been particularly dynamic or an activity personally meaningful, or they may have a negative predisposition because they have been coerced into attendance. These and other factors may influence their views and bias may result. Participants should be polled but need not be the only group to evaluate the effectiveness of the program.

Every programmatic intervention in an organization affects numerous important audiences. If these audiences are identified early, the practitioner can design appropriate evaluation techniques to gain their important feedback. The practitioner should consider the different vantage points of each group in order to understand just how the career development effort affects them. Some of the audiences that the practitioner will want to consider in determining an evaluation design include:

- Participants in the program: all those who have been targeted to attend the program.
- Managers of program participants: those supervisors or managers whose subordinates have attended the program.
- Top management: those at decision-making levels in the organization who approved the program and allocated funds.
- HRD staff: other human resource development specialists such as recruiters, and wage and compensation professionals, who may be affected by the program.

What? By polling the various audiences, the practitioner will learn what each audience will consider as evidence that the program has been successful. Once these "success indicators" have been collected, the list can be shaped further by considering whether or not a particular indicator is "measurable" either in a qualitative or in a more quantitative form.

Most practitioners have their own ideas of what should be evaluated beforehand, but it is best to move cautiously until all potential audiences and areas of evaluation have been studied. Some areas of evaluation for the various audiences have already been suggested in the preparation chapter (Chapter 2). Practitioners can develop their own list by questioning a random group of representatives of a particular audience about the indicators of success that are of importance to them. Practitioners can then decide what can feasibly be measured and what is useful to the organization.

When? Some evaluation activities can take place concurrently with the actual implementation of the program. Individual career development workshops can be evaluated at their completion and again, later on. Records can be kept on job posting systems as they are used and on the impact of their use on internal job changes over a certain period of time. Career development programs can also be evaluated in terms of short-term changes, three to twelve months following completion of the effort, or long-term, anywhere from one to five years after the initial implementation of the effort.

Determining when to gather data also depends on the kind of data one is going to collect. Initial reactions to the intervention, for example, are probably best collected immediately after the program has closed. On the other hand, data concerning learning and behavior change, as well as organizational and job change, is best collected after a certain time period has elapsed. Data on reduced turnover, improved performance, and so on is also best collected after a suitable period of time has elapsed.

Administering a pretest and a post-test with the same group would be ideal. Gaining information about a group prior to an intervention and then collecting data afterwards and measuring the change provides excellent data for evaluation. Preprogram data can be collected from any or all of the audiences or from a general sensing of the system.

Some organizations administer a climate study, a study that measures a wide variety of variables, several months prior to a program. The same study is then administered following the intervention. Companies using a climate study for career development then pay particular attention to the questions that address career development principles.

Evaluation should occur after the intervention and several times thereafter, covering a predetermined period of time. Practitioners are advised to recognize that the more they can evaluate at different points in time, the more chances they have to gain valuable data.

Where? Although the evaluation is conducted where the program has occurred, the practitioner should not forget that other parts of the organization will also be affected. A change in one part of the system will produce changes in other parts.

If a practitioner can utilize a control group, a group who has not experienced the intervention, and compare it to the group who has, the evaluation results are all the more credible valuable to the organization. In the preparation chapter, practitioners are warned to think carefully about where the effort should be launched, to start small, and to choose target groups carefully. Heeding these warnings will pay off in more effective evaluation at the Integration Stage.

How? There are a variety of methods for selecting data that can be used to evaluate the results of career development efforts. Using any one of them does not necessarily preclude the use of others. The method or combinations of methods that a practitioner selects will be contingent on the organization's specific informational needs and the results of the "who, what, when, and where" diagnosis.

Three approaches will be described briefly here: the use of records, observation techniques, and self-report measures.[2] The intent is not to describe every facet of these methodologies but to provide a summary of how each might be used in evaluating a career development effort.

Use of Records. Records are accounts of events that regularly occur in the system. When extensive records are kept as a matter of course, it may be easy for the practitioner to extract a substantial part of the data needed to determine specific activities that occurred, materials that were used, how and with whom activities took place, and changes that occurred over time. These records may include minutes of the planning and progress meetings; training sessions, or other developmental efforts; attendance records of development or administrative sessions; progress reports of subgroups and committees; and individual project or development plan progress reports.

This method yields credible evaluation information because it provides evidence of program events accumulated as they occurred rather than reconstructed later. They are also not affected by the experimenter's bias because they are independent of the career development practitioner. The major drawback of using existing records is that abstracting information from them and reorganizing that information into a usable form can be time consuming. Also, ethical or legal constraints are often involved in examining certain records. Some examples of existing records that might be used in evaluation efforts include documentation of instances in which employees (1) sought supervisory help or help from the personnel staff, (2) visited the career planning center, (3) updated their skills inventories, (4) used the job posting system, (5) requested tuition reimbursement for further skill training, or (6) sent unsolicited memos regarding their career progress or feelings about a particular part of the program. Another record would be the employees annual performance appraisal.

A format similar to Exhibit 7-1 for using existing records as a means of evaluation might be beneficial.

One might review the record and performance rating prior to the career development effort and again afterward to see if there have been any changes in the employees' performance in any number of evaluation dimensions as viewed by their managers. One could also record changes in employee-initiated grievances—these grievances *could* indicate a change in morale or a change in attitudes toward career paths and development possibilities. Asking to see records that are kept by the organization as a matter of course will usually not be seen as burdensome by those departments asked to share them. Often the extra burden of specially recording

Critical Characteristic	Record(s)	Available from:	Use
1. Level of Participation	1a. Roster of Program Participants	1a. CD Progress Office Files	1a. Overall numbers throughout effort.
	1b. CD Workshop attendance lists	1b. CD Program Office Files	1b. Specific workshop attendance. Consistency of attendance.
	1c. Training/ Development attendnace lists	1c. Training Department Office	1c. Specific training received by participants in skill development

Exhibit 7-1 Format for Using Records in Evaluation

events is the major drawback to fully using this particular evaluation device.

EVALUATION STEPS BASED ON THE USE OF RECORDS

1. Develop a list of critical features.
2. Determine what records are already being kept that are available (for example, performance appraisals—changes in performance appraisals might indicate behavior changes).
3. Match the critical features list with available records. For each type of record, try to find a critical program feature about which the record might give information. Think about whether a record will yield evidence of duration or frequency of an activity.
4. Prepare a sampling plan for collecting records and a plan for transferring data from the records examined.
5. Consider a means for obtaining access to records that does not inconvenience other people.

Observation Techniques. Using observation as an evaluation method requires that one or more individuals devote their attention to the behavior of current or former program participants for a prescribed time period. In some cases the observer may be given detailed guidelines about who or what to observe, when and how long to observe, and the method for recording that information. A tally sheet might be devised for such purposes. (If supervisors serve as observers they will need special training and guidance as the "halo effect" or the "horns effect" (a rating higher or lower than is fair due to predetermined biases) can impair their observations.

One way to enhance the credibility of observations is by demonstrating that the data from the observations is consistent, within acceptable limits, among different observers over time. An advantage of this method is that observations can be highly credible when seen as a report of what actually took place. Furthermore observers can provide a point of view different from that of staff members who are more closely connected with the program. (This is especially true if observers are seen as disinterested viewers.) One disadvantage of the observation technique is that awareness of the observers' presence may alter what takes place. Also much time is needed to develop observation instruments, to locate and train credible observers, and to organize schedules.

Events that might be observed during or after a career development effort are behavior changes toward colleagues and supervisors, the way employees apply to their present jobs the information they have gained, changes in the way supervisors guide their own subordinates, increased assertiveness, or requests for more responsibility.

> At Lawrence Livermore Labs, the case study is used to present a sample of participants after a program has been initiated. It is used to report participant actions and reactions and to note changes and impressions of individuals across time. The Lab has used these "scenarios" to describe the changes in the individuals who have moved through their career development workshops. The studies are prepared by the practitioner after long interviews with individuals and people who know them. They are used to convince management of specific charges occurring in individuals who participate in workshops.

EVALUATION BASED ON OBSERVATIONS

1. List the critical program features.
2. Prepare descriptions of positive actions, such as assuming more personal responsibilities or seeking on-the-job training that participants might demonstrate after the program.
3. Prepare descriptions of negative actions (alternative but undesirable program side effects, such as demanding promotion today or complaining about the transfer policy). Describe the most likely ways in which things can go wrong so that observers will know what to document.
4. Choose an observation method and decide how long each observation time sample should last in order to yield acceptable data.
5. Prepare a sampling plan for conducting observations.
6. Prepare observer tally sheets.
7. Select and train observers.
8. Try out the instrument.
9. Inform the program staff about the forthcoming observation.
10. Conduct observations, then score and prepare data for interpretation and presentation.

Self-Report Measures. Self-report measures are collected through interviews, questionnaires, logs, or journals. If collecting information from everyone who experienced the program is too time consuming, self-report descriptions can be culled from a random sample of participants. Since different groups of participants in a program might have divergent perceptions, the practitioner will want to gather self-report information from all levels of employees within the organization who have been involved in the program—nonexempt and exempt employees, first-line supervisors, middle managers, and members of senior management. Self-reports may also be solicited from members of the personnel staff who supported the program and from clients or organizational peer groups who may have experienced spinoffs of program results.

Data generated using self-report measures is best used to substantiate or enhance other more quantifiable findings. Using this evaluation method by itself, however, may leave the practitioner open to questions of data validity. Those who are closest to a program will be inclined to see such information as highly credible, while those more distant from the program (higher levels of management), are less likely to trust the self-reported information published by the practitioner's staff. They have a point. Sometimes those providing self-report information have a vested interest in making the program look good or bad, and they may not even be aware of it. If, as often happens, certain subconscious mechanisms reduce cognitive dissonance, individuals may overlook (or rationalize) program shortcomings or disregard potential problem areas. A great many programs are judged to be successful if participants have had a good time or have experienced a high energy, motivating presentation even though they have learned little that is of lasting value. The real test of a successful workshop or seminar lies in the amount of learning retained and the length of time that the information is retained by participants. Experiences that are enjoyable while imparting constructive knowledge will always rate high with participants, but first reactions often measure only the level of pleasure the program provided.

Self-report descriptions of a program are clearly second-hand accounts of what transpired—the evaluator tells a particular audience what people say they did! As a secondary source, however, they are still useful. With these cautions in mind, various self-reporting instruments are presented in this section.

The *questionnaire* method of self-reporting has several advantages—it can (1) provide answers to a variety of questions in a relatively short period of time (especially if questionnaires are precoded), (2) be given to many employees throughout the company simultaneously without having to train interviewers, and (3) present uniformly organized information by asking all respondents for the same information. Questionnaires allow the respondent time to think before answering, thereby, providing a chance for reflection and personal insight.

Questionnaires have disadvantages in that they do not provide the flexibility that interviews do. Some people are better able to express themselves in writing than others. And unless the wording of questions is carefully thought out and pilot tested for clarity, the practitioner is likely to

The Metropolitan Water District of Southern California used an evaluation which included surveys sent to participants and their supervisors. Supervisors were asked whether participants' performance had increased, decreased, or remained the same in the following areas:

—Quality of work   —Initiative
—Quantity of work   —Adaptability
—Dependability   —Attitude
—Judgment   —Potentiality

Among questions asked of participants were those relating to actions they had taken since the workshop. They were given a list of possible actions— ranging from discussing skills with supervisors to using new techniques at work—and asked which they had undertaken and how well those worked. They also were asked to list their career goals and indicate whether they had initiated action toward them. Finally, they had an opportunity to identify changes in certain personal attributes, such as self-confidence, feelings about their current jobs, relations with supervisors and coworkers, and attitudes about their career futures.

find that respondents have imposed their own unique interpretations on the questions, thereby providing little usable data for analysis. The unpredictable rate of return poses another serious problem of using questionnaires. A practitioner must plan several appeals for the return of questionnaires if this method is to be effective.

Interviews, on the other hand, are good for those who communicate best verbally. Interviews permit flexibility and allow the interviewer time to pursue unanticipated lines of inquiry. The interviewer can often gain a great deal of information. Disadvantages are, however, that interviewing is time-consuming and that sometimes the interviewers can by their nonverbal or verbal behavior unduly influence the response of the interviewees.

It is important to remember when conducting interviews to always ask open-ended questions. Questions that can be answered yes or no and those that imply a specific answer will not generate a great deal of information. Compare the following for the potential information they will elicit:

Closed Question	*Open Ended Question*
1. You are an accountant, right?	1. How would you describe the work you do here?
2. Did you like the career development presentation?	2. What are your feelings about the presentation?
3. Do you intend to go to more of them?	3. What would you like to see given in other presentations?
4. How many OJT programs have you taken part in?	4. Tell me about some of the OJT efforts you have taken part in.

It may occasionally be necessary to probe participants in order to gain additional information. The interviewer may need to encourage the interviewee to give additional information relating to the previous question. Probes might be statements such as, "Tell me more about that," "Expand on that, please," or "I find that fascinating." Questions might include, "What are some of those things that increase ability?" or "What are some of the likely long-range consequences of that action?"

The major drawback to using interview data in evaluating a program lies in the difficulty experienced when trying to quantify and summarize it. Although feelings, opinion, and experiences can be extracted, they seldom fall into any but the most generalized categories for quantification. It is possible, however, to ask quantitative questions and use the open-ended approach to provide back-up data.

Logs, journals, and diaries are less formal descriptions of activities, experiences, and feelings written by a participant either during or after a specific career development activity. Asking people to keep self-reports with accounts of their experience can be an effective data-gathering device, provided there is agreement from participants and an understanding between participants and their managers that this will not in any way affect job standing. When analyzed at the end of the program, these accounts can aid the practitioner in understanding the positive and negative experiences of participants with various components of the program. In addition the logs might reveal patterns of attitude change. Logs and journals can also be kept by managers to record changes in the work habits of subordinates who have been involved in career development activities. Diaries, on the other hand, are more private self-report instruments. They are kept by participants themselves and, while they cannot be collected and read by program evaluators without prior agreement, participants can be encouraged to review them prior to providing interview or questionnaire responses or to use them as a source from which to provide evaluators with representative quotes or extracts.

The advantage of these informal procedures is that they provide information about a person's experiences and feelings. The disadvantage lies in the problems of extracting, categorizing, and interpreting the information and in the ethical issues raised when using such information. To score and interpret information in this process also requires time and expertise. Accordingly deciding to use logs and journals and establishing plans for collecting and using the information they contain must occur at the beginning of the program if this method is to be used.

Clearly an advantage of this approach is that minimal demands are made on the practitioner's staff to record data. Furthermore by submitting these written reports, participants feel as if their experiences are noted and considered important, and they are more inclined to observe incremental changes in themselves and their behavior over time than they would be without this historical comparative data.

EVALUATION BASED ON SELF-REPORT MEASURES

1. List the program's critical features and the questions you want answered.
2. Decide if you already have the information in existing records.
3. Decide whether to distribute questionnaires, to interview, or to do both.
4. Write questions, based on the critical program features, that will prompt people to tell you what they said and did differently as a result of participation in the program.
5. Assemble the questionnaire or interview instrument.
6. Determine how many times to distribute questionnaires or conduct interviews, when to do it, and to which people/groups.
7. Try out the instrument on a small subsample. (Revise if needed).
8. Alert people that you will be requesting periodic information.
9. Administer the instrument according to a predetermined sampling plan.
10. Record data from questionnaires and interview instruments.

Prepare a data analysis summary.

Return on Investment—The Bottom Line

One of the most important, yet also most difficult, calculations about the effectiveness of a career development effort is the total cost savings for the organization. How can the organization put a price tag on the dollars that have been saved, and how does that compare with dollars that have been spent implementing the program?

Measuring the human return on investment of any program—be it a long-term career development effort or a one-time training endeavor—has been the subject of much debate and experimentation in business and industry. It requires that human resource costs be viewed as investments similar to capital investments and that the return on the dollars invested somehow be translated into quantifiable terms that can be compared with the investment expenditures.

One method for making such calculations is to compare earnings—the ultimate goal of most companies—with payroll expenses. Return on investment in human resources can be measured by dividing the total payroll costs (including fringes and training) into pretax earnings. A department that increases earnings faster than it increases payroll costs can be viewed as increasing its human return on investment. This may be due to higher employee productivity, increased employee skills, holding the line on salaries, or work force reductions.

When such measurements are taken before and after a program aimed at human resource development, they may indicate some tangible results of that program. However, several problems are inherent in this method of measurement. First, there are likely to be numerous confounding variables operating during the measurement period that make it difficult to determine whether or not the program concerned is responsible for the noted results. At any given time other factors may be occurring—such as the introduction of new technology or new operating procedures—that could also be responsible for changes in earnings and payroll.

Additionally not all units of the organization are directly concerned with earnings. Thus, staff offices such as personnel or accounting would need different methods for measuring return on investment in human resources.

One method of calculating the return on investment within the participating target group involves measuring changes in those cost areas that are most likely to be influenced by the career development program and other intervening variables. Three major areas that may be adapted to such measurement are reduced turnover, improved performance, and fewer grievances. Examples of cost savings calculations in these areas follow:

Reduced Turnover. The career practitioner should determine the employee turnover rates within the participating group before and after the career development intervention. The change, expressed as a percentage of the prior rate, is one measure of the program's contribution to reduced turnover. As an example, suppose the turnover was initially 10 percent per year, and the post-program rate drops to 8 percent; the turnover reduction is 2 percent per year, corresponding to an improvement of 20 percent. Of course, one obvious disclaimer is that the career development program is not performed in a vacuum; many outside factors will almost certainly influence the turnover rate, such as changes in the economy, management decisions, and variations in the demand for certain professional services.

The practitioner then computes all of the costs associated with turnovers within the target group. These include severance pay for the departing employees, lost productivity during the periods their positions are vacant, and the recruitment, selection, and training of their replacements. These costs should be expressed on a per turnover basis.

The resulting annual cost saving is simply the number of program participants, times the reduction in turnover rate, times the turnover cost. For example, the reduced turnover financial gain might be 300 participants times 2 percent less annual turnover times $10,000 replacement costs, which equals $60,000 per year.

Improved Performance. It should be stated immediately that increased productivity is difficult to quantify except in specialized cases, such is the case where there is increased sales volume or some other measurable quantity of work output, or, alternatively, the need for a smaller number of employees to accomplish a specific task due to increased efficiency, job enrichment, or newly acquired skills on the part of current employees.

An example of a case involving increased sales volume might be the case of a retail store where sales in a particular department increase by 5 percent, from $100,000 per month to $105,000 for a productivity gain of $5,000 per month, after the completion of a career development effort.

An example of a case involving increased work output might be the case of an organization where secretaries, having identified career goals in common with company needs, complete some basic accounting courses, saving the company $20,000 per year for a bookkeeper.

Fewer Grievances.   Improved compliance on the part of management with affirmative action goals may ultimately reduce the number of grievance actions with resultant savings in legal costs and back pay settlements.

For example, if the incidence of employee grievances drops by 25 percent within a minority target group, the company might reduce its affirmative action legal expenses by several hundred thousand dollars per year, with corresponding savings in settlement costs.

There are also many important aspects to a career development effort for which the return on investment (ROI) must necessarily be assessed in nonmonetary currencies. These can include:

- improved morale resulting from the feeling that the company cares about its employees
- appreciation of existing skills and their applicability to other job functions within the organization
- increased self-esteem and self-confidence
- identification of individual career goals and the means to achieve them
- heightened sense of community and the establishment of organizational support groups
- increased understanding of internal human resource development processes, such as performance appraisals

It is also important that the practitioner realize that the career development effort's payoff does not come only after the individual has moved through all six stages; there is substantial qualitative and quantitative return on investment for the individual and for the organization at the conclusion of each stage. During the preparation stage practitioners may have developed their own lists of return on investment factors for each stage (a good selling tool for top management), and they may now want to refer to it again to guide or check their program results. Exhibit 7-2 shows the potential return on investment (ROI) at each stage of the effort.

PREPARATION	• Increased organizational insight: Organization has assessment of how individuals view their careers and where the greatest problems lie. • Special selection of target groups: group needs are identified. • Formalized planning: Organization has a formal plan for developing its human resources. • Employee commitment to program and organization: Individuals are appraised of programs and have opportunity to affect what happens to them. • Increased management commitment to organization goals: Managers are prepared and apprised of their role in the process.
PROFILING	• Increased self-understanding: Employees gain understanding of their own personal, technical, and conceptual skills, their values and preferred work contexts. • Accurate self-appraisal: Employees seek opportunities to test the realities of their self-assessments in their professional and personal network. • Improved communication on performance appraisals: Employees will be able to determine their professional strengths and weaknesses and the areas that they wish to develop. • Increased organization understanding of employee proficiencies: Organization has documentation of employee skill areas needed.
TARGETING	• Employee understanding of organizational goals and directions: Future trends and their impact on career discussions and alternatives are clear to employees. • Flexibility in career goals: Employees have set a variety of career goals. • Matching of organizational goals and employee goals: Goals are viable and used by the organization in its human resource planning. • Increased understanding of promotional system: Qualifications for advancement and proficiency are clearly understood. • Increased employee understanding of organizational job requirements: Employees will have clear understanding of performance criteria and performance expectations.
STRATEGIZING	• Increased management employee interaction: Development plans are devised and commitment is strengthened by dialogues between manager and employee. • Training and development option studied: Individuals are aware of strengths and deficiencies and of resources offered by the organization to improve certain skill areas. • Training and development needs identified: practitioners are aware of the training and development that will be needed by employees and can formalize plans to offer such programs. • Goals and timetables developed: Affirmative action candidates develop action plans for mobility in the organization. These are in line with affirmative action goals. • Increased employee understanding of organizational direction: Individuals will be abreast of organizational directions and will be able to plan ther careers accordingly. Employees will meet career goals.

EXECUTION	• Improve selection of training and development activities: Employees are selective about the developmental options they enter.
	• Documentation efforts strengthened: Skills and competencies are strengthened by the organization as they are acquired by individuals.
	• Cost effectiveness in training and development: Training programs that are frills (not related to any specific career goals) are eliminated.
INTEGRATION	• Evaluation systems are developed: Support is provided for improvements.
	• C.D. efforts are documented: Practitioners can enhance and continue the career development effort.
	• Reward systems strengthened: Compensation systems support other directions besides upward mobility.
	• Increased mobility: A substantial number of individuals move vertically, laterally, and enrich their jobs.
	• Greater organizational flexibility: Organization will be able to keep abreast of and be responsive to changing work force trends and patterns.
	• Improved work climate. Organization will have a healthy growth climate and stable work force.

Exhibit 7-2   Potential Return on Investment at Each Stage

At Least Document

If serious evaluation is not possible, practitioners should at the very least document and report on the process. Documenting a career development effort details the way in which the various stages were implemented and makes results available to all those who need to use them further.

Few documentation efforts pay enough attention to the program processes that helped achieve certain outcomes. Although some reports might contain short descriptions of the program's major features, such as the workshops developed, the manager-employee interactions, the structural supports, and the special skill training programs, most reports leave readers with only a vague notion of how often and for what duration particular activities occurred or of how components combined to affect the daily life of employees in the organization. Few reports clearly picture what the program is actually like, and of those that do, most do not give enough attention to verifying the picture that is presented. Some form of final report is essential—it forces the practitioner to pay attention to all critical features, provides a way for others to continue the program once the first effort is completed, and helps the reader to understand the differences between a good and poor career development effort.

A report of program implementation should contain (1) a description in as much detail as possible of the interventions (such as workshops and counseling) and the structural elements (such as performance appraisal and job posting systems) that characterize the career development effort, and (2) a description of back-up data that comes from a variety of sources and ensures thoroughness and accuracy.

A Worthy Fuss.   It is important to record a description of the career development effort for internal and possible external documentation purposes. This kind of documentation can be useful to an organization in a variety of ways. However, the job is not easy.

Sometimes the expected outcomes of career development efforts are intangible and difficult to measure. Sometimes the outcomes are re-moved—they often occur after the program has concluded and the participants have moved on. (Career success stories, continued job mobility, and continued coaching of one's own employees are good examples). In such instances judging a program completely on the basis of immediate outcomes would be unfair. Even when career development activities result in intangible or removed outcomes, the practitioner must precisely specify the processes that were used.

A documented report may be the only description of the program that will remain after a particular career development effort has concluded. Reports should for that reason provide an accurate account of the program and include sufficient detail so that they can serve as a planning guide for those who might want to expand the career development effort to another division of the company. Furthermore, other professionals need to know the characteristics of the program—the materials, activities, interventions, and interchanges that brought about the program's outcomes. A docu-mented report about a particular effort can strongly suggest to organiza-tion decision makers that using similar processes for other programs or aiming toward other similar goals is a positive move.

Clearly, knowing how a report will be used will help the practitioner to determine how much effort to invest in it as well as what information about actions and changes will be most useful to top management or planners. If accountability is the major reason for the documentation effort, the practitioner should be ready to provide back-up data to show whether and to what extent particular events vital to the process occurred and were successful. The more skeptical the audience, the greater the necessity for providing formal back-up data to verify the accuracy of the program description. Sometimes reports must be backed up with measurement, such as coded observations by trained observers, examination of program output, structured interviews, or questionnaires. Carefully planned and executed measurement will allow the practitioners to be reasonably certain that the information they report describes accurately the situation at hand, especially if the practitioner expects to confront a serious skeptic.

A documentation report on the implementation of a career development program should include as a minimum the following five sections:

1. *Summary Statement.* A summary should give readers a quick synopsis of what is contained in the report—why the program was conducted, the type of evaluation mechanisms used, and the major findings and recommendations of the evaluation.
2. *Program Description.* A description of the program context should focus on the settings (off-site, on-site), the personnel involved, and special resources that were prepared and used. This section would also describe how the program was initiated, what it was supposed to do, and how resources were used. The origins of the program and historical background, the factors that went into preparing the program, and the selected target groups are all described in this section.
3. *Critical Features.* This section should describe the program's most critical features as prescribed by the original program design at the Preparation Stage. Here the practitioner could describe what the program was supposed to include, how much variation it allowed, its theory on philosophical stance, the rationale underlying the program, the provisions that were made for reviewing the program, and the results of planning meetings that helped to remedy programmatic problems as they occurred.
4. *Evaluation Measures.* This section should specify the focus of the evaluation, the range of measurement instruments for data collection, the checks that were made on validity and reliability, and the limitations or deficiencies that might be inherent in the sampling process.
5. *Program Results.* This section should describe the extent to which the program as implemented fits the design that was originally planned at the Preparation Stage. It should describe what was found through analysis, noting variations of the program across divisions or time. The report should conclude with an interpretation of the results and suggestions for further program evaluation or program development.

Tell, Tell, Tell. Career development practitioners have responsibility not only for documenting the results of their efforts but also for distributing the report to various organizational audiences. Publicity is necessary for future efforts. There is no such thing as an evaluation that is free of political considerations. Presenting evaluation information provides an opportunity to gain continued support for the career development effort. The desires of various audiences should be seriously examined, both at the beginning of the evaluation and throughout the evaluation process. The following key questions must be answered:

- Who needs to know about the program?
- Which groups and which key people need to have their specific needs addressed?
- What information must be provided to those people?
- What problems might be encountered in giving information to each particular audience about the career development efforts?

The career development effort has many audiences. Already identified are the participant, the participant's manager, the organization's top management, and the career development practitioner. Additional audiences might include a customer or client, a group or division that did not yet participate in the program, or other members of the human resource development staff anxious to see the results. Neglecting to correctly identify one or more of these groups is a common mistake, and an ignored audience may cause problems and be nonsupportive of future program efforts. Identifying the audiences who are to receive the evaluation report is critical if the practitioners hope that their findings will lead to approved continuation of the career development efforts.

It is also important to find out what information each group needs and why it needs it. This is a vital component in producing a good evaluation design and in reporting evaluation results. Different groups want different information—often even when they ask the same question. Some groups will be certain and candid about what they need because they want the evaluation of the career development program to support a particular point of view they hold. Other audiences will not know what they want until they *don't* see it. If the career development practitioner wants the audience to listen carefully to the findings, attention must be given to each group and their specific idiosyncracies. This understanding is especially important in anticipating the kinds of situations that will trigger negative responses from a given group. In reporting particular audience, the practitioner should plan a strategy beforehand: it is rare that the same report or manner of reporting will work for more than one group.

While evaluation methodologies can demonstrate some clear rewards to individuals and the organization, participants and their managers desire to reap more tangible rewards from their investment in the process. Therefore it is imperative that the Integration Stage also address organizational reward systems and ways in which those systems can inspire individuals to grow and inspire managers to assist in that growth. The next section of this chapter addresses that issue.

REWARD SYSTEMS

What is a reward?

To some it is additional money. To others a reward might be a pat on the back, an extra day off, a chance to attend a professional conference, a trophy or certificate on the wall, a promotion, or a job change.

A great many people and organizations get nervous when rewards are mentioned. They automatically think of pay systems and compensation programs that have been carefully worked out with unions and boards of directors and cannot be tampered with except under extreme conditions.

Practitioners attempting to find ways to encourage employee and management participation in career development programs will be faced with a host of problems when the subject of rewards comes up. What is a reward for one person may be laughed at by another; a suitable reward for one person may be no trouble at all, while the only positive incentive for another is something closely regulated by company or union policy—or even forbidden by state or federal regulations.

For these reasons providing rewards and recognition that are meaningful to the individual is a task that will require a great deal of thought and creativity.

Consider these cases:

- Martha Brown has been a secretary in the General Counsel's office for seven years. During the past year she has completed two college courses in paralegal techniques and has successfully carried out a lengthy legal research project. She can qualify for one of two paralegal positions in her office only after another year of college study. It is doubtful that one will become open immediately.
- Bruce Morse is a bookkeeper in a consulting firm. His supervisor, the firm's accountant, has encouraged him to further his learning by giving him increasing accounting responsibilities while he is beginning a series of adult education courses toward a Certified Public Accountant qualification. In the meantime he must still perform his bookkeeping duties for the firm.

Typically organizations want to encourage and retain valuable employees. But the ultimate reward of advancement to higher level positions may be a long way off. Management and career development practitioners must create a structure that will accommodate additional systems that provide incentives for employees to increase their value to the organization.

The organization's structural responses at the Integration Stage require a great deal of creativity—even risk taking. These responses may include rewards for employees who increase their learning and performance, rewards for caring managers who contribute to the development of subordinates, and the establishment of monetary and nonmonetary systems for determining and administering new forms of compensation and promotion opportunity. These options must be within the realm of practicality for the organization, and these creative devices must be supported by a system that monitors progress in order to determine responses that are perceived as equitable for all employees and as beneficial to the organization.

A Just Reward

For students of organizational psychology and managers of organizations the issue of appropriate employee rewards has spawned a great deal of head scratching and hand wringing but very little firm conviction. The question has been approached from angles as diverse as reward and punishment, job satisfaction, and punitive incentives. Research and experiments have attempted to shed light on the quagmire of confounding variables ranging from working conditions and fringe benefits to autonomy and participation in the decision-making processes of the organization. To date positive conclusions remain elusive, and the only clear answers seem to lie in understanding that different people feel rewarded by different things.

Several ideas if not concrete conclusions have emerged. First, it appears that for any organizational strategy to be seen as a reward, it must be both important to the individual and not presently being provided or available. For example, extra vacation days may be used as a reward; but for those who do not make use of currently available leave time, the need for time off will have little real impact as a reward. Bigger desks, private offices, and other prestigious benefits may be important for some and therefore rewarding, but those who attach little significance to such amenities will view them as no reward at all.

The immediacy of rewards is also important. Just as correction or reprimand must immediately follow the commission of an error, accomplishments must be rewarded as soon after the fact as possible to stimulate further achievement. Employees who complete a February training program that provides them with new skills will not necessarily feel rewarded by a bonus in December to recognize that particular achievement. Similarly if organizations desire to use time off as a reward for outstanding performance, they must make clear the restrictions attached to this time off. Some people want to save up reward days or compensatory time off and build minivacations with them. If this is contrary to the manager's personal desires or organizational policy, the refusal to grant such a minivacation becomes a punishment in the eyes of the employees, and the reward system has backfired.

Several additional conclusions stemming from research on reward systems are summarized as follows:

- Satisfaction with a reward is a function of both how much is received and how much the individual feels should be received.
- Overall job satisfaction is influenced by how satisfied employees are with both the intrinsic rewards (those associated with personal fulfillment, such as interesting work, responsibility, and opportunities for growth) and the extrinsic rewards (pay, benefits, status, and working conditions) they receive from their jobs.
- People differ widely in the rewards they desire and in how important the different rewards are to them.
- Many extrinsic rewards are important and satisfying only because they lead to other rewards.[3]

The Practitioner's Dilemma. Perhaps no function of the career development effort poses so great a challenge to the practitioner as determining appropriate rewards for employees who develop in other than clear vertical directions. There is no cookbook solution that can prescribe the precise ingredients or quantities which will be interpreted as rewards in any given organization or for any given employee. Those rewards outside the normal pay and promotion systems are especially difficult to design and deploy.

Clearly, the career development practitioner can best seek advice and support from the organization's compensation people and should, if possible, examine the problem jointly with them. Still, it is incumbent upon the practitioner to understand the basic concepts of how rewards work, to recognize the range of options for developing reward systems, to know what rewards are currently being used in the organization and with what results, and to continually seek to understand differences in employees' perception of what is rewarding.

Most reward systems contain four basic properties:

1. The system must make enough rewards available so that each individual's basic needs are satisfied.
2. The reward levels in the organization must compare favorably with those in other organizations.
3. The rewards that are available must be distributed in a way that is seen as equitable by the people in the organization.
4. The reward system must deal with organization members as individuals, recognizing their individuality by giving them the kinds of rewards they desire.[4]

Options for rewards other than pay and promotion fall into five categories: (1) Fringe benefits—such as leave time, pension profit-sharing plans, executive prerogatives, and insurance (this benefit is usually constrained by agreement with insurance companies and administrative problems). (2) Status—such as increased influence in decision making and greater personal autonomy. (3) Job conditions—such as bigger offices, longer lunch hours, and parking spaces. (4) Recognition—such as notations in personnel files, verbal praise, and formal employee award bulletins. (5) Bonuses—such as annual cash awards or a work group sharing in productivity savings.

When possibilities for movement within career development efforts—vertical movement, lateral movement, downward movement, job enrichment, and exploration—are weighed against these properties and possibilities, the complexity of the problem can be fully appreciated. A lateral move, for instance, may fulfill an individual's need for variety and growth, but may also cut down on time off and executive perq's, reduce status, make for less desirable job conditions, and provide less recognition. How then can an extrinsic reward be provided? Other than the intrinsic reward of growth what can be done to make persons who have made such a move feel that the organization endorses and supports their growth?

The practitioner seeking ways to reward individual career development should first assess what rewards are currently being used in the organization, who is receiving them, and why they are received. It may help to develop a complete picture of the organization's reward systems by completing a format such as the Reward Programs Survey shown in Exhibit 7-3.

In order to collect this information, the practitioner may need to ask departments to complete these or similar forms and to comment about the effectiveness of various rewards. Since reward systems often vary throughout the organization, this survey may aid the practitioner in discovering some highly effective reward strategies developed by only one segment (or department) that can be adapted for broader use in the organization.

Reward Programs Survey				
Type of System	Divisions or units using	Number of Eligible employees	Specific achievements rewarded	Frequency
Fringe Benefits (monetary or otherwise)				
Status (titles and other symbols of status)				
Job Conditions (environmental factors)				
Recognition (all approaches)				
Bonuses (monetary or otherwise)				

Exhibit 7-3   Reward Programs Survey

The next step for the practitioner is to determine what rewards now being employed might be valuable for wider use. Since rewards are highly personal, this may require collecting information about what is important to employees. Written surveys or group meetings with employees participating in the career development effort can often supply information that will lead to ideas for developing more effective reward systems.

Other Creative Options

Most current organizational reward systems rely on techniques that have been used for a considerable time, such as bonus pay, employee-of-the-month recognition, extra leave or vacation time, and an occasional pat on the back. Thinking beyond these, practitioners can expand the options into new and more experimental strategies that have only recently come into use.

One such option for offering rewards is the cafeteria style benefit package. By giving employees personal choice in how they apply a benefit bank account, this system allows them to select the reward(s) most meaningful to them. They may take a financial reward in the form of a lump sum bonus, increased medical coverage, paid leave, increased retirement benefits, or whatever makes most sense to them, up to the amount of the benefits they have earned. If cash rewards are to be offered as part of the career development reward system, these can also be flexible in order to accommodate different personal desires.

Job enrichment itself (a detailed discussion appears in the Targeting Stage Chapter) is an area of nonmonetary reward that is currently undergoing extensive investigation and experimentation. A convenient way to view the job's potential for enrichment is to think of two axes: vertical (the opportunities the job provides to participate in decisions affecting it and to take control over the various tasks involved) and horizontal (the variety and number of tasks involved). Efforts to enrich jobs on both dimensions have a high potential for being viewed as rewards by employees, as Exhibit 7-4 shows.

For example, by increasing supervisory task orientation to encompass entire projects rather than functional parts of many projects, an organization could increase variety on the horizontal axis. If greater autonomy over work scheduling were included, this would expand the vertical dimension. The organization must be careful not to simply add more tasks in the name of job enrichment. This horizontal loading has been attacked by unions as a method of increasing the quantity of work without increasing pay.

Performance feedback is yet another source of reward subject to much recent attention. Organizations are increasingly devising ways to guarantee adequate and timely face-to-face feedback from superior to subordinate.

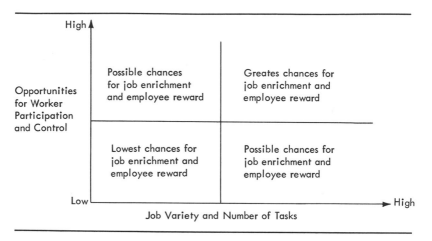

High

Opportunities
for Worker
Participation
and Control

	Possible chances for job enrichment and employee reward	Greates chances for job enrichment and employee reward
	Lowest chances for job enrichment and employee reward	Possible chances for job enrichment and employee reward

Low

High

Job Variety and Number of Tasks

Exhibit 7-4   Job Factors that Can Lead to Enrichment[5]

The strategies being employed include broader participating in the objective setting and review process, annual or semi-annual performance appraisal formats that require objective discussions of performance, and training in informal feedback techniques for managers. Employees can gain a substantial sense of reward through simple verbal recognition from superiors.

Finally, many organizations are looking to the provision of alternative work patterns as a nonmonetary incentive and reward system. One strategy in this area, flexible work hours, allows employees to choose when to arrive at and leave from work—generally with a core time during which they must be present and with requirements for total number of work hours per week. Other alternative work pattern experiments include the four-day work week, choices in when to take vacation holiday leave, and sabbaticals. While these arrangements can seldom be applied to reward individual performance, they can be adapted to groups of employees in the same function or unit.

A great many organizations that had previously opposed "flex time" and variable work weeks have found, as a result of the energy shortages in recent years, that a host of advantages can be derived from such innovative approaches to work schedules. One of the most creative approaches, devised by a large California manufacturing organization, is the Nine Day Week. Under this plan the work week is extended to nine days, employees choose, based upon such variables as car pools, family schedules, and personal preferences, which three days in a row they wish to have off. They then work six days in a row to have a three day week-end. At any one time two thirds of the work force is at the facility and one third is enjoying a three day weekend. Though the days off vary from calendar week to calendar week, employees found that they could accomplish more at work and in off-time as a result of the program. Some other organizations have experimented with the four-day week in which the work day is expanded to ten hours and the forty-hour week is accomplished in four days rather than five with equally satisfying results. Such arrangements must be worked out within the limitations of labor contracts in union environments but can be rewarding and highly motivating if properly approached.

The rewards discussed here are particularly relevant to those employees whose career development does not lead to vertical moves and perhaps not even to horizontal moves. Even without movement to another job, the career development participants must receive clear signals from the organization that their learning and growth is recognized and valued.

Compensating for the Past and Future

While traditional budget and job position classification systems constrain how closely pay and promotion can be tied to career development, it is true that in all organizations some people are being promoted and receiving pay raises every year. The trick is not to create a tandem relationship in which career development leads or is tied to higher salaries or higher-level positions but rather to ensure that pay and promotion systems can recognize career development as an integral part of compensation practice. At least career development should not be discouraged by pay and promotion systems that ignore learning and growth as vital factors in upward mobility.

Again the career development practitioner will need to review current practices (in consort with compensation administrators) and explore the need for change. Several initial questions are pertinent to this investigation:

- Are pay levels in our organization consistent with those for similar jobs in other organizations in the community? (Is there "external equity?")
- Are pay raises determined in a manner that is perceived to be fair to all employees? Do they encourage career development?
- Are promotion opportunities equally available to all employees who want them and are qualified for them?
- Do employees have a clear understanding of how and why pay and promotion decisions are made?

Pay Now, Buy Later.   There is an active and amazingly accurate inter- and intra-organizational grapevine that transmits information about who is being paid what and where. Effective recruitment and retention of employees requires "external equity" of pay for similar jobs in other organizations in the same community. Internal equity is often more difficult to achieve and requires more concerted effort to maintain. An ongoing compensation audit system can help ensure equitable pay by determining relative values for positions through ranking and classification methods that use point or point/comparison for positions through ranking and classification methods that are point or point/comparison systems. A system of fair and competitive compensation is an essential base underlying all future decisions about raises and promotions.

In many organizations the frequency and amount of pay increases are set more by policy than by individual achievement. This is done by determining a pay range for each position and a percentage step increase allowable within that range and deciding at what times these increases can be made available to employees. In such a system pay raises often become so automatic that they provide little or no recognition or incentive for individuals to achieve and are frequently looked upon as cost-of-living adjustments.

Many strategies have developed to break this mold and to increase the reward potential of pay raises that offer substantial promise for linking career development with decisions about pay. One such strategy gives each organizational unit extra merit budgets or slush funds to provide additional rewards for exceptional performance. Another allows for optional steps or grades at the top of the pay range. Still another puts a floor and ceiling amount on the steps themselves to create greater discretion for step increases.

Traditionally promotion decisions and sometimes even pay hikes have been cloaked in secrecy. Only a few higher-ups are privy to information about when promotions are available and how they are determined. Understandably this often leads to employee resentment as well as to arbitrary and inaccurate organizational decisions. Effective job posting systems can alleviate this problem by making job vacancy information available to all employees. This not only allows all qualified individuals an opportunity to apply, but also clarifies for others the types of jobs that are available and requirements for these jobs. This can have a positive impact on encouraging career development and setting directions for learning and skill building.

A New Day for Pay.   New concepts are beginning to affect methods of pay and promotion, most of them aimed at creating structures for increased equity and rewards.

Lump sum salary increases, for example, give employees a greater sense of managing their own financial rewards. Under this system employees individually decide when to receive their annual increase. It can be incorporated into regular paychecks or taken in one or more lump sums when it may be most needed—such as in April (to pay taxes) or in December (for Christmas). If the lump sum is received at the beginning of the year, it is considered a loan with whatever is still unearned to be repaid back if the employee resigns during the year.

Skill evaluation plans, another new concept in compensation, are used to pay employees for increasing their abilities whether or not they make a job change. This method focuses pay on the employee rather than on the job and generally ties pay raises to learning a certain number of new tasks. Obviously this encourages learning, although it does require a substantial organizational investment in training. Additionally employees can still become stuck or reach dead ends at the top of a salary range once they have mastered all tasks in their job area.[6]

Experiments are also underway to revise the ways in which promotion decisions are made. Peer review has replaced supervisory decisions in some instances with work groups deciding who among them should be the next to advance into an upcoming job opening. Some organizations now use committees drawn from subordinate, supervisory, and peer levels to review candidates for promotion. (Though these approaches may seem radical, organizations that have tried them have found employees more critical and reluctant to give rewards than management.)

The concept of dual promotion ladders has developed to take into account those technical specialists who may do superior work but do not desire promotion to management positions. Under such a system pay and technical responsibilities can increase as they would if the employee were a manager rising in the ranks, while the individual remains in a position to make the most beneficial technical contribution.

Rewarding Managers

Still another approach, not yet widely used but one that has potential, is to reward managers for the work they do in developing the careers of their subordinates. Under pressure for results managers become so concerned about operations that they can overlook opportunities to identify and develop talent. Their time, energy, and attention are devoted to increasing production, improving sales, streamlining inventory warehousing operations, and reducing costs, activities perceived as the most important ways to demonstrate dramatic and tangible corporate accomplishments. As a result opportunities that would lead to supporting the growth needs of employees and to discussing their career progress are often neglected. There is a natural reluctance of supervisors to allow their good people to move onward or upward. Why should managers cut their own throat by allowing the best worker in a group to move out? The only visible reward in such a case is the loss of a star performer and a decrease in group productivity.

Many managers still function as if conformity to rules, systems, and authority take presidence over employee expectations, needs, and skills. This is self-defeating in the long run. Proclaiming an interest or voicing a concern is not enough. Top management must demonstrate to managers and supervisors that success in career development carries weight in the appraisal of their performance in the distribution of corporate rewards. Most companies evaluate managers on their productivity—not on their ability to develop subordinates. Because of daily demands to get results that preoccupy executives, they have little time to devote to coaching employees and providing information about possible career paths. Furthermore, many managers regard the careers of individual as those individuals' own business and have actually been heard to say that they have enough trouble figuring out what to do with their own careers, let alone trying to assist others in developing theirs.

A few companies, however, have recognized that rewarding managers for coaching subordinates may go a long way toward encouraging career development and establishing credibility for the organization's interest in employee career development.

In one large Canadian computer company career planning is built into the managers' role. The manager is explicitly expected to develop employees and is rewarded in doing so. The manager is required to help subordinates plan for their next job in the company. Employees are aware that this policy exists, and they report that it is being well executed.[7] It would seem, therefore, that one way to reward managers would be to record the career progress of their subordinates in that manager's file. Another possibility would be for managers to file career development reports each year and in this way document the growth of employees who have been under their supervision.

In another company a production manager was successful in developing a number of his people. When opportunities for promotions arose, he was willing to release his subordinates for advanced assignments in other divisions, but he was penalized for doing so. The production manager was required to maintain his previous level of output despite the loss of two of his best men. He received little recognition from his superior of the pressure imposed by corporate action. Corporate expectations and demands were inconsistent with a system of rewards related to performance standards.[8]

Unless managers are held accountable and rewarded for creating an environment conducive to the growth of subordinates, they cannot be expected to commit themselves to a productive career management effort. Rewards must be clearly related to performance in meeting all organizational objectives.

Managers committed to working closely with employees know what it means to assist subordinates in their efforts to develop all of their talents. Managers should be rewarded for these efforts. Those who make a concerted effort to foster opportunities and production objectives, will be growing with their company in the very best way.[9]

There are a number of choices and much research to be done in this area. The career development practitioner's primary responsibility is to gather all available information about existing promotion and pay operations, to become aware of options for alternative systems, and to work with appropriate compensation professionals to develop structures that allow for integrating career development into decision making about pay and promotions.

Now What?

A completed and institutionalized Integration Stage in the career development cycle does not mean that the practitioners' efforts are completed and that they can sit back on their laurels. Completion of one cycle merely means that the time has come to begin again. The next Preparation Stage may be aimed at internalizing career development so that the organization, top management, individual managers, and employees can continue their efforts on their own. It may be that the time has come to expand the program. It may be time to try a different approach, one that is aimed at a different target group, one more adapted to the organization, or one that takes an entirely different tack.

Every organization is different. Managers will differ in their acceptance of and approach to career development, individual employees will want different outcomes and have different goals. Mistakes will be made, different barriers will be encountered, different aids and supports will be found each time a career development program is instituted. The first time around a practitioner may find it necessary to take each step carefully and weigh each move finitely. The next time around the process will be easier and will become more the personal property of the practitioner. Eventually, if all goes well, what develops may be totally different from what is suggested in these pages.

This book is not the be-all and end-all of career development; it is a guide, a starting point for those explorers and discoverers of the new lands and untapped resources that exist in every organization—the people who work, live and grow, there. When the journey of exploration begins, the pioneer explorer needs help. This book is intended to provide that help. Once the way is known, it should bear the name of its discoverer; it should bear the imprint of the practitioner who blazed the trail.

But what about the practitioner? Who looks out for that brave soul who has blazed this new and exciting trail?

ENOUGH ABOUT THEM—WHAT ABOUT YOU?

PARTICIPATING PRACTITIONERS

" . . . physician, heal thyself!"

Doctors are notorious for neglecting their own health while working feverishly to protect the well-being of their patients. Lawyers often become so embroiled in the legal affairs of their clients that their own personal matters become snarled. Nearly everyone has heard of certified public accountants who must hire other CPA's to mind their own books because they spend too much time looking after the financial affairs to mind their own.

Career development practitioners are no different from these other professionals. Just as doctors have excellent backgrounds, facilities, and opportunities with which to guard their own health, lawyers have the resources to keep their own legal affairs in order, and accountants have the ability to balance their own books, career development practitioners have by the very nature of their work exceptional opportunities to define and enhance their own career patterns. To ignore these opportunities is to miss out on a chance to greatly increase career satisfaction.

Practitioners know from experience how difficult it can be for busy employees to address career issues in a thoughtful and carefully planned manner, but they easily forget that the same constraints apply to their own lives and careers. In fact many practitioners seem to assume that since they have responsibilities for the career planning of others, they can pursue their own development by osmosis. The attitude seems to be: "I spend days and weeks dealing with self-assessment and the issues involved in setting goals, so I'm naturally aware of my own needs and options." But is that really the case? Many practitioners would be quite surprised to see how they score on the same surveys and exercises as are completed by program participants.

The practitioners' extensive knowledge of the organization as well as their grasp of career planning tools gives them a substantial advantage in making the career development process personally beneficial. And by using the resources so readily at hand for personal development, the practitioner is in a better position to understand and assist others.

The process available to practitioners and required of them in planning their own careers is exactly the same as that which is applicable to the employees they help. The same six stages can be used to plan and implement career goals and strategies. However, the practitioner is further aided by a fairly complete understanding of the organization and its resources, which often makes it easier to collect and analyze the information necessary to examine all options. This knowledge base provides a powerful career development tool for those professionals who are willing to practice for themselves what they typically have preached to others. (A practitioner with a well-managed career also models the process for employees.)

Something Gained

An excellent starting point is for practitioners to consider exactly what they have gained from their work in the career development arena—including professional skills, relationships with others, organizational knowledge, and personal reputation. Examining these factors can often stimulate a greater sense of extended alternatives than may have been previously recognized. Additionally this type of assessment readily leads to involvement in the stages of the career development process that practitioners can undertake to assure personally rewarding career movement of their own.

In general practitioners find that they can identify gains in three areas: professional skills, knowledge and information, and relations with others. The value of these are demonstrated in Exhibit 8-1.

Professional Skills. The skills that practitioners bring to bear in initiating and implementing career development programs can be transferred to a wide range of career options. For example, during the Preparation Stage practitioners may develop skills in planning, budgeting, and scheduling, as well as in negotiating with and gaining commitment from others.

As the career development program gets underway practitioners exercise a variety of additional managerial and leadership skills. They must become adept in areas such as program goal setting, program evaluation,

TYPE OF GAIN	VALUE TO PRACTITIONER			
Professional skills	Managerial skills	Leadership skills	Technical skills	Interpersonal skills
Knowledge and information	Knowledge of the organization	Information on career options	Knowledge of career development processes	Information on personal needs and goals
Relations with others	Personal support systems	Professional contacts	Identification of mentors	Visibility in the organization

Exhibit 8-1   Value to Practitioner of Career Development Effort

program monitoring, design of program elements, problem solving, decision making, and report writing.

Many practitioners are also involved in conducting meetings and workshops and thereby increase their skills in public presentation, training, and group leadership. The technical elements of the design and delivery of training sessions, program analysis, and financial management also add to the practitioner's skill repertoire.

It is important for practitioners to recognize the interpersonal skills they have acquired through contact with program participants and with top managers who need to be informed of the progress of career development efforts. These may range from individual counseling to communication and conflict resolution skills—the abilities required to effectively work with, report to, and assist others. Often these include skills in one-on-one negotiation, teamwork, and participative decision making.

Knowledge and Information.   Career development practitioners are in an ideal position to gather extensive information about the organization in which they work. They can then use this information to increase their own knowledge about options for personal career futures.

For example, by collecting and cataloguing information about the organization, its future, and its human resource needs, practitioners have been required to learn about every major unit and area of employment. It is likely that they now have not only substantive information about the organization but also a subtle intuitive sense of the informal system and probable future directions.

Practitioners have also gained a valuable understanding of exactly how the six-stage process of career development works and why it is important to move through the step-by-step procedures in careful and logical sequence. By assisting others in the process, they begin to recognize how the stages can be used to facilitate their own development. And it is likely that when practitioners are working with others, they are also using the process to define personal goals and to mentally determine strategies for achieving them.

Relations with Others. Throughout the implementation of the career development program, practitioners come into contact with individuals at all levels in the organization. Most practitioners also increase their contacts with individuals outside the organization, such as potential providers of resources from educational settings, other career development practitioners, and training and HRD professionals from other organizations.

It is essential that practitioners recognize the support and assistance they can receive from these persons for their own career development, and it can be useful for them to develop a contact list or file of names for that purpose. These new contacts may be mentors who can offer advice based on their own experience, top level managers in a position to make decisions that assist practitioners' achievement of goals, or colleagues who can offer information and encouragement. Practitioners, because of the wide range of relationships developed through their work, are in an excellent position to form a network of resource persons who can greatly enhance movement toward career goals.

Another benefit is the visibility practitioners gain throughout the organization. The expertise that they have the opportunity to demonstrate becomes widely known, and successful practitioners are recognized as people who can plan, organize, and implement a vital, large-scale program with significant impact. Therefore, in attempting new endeavors, practitioners generally will not be required to first prove themselves competent for the task.

Plugging It In. These substantial advantages enjoyed by career development practitioners imply a great many opportunities for their career futures. Many will move up in the organization to general management positions; others will move up in the field of human resource development or personnel. Some will use their new skills in program management to move laterally to other departments that deal with completely different substantive issues.

It is up to the individuals involved to capitalize on the experiences and knowledge that have been available. This implies a call to action on the part of practitioners in the form of an increased willingness to move through the career development process in the same concerted manner required of program participants.

The Process Revisited

Practitioners who set out on their own six-stage process will find (as do employees) that at times the endeavor is more difficult than anticipated.

These difficulties often result from the need for practitioners to be their own sources of advice, encouragement, and ideas. Whereas other participants can turn to their practitioner for assistance, self-directing career development people have no such expert resource readily available. For this reason it is often advisable for them to enlist others—on the career development program staff in other areas of human resources development—to undertake the process with them. This can provide an exchange of information and a shared commitment to continue working toward goals.

Practitioners must also resist the temptation to take short cuts around certain elements of the process. For instance, it may seem unnecessarily tedious to actually complete various profiling surveys, especially for practitioners who assume they already know enough about themselves. However, skipping this stage denies them valuable information that may lead to surprising personal insights. Likewise, practitioners may be tempted to only mentally note goal statements rather than to write them out and share them. Taking this short cut neglects the need for personal commitment and evaluative reference.

At some points in the process practitioners may find the task to be easier than anticipated—especially when information is required that has already been gathered or when necessary skills, such as writing goal statements, have already been learned. It is the responsibility of individual practitioners to candidly assess how quickly they can move through the six stages and to ensure that each stage has been successfully completed before moving on to the next.

It might be useful for practitioners to at this point review the six stages of the career development process with a view toward determining how those stages can apply to their own personal cases.

Stage I: Preparation.   This stage in the career development process is really an organizational activity that is undertaken prior to the start of individual activities. If practitioners have adequately assisted the organization in preparing for the career development program, that preparation will eventually facilitate the practitioners' own career development.

Practitioners' own endeavors toward personal career development provide a good check on the completeness of the overall Preparation Stage. Whether or not the organization's existing human resource activities are appropriately linked to the career development program and whether or not responsibilities and resources have been adequately assigned will become readily apparent. In addition practitioners should consider ways in which those people and projects in their immediate working environments might need to be more thoroughly prepared so that they might enhance career development activities.

Stage 2: Profiling.   The challenge for practitioners during the Profiling Stage is the active pursuit of self-understanding. This means answering the "Who am I?" question by gathering new insights rather than by simply guessing from assumptions based on old material. New insights should include knowledge about interests, abilities, attitudes, opinions, values, and preferences in work contexts. The identification of these assets can be greatly facilitated by the broad experiences that have been undertaken in administering the career development program.

During the identification phase of the Profiling Stage, practitioners should use the same surveys and assessment instruments provided to career development program participants. If at all possible they should find opportunities for group settings where the results can be exchanged and verified. It is extremely important that practitioners actually put pen to paper at this point in order to spark their own enthusiasm and commitment.

During the reality-testing phase practitioners will need to solicit feedback from colleagues and others to check on the findings that have surfaced. It can be especially useful for them to discuss profiling information with their own managers who may be familiar with the practitioner's work both before and after the inception of the career development program. Managers can point out new strengths and needs for continued development. Valuable and objective feedback can also emanate from career development program participants who do not see practitioners in other contexts. While they may not be able to discuss the specifics of the practitioners' planning or monitoring abilities, they can relate perceptions about interpersonal skills, such as group leadership and counseling.

Stage 3: Targeting. The Targeting Stage is generally facilitated for practitioners by the knowledge of organizational goals and future intentions they have acquired. For instance knowledge of top management's commitment to human resource development allows practitioners to determine realistic personal goals in that area. Similarly information about new corporate plans in product development or marketing may indicate appropriate goals concerning those opportunities. Practitioners' responsibilities at this point are to link both profiling information and organizational information into clear goal statements.

Again practitioners may be tempted to take short cuts in the process—especially the exploration phase. This phase requires that they develop goals in all six career alternative areas (vertical, lateral, realignment, relocation, job enrichment, and exploratory). It is important to pose options in each of these areas as a means of visualizing all possible alternatives and of determining back-up goals if one or more should prove unfeasible. Goals in each area should be written and discussed with colleagues, supervisors, and friends and family.

At the specification phase practitioners will need to practice the goal statement writing skills that they have taught to program participants and to test these statements against the key characteristics of action-oriented goals. Once the goals are finalized and committed to paper, they should be shared with others. At this point practitioners from other organizations or colleagues who are familiar with the career development process can be valuable resources. They are generally knowledgeable about the requirements for well-stated goals and can give useful feedback about the possibilities for goal attainment.

Stage 4: Strategizing. Again at this stage practitioners' tasks are made easier by the organizational understanding they have already acquired. Through work with a variety of different units and individuals, practitioners have developed an inside knowledge of the culture and politics of the system. This will enable them to perceive the realities of what is required to act upon their goals.

Specifically the understanding of the system that is required at this stage is often simplified for practitioners who are already familiar with the constraints and opportunities existing in the organization. Nevertheless the process of brainstorming can result in valuable input. By working through an exercise such as Force Field Analysis, practitioners can clearly visualize what personal and organizational constraints may need to be alleviated and what contributing forces can be brought to bear on their own career goals.

The synthesizing phase requires of practitioners the same type of action planning that is required of program participants—taking into account needs and desires, actions, resources, and deadlines. Needs and desires are particularly relevant for practitioners who want to move up or move to a different substantive area within the organization. While such moves may build on existing abilities, they typically also indicate a need for new or improved skills, such as knowledge of new areas (for example, marketing or public relations) or increased managerial abilities. Once these are identified, practitioners can draw on their knowledge of organizational support programs (such as tuition reimbursement, training, and job rotation) in order to specify the actions to be taken during the next stage.

One valuable byproduct of active involvement at the Strategizing Stage is the personal experience of the practitioners as they test the adequacy of organizational structural supports, such as career paths or career counseling. Often it is assumed that these have been adequately linked to the career development program until personal experience indicates weaknesses that had not been recognized earlier.

Stage 5: Execution. For practitioners, as well as for other employees, the Execution Stage is the skill acquisition point in the career development cycle. Practitioners now have an opportunity to use the resources that have been developed to help link the organizations' training efforts to the career development program—from specific seminars and courses to mentor arrangements and from tuition reimbursement plans to professional organization memberships.

Because part of their job has been to know what career development resources are needed and available and to encourage the organization to provide a full range of skill building and experiential opportunities, practitioners are in a good position to select the best resources for their own development. By doing this, they can simultaneously evaluate the developmental resources offered. They may soon discover that the criteria for tuition reimbursement eligibility are too narrow or that the selection process for job rotation is inconsistent. It helps to be personally involved if one wants to thoroughly examine such programs.

Practitioners are also likely to experience the same difficulty that many employees face in working their current jobs and pursuing developmental experiences at the same time. Attending classes, taking on new projects, or even meeting with mentors is time consuming; and once the Execution Stage has begun, it may be necessary to revise the deadlines posed in the action plan. A significant advantage is that practitioners' first-hand knowledge about the variety of developmental resources limits the likelihood of their floundering and selecting the wrong resource to help meet their career goals.

Stage 6: Integration. Like the Preparation Stage the Integration Stage is largely an organizational rather than individual activity. Two major factors are evaluating the program and rewarding those who participate.

Personal experience helps practitioners evaluate the program results. If the program is meeting practitioners' developmental objectives, and if these objectives are contributing to organizational objectives for human resource development, it is likely that a formal evaluation will indicate a high degree of program success.

For practitioners one important source of reward is getting personal, first-hand knowledge to prove that the program benefits both individuals and the organization. Personally experiencing these benefits is professionally satisfying to those whose efforts helped to set the career development program in motion.

During the Integration Stage practitioners will have to decide how to continue their own development and at the same time improve the program so that others can reap even greater benefits from it.

A Future without Shock

There is evidence that human resource development is a growing concern in organizations throughout the country. Workers are asking for more than a paycheck and a place to locate themselves from 8 AM to 5 PM.

Increasingly they want the challenge of new experiences and the stimulation of opportunities for growth and advancement. Organizations are responding with programs and policies that encourage employees to learn and grow on the job and to strive for future opportunities.

As an essential part of this new thrust, the career development practitioner is in the forefront of a movement that presents excellent possibilities for professional challenge and growth. Organizations are increasingly ready to listen to the ideas of creative professionals in the human resource development field and to allow them to assist in responding to employee needs and demands.

These circumstances create excellent opportunities for practitioners who are concerned with their own career development. They are in a position to experiment with new organizational strategies, to manage new programs, and to lead the organization to a new level of commitment to human resource development. Success in these endeavors opens doors to wide-ranging career futures within and outside of the organization.

notes

Chapter 2

[1]James M. Kouzes, Chairperson, National Organization Development Network Conference, Fall, 1980, and Bill Allin, Chairperson, The Committee on Organizations in 1990, Organization Development Network Conference, Fall 1980.

[2]*Los Angeles Times,* August 5, 1980, Sec. 2, p. 5, "Are the Managers Mismanaging?" by Robert J. Samuelson.

[3]Adapted from an article by John Glover, Ralph Howes, and Renato Tagiuri, *The Administrator: Cases on Human Aspects of Management,* 5th ed. (Homewood, IL: Richard D. Irwin, 1973), pp. 204-206. © 1973 by Richard D. Irwin, Inc.

[4]Donald Schon, *Beyond the Stable State* (New York: W.W. Norton and Company, 1971), pp. 48-60.

[5]Adapted from an article by John Glover, Ralph Howes, and Renato Tagiuri, *The Administrator: Cases on Human Aspects of Management,* 5th ed. (Homewood, IL: Richard D. Irwin, 1973), pp. 204-206. © 1973 by Richard D. Irwin, Inc.

[6]Thanks to Jane Gouldner of Richway Department Stores, Atlanta, GA.

[7]Richard L. Knowdell, "The Implementation of a Career Life Planning Program in an Industrial Setting," ASEE Annual Conference Proceedings, 1978, p. 2.

[8]For further information contact Walter Berg, Manager, Personnel Development and Organization Effectiveness, Electro-Optical and Data Systems Group, Hughes Aircraft Company, Culver City, CA.

[9]Paul Ferrini and Alan Parker, *Career Change* (Cambridge, MA: Technical Education Research Center, 1978), p. 49.

[10]*The Career Development Bulletin,* (Vol. 1, No. 4, 1980), pp. 1-2. For further information write Marlene Thorn, General Accounting Office, Washington, DC.

[11]John E. McMahon and Joseph C. Yeager, "Manpower and Career Planning," in Craig, *Training and Development Handbook,* 2nd ed., ed. Robert L. Craig (New York: McGraw-Hill, Inc., 1976).

[12]Robert D. Melcher (MRG Associates, 10801 National Boulevard, Los Angeles, Ca 90064), "Roles and Relationships: Clarifying the Manager's Job," *Personnel* Magazine, May/June 1967, American Management Association, Inc.

[13]Paul Ferrini and Alan Parker, *Career Change* (Cambridge, Mass.: Technical Education Research Center, 1978), p. 33.

[14]*Career Planning and Adult Development Newsletter,* (Vol. 2, No. 8, August, 1980). For more information write Zandy Leibowitz, Goddard Space Flight Center.

[15]For further information contact Dave Nicoll, Kaiser Permanente Organization Development Department, Los Angeles, CA.

Chapter 3

[1]Henry Mintzberg, *The Nature of Managerial Work,* (Englewood Cliffs, N.J.: Prentice-Hall, Inc., 1973), p. 188.

[2]Robert L. Katz, "Skills of an Effective Administrator," *Harvard Business Review,* September-October, #74509, 1974, p. 24.

[3]*Ibid.*

[4]Paul Hershey and Kenneth H. Blanchard, *Management of Organizational Behavior: Utilizing Human Resources,* 3rd ed. (Englewood Cliffs, N.J.: Prentice-Hall, Inc., 1977), p. 7.

[5]*The Career Development Bulletin,* (New York: Columbia University School of Business, The Center for Research and Development, I, no. 2, (Spring, 1979), 1-2.

[6]Richard Knowdell, *Career/Life Planning for Adults* (San Jose, Calif.: Career Research and Testing, 1979).

[7]Suzanne Bryant, "Building Up to Career Goals", *Career Management Workbook,* (Los Angeles, Calif.: Security Pacific National Bank, 1977).

[8]Cary Barad, "Developing and Using an In-House Interest Inventory", *Personnel,* 54, No. 6, (December, 1977), pp. 51-57.

[9]Information supplied by Karen Hemphill of the Honeywell Corporate Human Resource Development Staff, Minneapolis, Minnesota, 1980.

[10]Donald Miller, *Personal Vitality,* (Reading, Mass.: Addison Wesley Publishing Co., 1974), pp. 239-240.

[11]For more information write Zandy Leibowitz, Goddard Space Flight, Career Development Center, Greenbelt, Maryland.

[12]Beverly Kaye, Shelley Krantz, *The Win/Win Approach to Performance Appraisals,* (Los Angeles, Calif.: In-house publication, The Broadway, 1980.)

[13]For more information write Janet Duprey, Internorth, Omaha, Nebr.

[14]For further information on skills inventories see Richard Kaumeyer, *Planning and Utilizing Skills Inventory Systems,* (New York: Van Nostrand Reinhold Co., 1979).

[15]Paul Scheiber, "A Simple Selection System Called Jobmatch". Reprinted with permission *Personnel Journal,* Costa Mesa, Calif. © January 1979.

[16]William H. Bright, "How One Company Manages Its Human Resources," *Harvard Business Review,* January-February, 1976. Reprinted by permission of the *Harvard Business Review.*

Chapter 4

[1]For more on levels of incompetence, see Laurance J. Peter and Raymond Hull, *The Peter Principle* (New York: William Morrow and Co., Inc., 1969).

[2]Paul Ferrini and L. Allen Parker, *Career Change* (Cambridge, Mass.: Technical Education Research Centers, 1978), p. 63.

[3]*Ibid.*

[4]Douglas T. Hall, *Careers in Organizations* (Pacific Palisades, Calif.: Goodyear Publishing Co., Inc., 1976), p. 164.

[5]*Ibid.*

[6]J. Richard Hackman and J. Lloyd Suttle, "Work Design," *Improving Life at Work* (Santa Monica, Calif.: Goodyear Publishing Co., Inc., 1977), p. 129.

[7]Parts of this section appeared in an article by the author entitled "How You Can Help Employees Set Career Goals", *Personnel Journal,* (May 1980), pp. 368-372.

[8]William E. Bright, "How One Company Manages Its Human Resources," *Harvard Business Review,* (January-February, 1976), pp. 81-93. Reprinted by permission of the *Harvard Business Review.*

Chapter 5

[1]Hugh R. Raylor, *More Power To You!* (Work in progress on the sources of interpersonal power, politics, and persuasion. Unpublished.)

[2]Rosabeth Moss Kanter, *Men and Women of the Corporation,* (New York: Basic Books, Inc., 1977).

[3]Nicholas W. Weiler, *Reality and Career Planning: A Guide for Personal Growth,* (Reading, Mass.: Addison-Wesley Publishing Company, Inc, 1977), p. 22. Reprinted with permission.

[4]Gerald R. Roche, "Much Ado About Mentors," *Harvard Business Review,* (January-February, 1979), p. 15.

[5]Roger Harrison, "Diagnosing Organization Ideology, *1975 Handbook for Group Facilitators,* John Jones and William Pfeiffer, eds. (La Jolla, Calif.: University Associates Publishers and Consultants), p. 101- 107.

[6]Suzanne Bryant, "The Market Environment" *Career Management Workbook,* (Los Angeles, Calif.: Security Pacific National Bank, 1979), p. 84.

[7]James W. Walker, *Human Resource Planning,* (New York: McGraw-Hill, Inc., 1980), p. 313.

[8]Harry L. Wellbank, Douglas T. Hall, Marilyn A. Morgan, Clay W. Hamner, "Planning Job Progression for Effective Career Development and Human Resources Management," *Personnel,* (New York: AMACOM, a division of American Management Associations, March-April, 1978), p. 57.

[9]Gerald A. Vastano, *Career Path Handbook,* (Hartford, Conn.: Aetna Life and Casualty, Human Resource Development, 1979), p. 1.

[10]Robert E. Hastings, "Career Development: Maximizing Options," *The Personnel Administrator* (Berea, Ohio: American Society for Personnel Administrators, May 1978), pp. 58-61.

Chapter 6

[1]*G.E. Training and Development Guide,* San Jose, Calif.: General Electric Co., Relations and Utilities Operations, Training and Development Dept., 1979). Thanks to Pam Jones.

[2]Lester Digman, *How Well-Managed Organizations Develop Their Executives* New York: Organizational Dynamics, Autumn, 1978), pp. 63-77, 69.

[3]*G.E. Training and Development Guide,* (San Jose, Calif.: General Electric Company, 1979).

[4]Thanks to Hugh R. Taylor, CDR, USN (Retired).

[5]*The Career Development Bulletin,* (New York: Columbia University, No. 2, Spring, 1979), p. 3.

[6]For more information on this particular type of organization structure see John F. Mee, "Matrix Organization", *Business Horizons,* VII, No. 2, (Summer 1964), pp. 70-72.

[7]Mohammed Fazel, "Taking the Mystery Out of Career Development", *Personnel,* (March-April, 1978), pp. 46-53, 49-50.

Chapter 7

[1]James W. Walker and Thomas G. Gutteridge, *Career Planning Practices,* AMA Survey Report (New York: AMACOM, a division of American Management Associations, 1979), p. 34.

[2]Many of the ideas expressed on this section were influenced by the excellent work of Lynn Lyons Morris and Carol Taylor Fitz-Gibbon, *How to Measure Program Implementation,* (Beverly Hills: Sage Publications, 1978) (Developed by the Center for the Study of Evaluation, UCLA).

[3]Edward E. Lawler III, "Reward Systems," *Improving Life at Work,* ed. J. Richard Hackman and J. Lloyd Suttle (Santa Monica, Calif: Goodyear Publishing Co, Inc., 1977), pp. 164-166.

[4]*Ibid.*

[5]Katherine C. Janka, *People, Performance...Results: A Guide to Increasing Employee Effectiveness in Local Government* (Washington, D.C.: NTDS Press, 1977), p. 31.

[6]Edward E. Lawler III, "Reward Systems," *Improving Life at Work,* ed. J. Richard Hackman and J. Lloyd Suttle (Santa Monica, Calif: Goodyear Publishing Co., Inc., 1977), pp. 183-185.

[7]Douglas T. Hall, *Careers in Organizations,* (Pacific Palisades, Calif.: Goodyear Publishing Co., Inc., 1976) p. 156.

[8]Verne Walter, "Self-Motivated Personal Career Planning: A Breakthrough in Human Resource Management", *Personnel Journal* (March, 1976), 112-116.

[9]*Ibid.*

index